Advance Praise for *To Be or Not To Be Sociological*

'As an engaged teacher, creative researcher and exceptional writer, Dev Nath Pathak interrogates the culture of academic conservatism, methodological rigidity and associated intellectual insecurity prevalent amongst the priestcraft of formal and institutionalised sociology in India. The book, written with philosophical depth and heightened sensitivity, is bound to make one reflect on the efficacy of epistemological pluralism and self-reflexivity.'

Avijit Pathak
Sociologist and public intellectual; former professor,
Jawaharlal Nehru University, New Delhi, India

'Masterly and witty, this book is a new and wonderful addition to the pedagogical literature on sociology. It offers a genealogy of sociology's precursors, foundational thinkers, as well as critics within the discipline, who have taught generations how to see like a sociologist. The account gives space both to the raw and the cooked—the field notes and unedited reflections as well as the finished, sanitised and edited products, so that the book is one that teachers and students can equally enjoy.'

Swargajyoti Gohain
Associate professor of sociology and anthropology and
assistant dean of faculty, Ashoka University, Haryana, India

'A bold, provocative and sharply polemical book that, while acknowledging the scientific spirit of seeing the social world, challenges the epistemic authority of science itself. Taking a postpositivist perspective, it calls for freeing sociology and social anthropology from their methodological rigidities and disciplinary boundaries and returning to reflexivity about the compelling phenomenon of "experience". It brilliantly traces the historical trajectory of the "sociological", the transition from what is considered philosophical to "social", critiques of classical epistemology, particularly through the lenses of feminist and subaltern epistemologies, and the plurality of the ways of capturing the social. It also exemplifies how a teacher could engage with students to intellectually provoke them to chart their own pathway of knowing the world rather than mechanically following the "established" methods and techniques that have become formulae for quick academic success. In summary, this book is an important addition to the literature on methodology and is essential reading for students and practitioners of sociology, anthropology and other social science disciplines.'

Pushpendra
Sociologist; former professor and dean,
Tata Institute of Social Sciences, Maharashtra,India

'*To Be or Not to Be Sociological* challenges established debates and methodologies within the fields of sociology in India and South Asia. By integrating diverse materials, Dev Nath Pathak provokes new lines of inquiry. He disrupts conventional approaches, implying that methodologies in sociology should remain open-ended and adaptive rather than static. The book proposes that experience itself can serve as a rich source of knowledge, encouraging a reflexive, self-critical approach to research. The book is an essential reading for students and scholars of sociology.'

Satendra Kumar
Social anthropologist and senior fellow, Institute of Asian and Oriental Studies, University of Zurich, Switzerland

'Brilliant work. The narrative flows like a river. It's a genre that is trying to dismantle the cobweb of a purist's pretensions and academic arrogance. The book is a pathbreaking work for our time. Simply unputdownable. I strongly recommend it to anyone who cares for and has an interest in the world of letters and philosophy.'

Santosh Kumar Singh
Sociologist, poet and public intellectual; associate dean, Dr B.R. Ambedkar University Delhi, New Delhi, India

TO BE OR NOT TO BE SOCIOLOGICAL

TO BE OR NOT TO BE SOCIOLOGICAL

Methodological Ways of Seeing

Dev Nath Pathak

B L O O M S B U R Y
NEW DELHI • LONDON • OXFORD • NEW YORK • SYDNEY

BLOOMSBURY INDIA
Bloomsbury Publishing India Pvt. Ltd
Second Floor, LSC Building No. 4, DDA Complex, Pocket C – 6 & 7,
Vasant Kunj, New Delhi, 110070

BLOOMSBURY, BLOOMSBURY ACADEMIC INDIA and the Diana logo are trademarks of Bloomsbury Publishing Plc

First published in India 2025
This edition published 2025

Bloomsbury Academic India
An imprint of Bloomsbury Publishing Plc

ISBN: HB: 978-93-56409-68-2; eBook: 978-93-56408-96-8
2 4 6 8 10 9 7 5 3 1

Typeset by Manipal Technologies Limited
Printed & bound in India

To

Priya, Prabuddh and Nargis

for living with the unbearable heaviness of my being and tirelessly trying to change it into an amicable lightness of existence

CONTENTS

PROLOGUE: A PROVOCATION FOR PLURALISM IN THE WAY OF SEEING IN SOCIOLOGY

What shall a methodology book do for a sane society? If we recall the ideas of Eric Fromm, the Marxist psychoanalyst and proponent of the sane society, methodology shall mirror the ubiquitous pathologies of social minds. In research terminology, it shall divulge the concealed aberrations of the sociological ways of seeing and related practices. The methodological sanity of the community of social scientists solicits a self-critical diagnostic understanding and revisiting of the canonical deliberations from the texts usually prescribed for techno-managerial readings. Only then can we understand how much (un)freedom prevails upon sociological ways of (un)seeing. We cannot be called 'sane' only because we all share similar pathologies. Instead, a methodology book aids us in getting to know how much we are free and unfree, certain and uncertain, in our experience and knowledge, towards ensuring a sane society of professional social scientists. Other than answering the usual questions about ways of seeing at the points where science and social science meet, such a book brings about a much-needed realisation that we know and hence, we are free. And, paradoxically, the more we know, the more acutely we realise the presence of our ignorance that spectrally surrounds our knowledge. No methodological route provides for an absolute truth claim. It is somewhat akin to the fact that the more we are mindful of our breath, the more intrigued we grow about the ever-changing shades of the breath. In other words, a methodology book shall aim at translating the following verse from *Isha Upanishad*[1] into a sociological ambiguity:

Into blinding darkness enter
Those who worship ignorance
Into as if still greater darkness enter
Those who delight in knowledge!

Into blinding darkness enter
Those who worship the unmanifest
Into as if still greater darkness enter
Those who delight in the manifest.[2]

This is philosophical as well as political insofar as there is an assertion of humane hermeneutic aspirations to break free from silos of minds. The straightjacketed minds pertain to the rigid scheme of cognition in which experiences such as darkness, ignorance, knowledge, the manifest and the unmanifest are unequivocal. Intellectual explorations in sociology, in particular, and the social sciences, in general, can benefit from a creative epistemological ambivalence, which can then allow the teacher and student to admit the co-terminus presence of knowledge and ignorance. Research thereby becomes an intellectual political act to realise the aspiration of creating hermeneutic ruptures. Uncertainty is thus an essential twin of certainty of knowledge.

Using a sense of freedom in the Prologue of this book, I attempt to elucidate the crux of the rules underpinning the present book. And yet, while following these rules, I seek to demonstrate how a modicum of freedom amounts to a variety of intellectual politics. This intellectual politics is not the same as the electoral politics in a democracy, nor is it guided by the prevalent political correctness. It is a politics in which contestations and negotiations among the ways of seeing are key characteristics. As in intellectual politics, so in spiritual and meditational politics, the combination of freedom and rule augments consciousness. The amalgamation of rules and freedom unfolds in a fundamental lesson one can learn from Vietnamese monk and peace activist Thich Nhat Hanh:[3] 'I am breathing in, I am breathing out'. That the present moment is wonderful; that I am calm; and that I am free are the virtues of mindfulness in breathing, doing and being. There is a rule in Thich Nhat Hanh's meditative practice that leads to freedom, and, in turn, freedom adds more peacefulness to the rules. That is the aspired mindfulness at the core of the book—so mindful, in fact, that a breath can become a telos of meanings. A breath that can escape our daily attention indeed was the fulcrum of poetic meditation for the thirteenth-century poet Jalaluddin Rumi[4] as well as twenty-first-century Thich Nhat Hanh.[5] Many mystics have emphasised breath as a key to freedom. This book presents methodological discourses as that inescapable breath most social scientists may neglect thinking of it as a given. Thus, we tend to abandon our sources of freedom, despite having read several critical educationists who centralised love as a key method of teaching and learning. Never could we forget Paulo Freire to bell hooks, emphatically telling us—to educate is the practice of freedom. To learn and practice sociology in academic or in everyday life solicits the freedom of the mind, owing to the mindfulness about the visions, spectacles, optics, lenses, perspectives and overall ways of seeing that condition us.

bell hooks, deeply influenced by both Freire and Thich Nhat, informed us about the value of excitement in an act of teaching that sets off a series of transgressions—'to enter classroom settings in colleges and universities with the will to share the desire to encourage excitement, was to transgress' (1994, 7). She had witnessed both kinds of classrooms, one in which freedom was non-existent and another in which classroom and curriculum were subject to the pedagogic pursuits of freedom. It was a classroom inclined to freedom that enthused students and teachers to unravel their dispositions as well as academic and scholastic conditions, which made them mindful of the text and contexts, constraints and liberties. This book entails that larger agenda of recapitulating episodes from the diverse texts to enliven a context for intellectual freedom. Let's ruminate further on what is and what could be—some bitter realisation and some wishful thinking. This is against the backdrop of the predecessors' insightful offers, though minimal on the practical moribund, that is, citations, quotations, references and footnotes. As the book unspools, we meet some of those predecessors, philosophers and historians, sociologists and anthropologists, thinkers and polemicists. Some of them will make cameo appearances while others will hold our attention for a longer duration. In short, the discussions in the book dwell upon an interdisciplinary framework in which the meanings of methodology are plural.

Relevance

These days, there are a large variety of students in a classroom. Most seek from a teacher a well-crafted way in and out of the academic world. They surrender themselves to the ruthless manipulations of a teacher who may misguide and instigate students. In a few rare cases, some also seek to be exceptional 'Alices in Wonderland' in the pursuit of lessons and discourses in the classroom. Many grow complacent and arrogant to the extent that they reduce a teacher to a mere professional agent, a service provider. And still, some find a friend in a teacher and join in endless dialogues, somewhat in the spirit of the Upanishad or in the manner of Rumi listening to his beloved mentor Shams of Tabriz. Both teachers and students refer to the books.

A teacher needs a book and so does a student, for purposes larger than what may initially be apparent. At face value, a book that puts together scattered materials, theories and debates could be judged with sheer utilitarian logic of the immediate kind. And with this logic, the question would be: how much of the syllabus of a particular course is covered by the book in question? This query has many underlying facets, about the ability of a book to help a teacher teach and a student learn. We often wonder how a book enables students to score well in the examination and aids teachers in smoothly finishing the curriculum. The utilitarian logic behind selecting, using, admiring or rejecting a book is fine for the rational purpose—obtaining good grades. Such practices are commonplace in classroom deliberations, in poring over the books in the library, and in the essays that young scholars write to fulfil a technical requirement in a course. At the end of the day, the teacher will evaluate a student based on the written essays. But this is very a narrow, reductive logic, which is often used by book manufacturers and sellers as much as the buyers. Thankfully, this narrowed version of logic does not govern all the sellers and buyers. And it certainly does not apply in entirety to teachers and students, or so we wishfully think. The very purpose of utilising a book, through critical reading and nuanced engagement, is to go *beyond* a book. This particular book operates with the idea of enabling the teachers and students to read it, put it aside and think beyond it. In short, in the larger logic of utility, this book invites meditations, ruminations and debate. It is hence not a simple guidebook, nor a typical textbook, that can be reduced to the narrow sense of utility. While it tries to give comprehensive presentations on a variety of themes, issues and pre-existing debates, the book asks for a favour from the readers, the teachers and students don't take the book for granted.

This is very much in tune with what I tell my students in the classroom. My lectures are not an end by themselves; they are only the means for further explorations by students. That is, however, easier said than done, since a lot of essays written by students simply reproduce from the notes they take in class. Despite a constant reminder that class notes are supposed to merely provide an inroad into the world of books, the students do not venture beyond the class lectures, notes and discussion. Yet, as a diehard pedagogue one keeps reminding and persuading students to take notes not in order to reproduce them in the answers to the questions in examinations. Mere reproduction can make them secure some grades. But it does not serve the purpose entailed in the teacher's pedagogy. Any teacher would be more delighted to see that a student is engaging with the class lectures and coming up with original propositions rather than mere reproduction. Teachers delight in being instigated by students' critical engagement with the texts, prescribed as well as non-prescribed (or even prohibited) and anchor the discussions in the classroom beyond the set parameters. Moreover, students bring in the influences, information and interpretations from their contexts that aid in enlarging the textual framework of discussions in a curriculum. For their part, the students too make, unmake and remake the teacher with their nuanced interjections. All credit, congratulatory or otherwise, is due to the students if a teacher performs or does not perform well. And this book is therefore a tribute to the students who make it difficult for a teacher to be a docile vehicle of texts, complacent consumer of research findings and virulent vendor of politically (in)correct ideologies. This book anticipates that students and teachers mutually set each other free. Therefore, they make themselves available for ruthlessly dissecting a much-taken-for-granted episteme called experience which is central to this book. After all, across methodological debates in sociology, the category of experience is a real apple of discord or epistemological accord. The more we know our methodology the more we sense our wariness about the nature and scope of experience. This is just like the lesson from the Upanishad: Those who delight in knowledge tend to enter, as if, still greater darkness.

Methodology as Ways of Seeing

This book is also driven by a personal anxiety of public significance. This is an anxiety about the reduction of methodology into mere methods, techniques, tools and deliberation on the types of research—qualitative and quantitative. Needless to say, an awareness of methods, techniques and tools in qualitative and quantitative researches in social sciences is important. Every student learning the fundamentals of research and planning a project might need such awareness. Indeed this is the case with many professional sociologists and anthropologists. But then, methodology is more than these tangible outputs. Methodology in social sciences is a discursive realm entailing myriad ways of seeing the objects, subjects and fields with wide eyes as well as partial vision, and with sensorial experiences in which time and space, history and polity determine the hierarchy of sensory organs. Methodology entails a diffused power structure that contains seeing as well as not seeing, hearing and not hearing, feeling and not feeling. Even though it tends to be holistic, there is an inevitable possibility of skewed vision and partial understanding. Unwittingly, it alludes to inclusion and exclusion, choices and preferences, pride and prejudices in spite of sophisticated claims of neutrality and objectivity of research. The debates on and about methodology thus could aid in the first step, a profoundly Socratic one, 'to know that one does not'. Or it could give us a return to the verse from *Isha Upanishad*, noted at the onset of this Prologue, unspooling creative ambivalence as a pertinent aspect of our ways of seeing. Methodology thus assumes a radical significance in the politics of research in social sciences, which could be realised if and only if social scientists allow the philosophy of social sciences to have a say.

It is lamentable that we tend to dissociate methodology from epistemology, philosophy and theories. Methodology is, in the ultimate analysis, an orientation fraught with values. And this is not a monolithic orientation that is immune to changes. Just like no value orientation is pristine and persistent. Just like our knowledge of mythology is subject to our time and space and so are our ways of seeing. And concomitantly, as mythology becomes mythologies, value-orientation becomes value-orientations and methodology becomes methodologies. If there is truly pluralism about everything, how can we be silent about it in social science orientations? And if we are not silent about it, how can we tend to take sociology as one unchanging entity? There are bound to be 'many sociologies', and many ways of being sociological. The case of 'many sociologies' is also appropriate in the wake of a crucial realisation about the genesis of all modernity. Elsewhere we have derived a conclusion, more or less a foregone conclusion in our times, that there are multiple modernities. Many historically informed philosophical ruminations aid in accepting the variegated images of modernity. And if sociology is a brainchild of modernity, to gloss over a rich debate, one can suggest, in the same breath, that there are 'many sociologies'. And this cannot be mistaken for the relativist conceptualisation of sociology since there is no intended nihilism. No one is arguing for the death of sociology akin to the death of god. Instead, the imminent and immanent pluralism of sociology shall be taken to be a fertile ground to rethink the ways we adopt to become 'sociological'. If this is so, one cannot become 'sociological' just by using some method, technique, or formula of doing research or sociological theories. One need not be called sociological just because of the presence of some of the thinkers taught in certain universities at certain times. Likewise, merely putting indicators of social stratification such as caste, class, gender and so on would not amount to being sociological. Many good scholarships in literary studies, performance and visual studies, among others, also do the same, and yet they are kept out of the pale of the sociological. It means there is something more crucial about being sociological. This book proposes that being located in the ferment of philosophy and history of science, sociology of knowledge and hermeneutics, positivist and post-positivist theoretical debates suffice for the value orientation that could be deemed sociological. Being sociological is, in a nutshell, about harmonious contentment with the discontented terrain of thinking on a particular question—how do I know what I know? In sum, it is about placing the researcher and the researched in the cauldron called methodology.

Having said that, this book is not about delivering yet another formula, another prescription coming from the ivory tower to be translated into doables and deliverables. The complex terrain of methodology cannot be summed up in another profound sermon handed down by the owls of Minerva. Methodology is inherently praxiological, imminent ways of seeing, arising from what a researcher does and what she avoids doing. In the case of methodology, the course and in-depth supervision by a senior peer are not sufficient to guide a young scholar. The latter is left alone in the vortex of experiences, in the field of research in the library or in everyday life, dealing with the intricacies of seeing and not seeing. Also, unlike the funding agencies or the formal institutions, learners, be they teachers or students, do not operate with the idea of doables and deliverables. Learning is perhaps a high-electric domain where one encounters a perpetual short circuit of utilitarian goals. At times, it is precarious to forget such goals while drunken on the soma of transactions inside and outside the classroom. This is akin to an aesthetic challenge to an artist that leads him or her to become playful with uncertainty in the art practices. It is challenging to develop an iota of ease with the unpredictable process entailed in the making of an artwork. A scholar, young or old, faces this similar challenge of the unpredictable situations in which methodological certainty is obscured. That is when a scholar, like an artist, opens up to the difficult realisations in the field of methodologies. A methodological playfulness with uncertainty appears to be a foregone conclusion. And hence, in this book, one can encounter a dilemma, whether to tell a story or speak through exegeses. The dilemma could appear as a stylistic aberration to the professional editors in a publishing office. But it is not since it is geared towards persuasion and perspective at once. The readers of the book shall juggle with intrigue, insights, enchantment and arguments. In a way, the ideas of methodological ways of seeing also shape the way chapters are written, fusing facts and fiction, certainty and uncertainty. As a praxiological entity, methodology is a deliberate tactic, at times seamlessly performed, and at other times, left with rough edges for the inspectors to find the culprit of the crime. In short, there is an attempt to maintain some method behind the madness, so that a methodologically conditioned readership is not totally annoyed.

Methodology as Intellectual Politics

At a challenging time for academic politics, when anyone with the slightest of interest in the topic can potentially fall on the radar of institutions and society, discussing methodology amounts to a kind of creative intellectual politics. However, it merits knowing what kind of politics is inherent in methodology. Arguably, it is an emancipatory intellectual politics because a discussion on methodology makes one aware of the various ways of seeing. Such politics is essentially premised upon a classroom egalitarianism that allows both teachers and students to get into endless dialogue. The dialogic partners point to each other, the coexistent seen and unseen, knowledge and ignorance, light and darkness. To reiterate a point made earlier, what one sees and decides not to see—the seen and unseen—become crucial components in the intellectual politics of methodology. It is not a neutral process, loftily called research. A whole gamut of inclusion–exclusion is entailed in the process, starting with the selection of a topic to the research design and execution for data collection, and, finally, the endeavour to interpret, explain and understand. The researcher has the preferences, likes, aversions and visions that unfold in the process of research. Since research is not divorced from the researcher, his or her way of seeing, with inherent omission and commission, seeing and not seeing makes a profound intellectual politics.

However, we cannot forget to mention a prevalent tendency among students. Many of them speak platitudes about academic freedom but many get jittery when it comes to handling freedom. If provided with cues and aids to traverse alone, they begin to demand for categorical definitions, recipes for doing, maps for navigation and formulae for actions. They seek from their teachers and research guides not only research topics, questions and field sites, but also overall methodology. They aspire to be mimetic and willing to surrender their agency. In the classroom, they have started asking for class notes on PowerPoint slides. They have started saying that they don't want a professorial lecture which could enable them to craft their own pathways. Rather, they want the professors to deliver them the pathways on which they can comfortably walk. There is a hesitation to explore the unfamiliar, step out of their comfort zones and undertake much-needed intellectual risks in seeing the world from their particular perspective. They borrow visions from the textbooks, the market and dominant institutions. Sometimes, such visions are heavily conditioned by self-proclaimed progressive ideologies, and some other times, by conservative forces. They are reluctant to see the world independent of such forces, authorities and the determinant models. There is, in fact, a fear of freedom. A psychoanalyst who worked on such fear like Eric Fromm[6] will feel vindicated. This fear is dramatically articulated during open-book examinations. Students used to complain about the conventional examination format where they had to rely on their memories and rote learning. Such examinations were sites of unfreedom, so to say. But when it is an open-book exam with the liberty to return the answer script in twenty-four hours, the students become far more helpless. They invariably end up reproducing familiar texts, devoid of their ability to reason, in their essays, which are less about answering the questions and more about filling up the pages of the answer sheets. Given such an uncanny paradox, many students find it difficult to handle the philosophy of social sciences, let alone the complexity of methodology. They are mostly complacent with a textbook-based method course, which is invariably taught without showing the relationship with epistemological challenges. The whole methodology is reduced into a 'how to do' discussion on methods and techniques of social science research. Methodology thus practically means nothing more than methods and techniques. This is far from the intricacies of the ways of seeing that underpin methodology in social sciences. The status quo neutralises the intellectual politics of methodology that can deliver to the world fresh perspectives and novel ways of interpreting and understanding. This is anti-politics of the status quo, a professionalised sociology that this book seeks to expose while highlighting the politics of experience in the methodological debates in the social sciences.

The intellectual politics of methodology is necessary to realise the goals set by the Gulbenkian Commission Report (1993).[7] Formed by the Calouste Gulbenkian Foundation,[8] the commission was led by Professor Immanuel Wallerstein,[9] an American sociologist known for world system theory, and comprised scholars from the world of social sciences, natural sciences and humanities. The report unearthed currents that solicited adequate counter-currents in the social sciences. It discussed the fragmentations of the disciplines in the name of standardisation and professionalisation, leading to distinct modern intellectual cultures. Natural sciences, arts and humanities were separated from each other. Also, the report elucidated how social sciences were neatly divided and segregated from sciences and humanities in the nineteenth century. Institutionally, there was a consensus about such segregated existence of the branches of knowledge, only challenged in the 1960s, and yet to be materialised fully at the levels of institutions of teaching and learning. The report argued that the present structure of the social sciences creates unreasonable blocks to intellectual development and the consequent need for restructuring. Reading such a report and listening to some of the conscientious teachers' critical remarks about sociology makes sense. A teacher frequently observes that sociology is far behind the fast-changing social world. Preoccupation with methodology in sociology is primarily aimed at maintaining disciplinary distinctions, gatekeeping and perpetuating disciplinary parochialism. It is a regressive variety of intellectual politics that has made even progressive values a stooge in the manipulative maintenance of the status quo. The transformative capacity of social sciences, as the report observed, has to be realised through methodological ruptures at three levels (1993, 74–77). One, it requires re-enchantment rather than disenchantment of the world to be the central objective in our way of seeing. This is imperative to further the liberation of humans—by adhering to the wholesomeness of experience rather than fictive objectivity. Second, it means to reinsert time and space as integral variables constitutive of our analysis. Rather than an elusive objectivity-driven positivist way of seeing, there is an urge to see social reality as an ongoing accomplishment, sensitive to time and space. Third, it means overcoming the artificial disciplinary distinctions created in the nineteenth century. A lot of intellectual energy is exuded just for gatekeeping and guarding the boundaries of knowledge. Overcoming this will mean better utilisation of our analytical capacity. When multidisciplinary orientation becomes institutional and practical, scholars won't be uncomfortable with the ideas and insights, concepts and theories and all the varied ways of seeing coming from diverse sources. There will be a happy admission of what Karl Popper had to put across while deliberating on the philosophical nature of science. A problem leads to another problem through a process in the picture. A research question need not be defeated with an answer. Instead, through one question, following research, one may arrive at an answer that is only the beginning of a new set of questions. Perhaps, Popper's emphasis on an open society (guided by critical rationalism) was an anticipation of the Gulbenkian Commission report's invitation to 'open' social science.

Conclusion: A Way Forward

In the end, one ought to reiterate Fromm, who had observed, and so do we in our common-sense world, that inmates of an insane asylum are convinced that everybody else is crazy, except themselves.[10] Methodologically, we are perhaps more in the practice of concealing our failures than acknowledging and undertaking risks to find ways out as well as ways ahead. Everyone, for example, would like to locate bias, prejudice and subjectivity in the other: I am not crazy, someone else is! I am not biased, someone else is!

When intellectual sanity is alluded to in dehumanised data, rather than mindfulness of the methodological–experiential nuggets, we are most certainly not sane. The young scholars trained under our wings begin to clone the insane average, the predominant ways of seeing and doing and yet we don't seem to see the adversity of our doings. Unfreedom breeds unfreedom in academic practices and yet we join in the rhetoric of academic freedom without adequate wherewithal. Worse, rhetorical chanting of academic freedom gives birth to manipulations by senior peers, teachers and supervisors and mislead young scholars into some or other kinds of victimhood. Since the art and craft, skills and substance of practising freedom through methodology, as a socio-political praxis, is conspicuously absent, our rhetorical politics resorts to the lowest common denominators. Our realm of practices summons epistemological courage to take note of what is more or less a truism in the methodological debates—the way of seeing has been subjective all along. That the truth has been partial all along emerges vehemently in the trajectory of what we have conveniently and yet gingerly, termed post-positivist in this book. Be it in the wake of a successor science informed by feminist epistemology or even before the advent of critical departures in the post-Second World War social sciences, there are ample possibilities.

We need to find cues from the polemic outcry that also had reasoned arguments. We often read and teach them and yet do not deliver them into our practices. They are not only the likes of Alvin Gouldner, C.W. Mills and Pierre Bourdieu, but also several pioneers in sociology in India. They had valid concerns about the way of seeing and what all the sociologists shall be seeing. There are abounding methodological insights in a vast panorama of colonial and postcolonial India, be they the doyens in central India such as Patrick Geddess, G.S. Ghurye or Radhakamal Mukerjee, D.P. Mukerji and A.K. Saran at Lucknow University. They have been subject to readings intended at unmasking to debunk rather than understanding to marshal the ways of seeing. The book shows that it is not wise to throw the baby away with the bath water; the methodological content of the pioneers of sociology must not be trashed with a critical comprehension of the ideologies therein.

Though the book offers condensed contents from philosophy to the history of sciences, the intellectual history of social sciences and sociology, it is still not a satisfactory fulfilment of a significant objective. As far as exploring the methodological strands in contemporary sociology is concerned, the book does not cross a threshold. It only provides young scholars and researchers sufficient ground to do so. There are various cognates fields of study, which may provide deep and detailed deliberations on methodologies. They deal with issues pertaining to visuals, humour, sensorial, emotions, art and performative inter alia. In such fields of study, we encounter departures of methodological significance. The book will enable those who wish to go beyond in furthering the explorations of methodological departures. Indeed, the book will upset those practitioners—and there are many—who wish to play it safe and cast the methodological imperatives into oblivion. The mirror the book holds up reflects disturbing images and reveals the insanity of uncritical mimesis that is somewhat normative in social sciences.

The long deliberations, comprising the relevant slices from diverse sources, in this book, are not aimed at undermining the significance of scientific epistemology, or the imperative of science. Instead, it is a response to the many ways in which our way of seeing could be scientific, somewhat in the manner in which Isabelle Stengers (2018), the Belgian feminist philosopher of science, had suggested, 'another science is possible'.

References

Fromm, E. *The Sane Society*. New York: Routledge, 1955.

Hooks, Bell. *Teaching to Transgress: Education as Practice of Freedom*. New York: Routledge, 1994.

Katz, V., and T. Egenes. *The Upanishads*. New York: Penguin, 2015.

Stengers, Isabelle. *Another Science is Possible: A Manifesto for Slow Science*. Cambridge: Polity, 2018.

Wallerstein, I. *Open the Social Sciences: Report of The Gulbenkian Commission on the Restructuring of the Social Sciences*. Stanford, California: Stanford University Press, 1996.

PART 1

DAWN

1

THE ORDINARY AND THE EXTRAORDINARY IN THE SCHEME OF THE SOCIOLOGICAL

Often, the way of 'seeing' in modern academia tends to be an area of utter fogginess. There are, in fact, many jokes about the way sociologists and anthropologists see their object of study that are part of academic folklore. Embittered derision accompanies our laughter at how the term 'sociological' is employed like a talisman in judging a piece of research and writing amongst the scholars of sociology. Even in daily banters of sociologists and their interjections in a public forum, we often hear, 'How is that work sociological?' Everyone seems to worship an extraordinary disciplinary boundary despite the fashionable mention of interdisciplinarity here or multidisciplinarity there. The strict gatekeeping by senior peers in sociology ensures the exclusion of outsiders and the inclusion of insiders of the discipline, simply by citing professional objectives. This is hitherto so even though there could be sporadic moments of radical celebration of post-disciplinary or transdisciplinary academic interests, inside and outside the classrooms. It is in this wake that this book brings forth a fundamental question for deliberation that was flagged in the Prologue. To reiterate for the convenience of comprehension: 'What is that way of seeing responsible for a work to be called sociological?' The question centralises an apple of discord rather than a contract for consensus and so does the book. For this is not a book to promise a fine, balanced, calm and clinical work. The chapters shall unspool ample evidences of polemic and poetics, prejudices and politics. On the whole, the book executes a 'performative communication' in order to engender a conversational trope.

A book that a teacher and students of sociology could read together cannot afford to be a dry perusal of pre-existing discussions or a clinical reproduction of the answers to some of the textbook questions: What is sociology? What is sociological? What is sociological methodology? Teachers and students converse with as well as without references, footnotes and citations. In the mode of conversation, they critically engage with the textual and the contextual, the given and experienced, and the cleanly explained and creatively ambiguous. Curiously, some raw and some cooked content blend in the mode of conversation. To indulge in some creative mischief, one can recall a significant imagery of cooked and raw food in the famous structuralism of French anthropologist Claude Lévi-Strauss. Anthropologists in South Asia have spoken of the distinction between the two, raw and cooked, in the institutions of hierarchy. The folks with equal status can share raw food while those with unequal status have no choice; they ought to be sharing only cooked food. In a caste society, the lower caste can invite the upper caste to eat only well-fried puri-jalebi (metaphorically, deep-fried caste pollution). The conversation between teachers and students inside the classroom, as well as outside, defies the distinction between raw and cooked food. Or so we think! But if such defiance does take place, unwittingly it amounts to partaking on both well-cooked juicy meat and a half-cooked or maybe fully uncooked smelly flesh. One can play with the idea that this conversational defiance is indeed detrimental to the hierarchy of purity and pollution, experienced and naïvete, rational and emotional. The following is a presentation of a conversation, occasionally loaded with references, and yet explicitly using unverified stories. This is, in other words, fraught with hogging cooked stuff, properly referenced contents in the available prescribed texts that a teacher and student encounter in the curriculum. And in the same breath, this shows an inclination to seriously toy with raw material that is yet to go through serious research verification. Free from puritanical anxiety, a pundit's apprehension of the imperfect, this book serves the teachers and students in bringing to attention the significance of both, the canonised as well as the orally transmitted tales, gossip, hearsay, legends and so on. This combo offer, of putting together the raw and the cooked, is conducive for a discussion that seeks to broaden the scope of the sociological, a usage in sociological discourse that leads to unravel sociological ways of seeing. Thus, it is in the spirit of the book to start with a couple of tales, orally told of unknown provenance at once that sets the tone of curiosity.

This chapter unravels the basic premise of the book in which the endeavours of some of the key sociologists from various locations around the world, including India, are critically revisited to unsettle the conventional idea of 'sociological'. In the format of a polemical debate, with methodological posturing, the chapter tries to invade the disciplinary fort to establish the significance of reading, and perhaps rereading, theories, for unravelling methodological perspectives. This is largely to suggest that if there is a merit in the 'extraordinary' character of sociology, there is also a reason why sociology could be deemed logically ordinary.[1] In doing so, the chapter seeks to situate the discussion on methodology (in plural) between the domains of ordinary and extraordinary.

Two tales from oral traditions are befitting to commence the narrative. The first one goes like this:

> A guru sent ten of his disciples to collect dry logs in the forest across a river. On the way back, after having collected the logs, the disciples began to count themselves to ensure that no one was left behind. Each counted and found that they were only nine since each did not count oneself. Each came to the same conclusion that one was left behind. They rushed to the guru and recounted their apprehension. The guru counted them all and informed them that all ten had returned.[2]

It is all about individual perception in the above tale. Moreover, the truth perceived by apprehensive disciples and an interrogative guru eventually converges. It invites us to engage with the key problematic: our way of seeing that is inclusive of preferences, perspectives and intellectual schemes of inclusion and exclusion. The act of perceiving is loaded with both the object of perception and the subject that perceives. For example, even the mathematical calculation is often riddled with the way we tend to see things. Before we arrive at a foregone conclusion, such as 3 + 3 = 6, we have a perspective in place that enables as well as disables (more appropriately, delimits). The problematic flagged in the above tale is reaffirmed in the following tale, once again reproduced from memory though it could have emanated from one of the ancient texts of the subcontinent.

> Shiva, the bridegroom, prepared himself and his entourage to reach the castle of the king father of Princess Parvati, the bride-to-be. The entourage included ghosts, goblins, aghoris, mendicants, and such outlawed while Shiva himself resembled one of them. Upon a glimpse of the bridegroom and his entourage, all amongst the host including the parents of Parvati began to wail and faint. How could they marry off their dear daughter to such an uncouth bridegroom? When Parvati requested Shiva to be a little kind, he changed his look and that of his entourage, and thus was happily greeted by the host.

And one can go on reproducing many such tales to place for consideration one basic idea: it's all about the way we see things. A seemingly innocuous entity, way of seeing, thus solicits creatively curated complication. An apprehensive moral authority, the father of Parvati, seeks to see an ideal groom in Shiva, while Parvati's perception is free from any such apprehension. The daughter sees through the emotion of love, whereas the father through the emotion of care, to make the matter over simplistic. While it is about seeing, one can notice the flip side, the way of showing. In the end, the seen is an interactive yield. And hence, one interrogates the way things are shown to us while asking a few questions about the way things are seen.[3] As it is in everyday life, so is it in sociology—the terrain is fraught with the complexity of seeing and showing, and the provisional finality of the seen. But how often do we have the luxury of interrogating our way, or ways, of seeing and showing? It is one of the most, among many others, taken-for-granted ideas. If mythologies and folklore of yore condition us to take our way of seeing for granted, so does common sense masquerading as scientific conclusions or science as common sense. This is not to dismiss or celebrate the importance of common sense, scientific conclusions, or mythology and sacred injunctions. There is no 'anything goes' invoked as a new sacred here. The objective is to emphasise the all-pervasive, and frequently overpowering, ways of seeing and showing, being seen and shown, in various domains of reasoning. We are, the way we are, as per the way we and they, you and I see things in and out, about and around. If we say, and believe, that we are sociological, it must be owing to a way, or many ways, of seeing that enables us to make the claim. It gets far more melodramatic in science, and sociology, as in art and philosophy, given the pretences, prejudices and preferences of certain kinds reigning high. The complexities unfold in the various chapters in this book so that we can get a sense of an all-pervasive noun, namely, ambivalence. It is a kind of aesthetic of ambivalence that allows anyone traversing through the discursive trajectory in this book to whisper and whisper to raise a crescendo of whether to be or not to be sociological.

Ways of Seeing: An Inquisitive Preamble

The way we see things in science, sociology or our everyday life is important. And perhaps this is more pronounced in the history of sociological reasoning. What could be, thus one can ask, sociological way(s) of seeing? What about the scientific way(s) of seeing? This is an important question since sociologists began to await an Isaac Newton of their own in the late nineteenth century. After all, August Comte was committed to developing a discipline through *The Positive Philosophy* that he deemed to be social physics, interchangeably named, sociology. The classical sociology of the early twentieth century continued to engage with the question of the ways of seeing in sociology by way of discussing the rules, methods, rationality and science. Many such questions are crucial throughout this book, taking epistemological, philosophical and methodological routes of reasoning. The subsequent chapters enable one to debate and think aloud for restless curiosity. In so doing, as well as to do so, the various chapters in this book envisage a conversational trope, a discursive trajectory, rather than smart answers to technical questions. One may, however, stumble upon some of those answers by engaging with the discourses. And for that utilitarian objective, there is a conscious effort to avoid making things too confusing, or as we say with due sarcasm, intellectually profound. Explicitly, the chapters work towards bringing about an intimacy with the aesthetic of ambivalence that runs through scientific and sociological epistemology and ontology.

The question about the way of seeing borrows an insight from John Berger who passed away in 2017 and contributed an enriching television series titled *Ways of Seeing* on the British Broadcasting Corporation. In a book based on the show, with the same title, Berger starts the discussion with an apt provocation, 'Seeing comes before words' (1972, 7). There is a preference for seen over heard; however, he goes on to acknowledge a tense relationship between 'what we see' and 'what we know'. But what is more important—seeing or knowing, visuals or words, feelings or explanations, and so on? Berger conjured a creative and convincing imagery when he said, 'Each evening we see the sun set. We know that the earth is turning from it. Yet the knowledge, the explanation, never quite fits the sight' (7).

One of the reasons why the relationship between the seen and the known is not settled is because of the historical and sociocultural determination of the ways of seeing. We seldom freely see, our sights are rarely neutral, and we tend to see through many considerations. 'The way we see things is affected by what we know or what we believe. In the Middle Ages when men believed in the physical existence of Hell the sight of fire must have meant something different from what it means today' (8).

Likewise, along with historical epochs and thereof ideologies and utopias, our emotions add colours to our vision. When we look at someone lovingly, we see not only the loved one, we also envision an uncanny completeness. The images and things that we see thus become a bridge between the visible and the invisible and the knowable and the felt. An artist, a photographer, as well as a wordsmith, play with the immense possibility offered by the complex practice of seeing. Besides, an artefact, an output of an artist's practice has its journey. The creative output of an artist is subject to historical, social and material vicissitudes. An anthropologist of visuals, Professor Marcus Banks[4] taught many such lessons through his research and writings to the learners of visual anthropology and sociology. One such axiomatic lesson is about the perpetual passage, of time and space, of discourses, in which a photograph is located. A visual, unlike a *Tabula Rasa,* receives inscriptions of experiences even though it seems to be already inscribed with an intended meaning. A photograph assumes the significance of a meta-narrative, with layers of social life entrapped within. Be that a photographic image of a postcard written by a dear one, or of bustling streets with humans as well as dotting visuals within the photograph, such an abundance of life that we see some things, and yet, we also don't see many others. Thus, the seen and the unseen both unfold at once in an act of seeing! No wonder why there has been a persistent call for rethinking within visual anthropology.[5]

How does this all surface when we think of a way of seeing in sociology? What all come to constitute the sociological way of seeing? And in short, what makes us sociological? Such questions make more palpable sense if located in the matrix of the being and becoming of a sociologist or an anthropologist. For example, Marxist sociologist Michael Burawoy's[6] quest for public sociology was simultaneously his biographical, experiential, intellectual and emotional becoming, to the extent that he said, 'One is not born a sociologist, one becomes a sociologist' (Burawoy 2021, 43). It makes sense when read against the backdrop of the decade of the 1960s, which was deemed to be the decade of sociological promises globally as well as in India. A difficult but relevant question across this book is one raised by Burawoy: 'Knowledge for whom? Knowledge for what?' (162). He undertook a journey of becoming, in which his readings and writing, research and teaching, ideological standpoint and practical experiences underwent historically significant shaping and reshaping. There was a great deal of intellectual freedom that enabled him to see things in sociology through the prism of his being and becoming.[7] One wonders why every young scholar of sociology in South Asia cannot!

Likewise, Burawoy's friend and colleague, eminent Marxist sociologist Eric Olin Wright, known for his consistently developed ideas on the 'real utopias'[8] and a manifesto for an anti-capitalist practice in a capitalist society, wrote *Stardust to Stardust: Reflections on Living and Dying*.[9] The end was an invitation for a retrospective journey to understand that even in the Marxist sociology of Eric Wright, a very personal orientation was palpable. At many junctures in such a quest, there arises a peculiar realisation—to be sociological also means to be anti-sociological. Anti-sociological depicts the counterintuitive world. It seeks to broaden the intellectual horizon of a discipline rather than reproducing the tried and tested. Hence, an anti-sociological stance is profusely useful for sociology. Suffice it to say, those who are well-versed in sociology seek to undo the prevalent sociology in a time and space. After all, not worshipping the same god as others does not amount to heresy in a polytheistic religion. One can find a god of their own, irrespective of the hierarchical position of the god. Simply put as creatively ambivalent, this amounts to a dramatic expression, to be sociological or not to be.

The context of provocation is not unfamiliar to most of us in the profession, or vocation in an ideal sense, of sociology in the larger context of the South Asian region. Many of us encounter the question: How is your work sociological? Students face it in front of the community of academics while defending their research proposals or their dissertations and theses. Scholars face it too while proposing research to a funding agency. Or we encounter the barbed wit of our peers along this line. And, in response, we dutifully subscribe to the 'accepted norms' of doing sociology, more often than not. Does this mean we are very sure about what the usage of the term 'sociological' means? By and large, we seem to remain foggy about it while we tend to sail through various testing waters by simply resigning to the dominant expectations. We do tweak our research plans, our analyses, our data, findings and so on in order to become acceptable to our peers (anonymous as well as not-so-anonymous reviewers). But we never dare to ask: what did you exactly mean by sociological? This is so, perhaps, due to the professional hazard, as much as due to our intellectual laziness, so to say. The chapters in the latter part of this book make an attempt to answer this question, discursively, by curating a debate on the category of sociological within the disciplinary framework. Most of the theoretical, philosophical and methodological discussions in sociology aid in this debate and offer various avenues to critically reason with the idea of sociological.

The complexity of the key issue, what is sociological, summons some wild guessing laced with polemics. Perhaps what makes a work sociological are some of the most familiar methods, techniques, theories and concepts. Maybe it also means to suggest that a work has to address some of the necessary indicators of social stratification such as caste, race, tribe or gender. And most importantly, perhaps it also means showing a stakeholder's engagement with the predecessors' works. This is an important aspect leading to the planes of debates on the politics of being sociological. And it is not merely a wild guess as many of us do notice this tendency in our peers who evaluate our works—they straight away turn to the last pages of our writings and check if we have engaged with the 'important works' of 'important predecessors'. If we have, we are likely to earn the epithet of sociological (a loaded prefix) for our works. And if we have not, we are disciplinary outcasts. To illustrate this point from a personal experience, a so-called expert in a committee meant to evaluate the promotion of a teacher in the department of sociology of a top-ranked university asked the candidate—have you read the books I have written? If you have not, how could you be considered a sociologist? Such power play, between those who evaluate and those who are evaluated, can result in a funny line of thinking—my writing, my book, my essay, and my research project. The my-ness is perhaps an Achilles heel in the body of sociology that ought to be unravelled.

This is the provocative context in which it becomes imperative to enquire about the meanings of the usage of the word sociological. What does it mean in terms of course curriculum, pedagogy, predominant themes of research in a particular historical milieu, the theoretical debates on/about sociology, philosophical deliberations on the nature of science, ideological and utopian constitutions of the discipline and its boundaries? By calling for a debate, with reference to the appropriate works (literatures) in existence, it would be possible to arrive at an understanding of the meanings of 'sociological'. But why do so? There are plenty of textbooks which amply serve somewhat similar purpose.

The importance of this book lies in the key argument, a hinge, as it were, for the whole book—sociology, while creating boundaries, is sufficiently porous to allow novel osmosis. The disciplinary boundaries are obstacles for intellectual progress. Yet, there are struggles against the boundaries that lead the discipline to explore new horizons. Indeed, this requires an elaborate debate, which this book is geared towards. But it could suffice to make a benign observation to strengthen the merit of this book. It is not farfetched, as we traverse through the dense terrain of theories and methodological discussions, that sociology is more than what 'sociological' can represent at any time in any context. And the potentials of intellectual promiscuity, of a very fecund kind, rest in the genesis of discipline, be it in Europe or India, the two key cartographic locations mapped in this book. These two locations are heuristically important: one is where the sociology dawns and the other is where the author of this book is located. The historical milieu of socio-political ferments in France and the advent of sociology, or the fraught encounter with the colonial regimes in South Asia and the advent of social anthropology, summon academics to create a discerning discourse. The latter alludes to the possibility of locating the fertile seeds of intellectual promiscuity, which was conducive to the growth of this modern discipline in responding to the historical upheavals in the respective cartographic locations. Perhaps that was the reason how, and why, a physicist such as August Comte, or a priest such as Saint Simon, often appearing as the founders of the discipline in sociology textbooks, assumed titular significance. Perhaps this is the reason why many textbooks don't shy away from getting lost in counting the names of the forerunners of sociology including Rousseau, Burke, etc. Sociology thereby seems to be wooed by suitors from diverse backgrounds, be they conservatives, romantics, radicals, progressive or the Enlightenment rationalists. This indeed underlines the broadness of the nature and scope, which, however, begins to dwindle as the discipline progresses to what many term 'classical' sociology. But did it really dwindle? If that had been the case, Marx would not have been counted, along with Durkheim and Weber as one of the typically known sociological trinity. It is a foregone conclusion that Durkheim and Weber, formally committed to the disciplinary framework of sociology, unlike Marx, contributed to the sharpening and narrowing of the disciplinary focus. But did they not read, in their process, many texts from religions, history, education, and philosophy among other sources? The trinity of Marx, Weber and Durkheim and their engagement with positivism led to the strengthening of the 'scientific' bedrock of sociology. As the chapters in this book elucidate, the story only unravels with more twists and turns. In relation with scientific epistemology, early sociology developed positivism, which turned into a domain of disputes post the Second World War. This was a natural consequence since science had become a bone of contention amongst the philosophers and historians of science. The crying question was whether sociology could be a victim of scientism? The apprehension was correct and therefore we find a severely critical debate on the relationship of sociology with science and arts during and after the Second World War in the history of social sciences. Against such a backdrop, the idea of 'sociological' assumed a more profound type of complexity. This led to exploring whether sociology was science in one sense, but it is primarily an art form. Then again, it also paved the way for an apprehension of the coming crisis in Western sociology in the wake of interpretative, hermeneutic, subjectivist, and, to sum it all, anti-foundational sociology. The latter part of this book unfolds the discursive drama in which crisis of Western sociology and its aftermath delivered new promises. The fixed notion of sociological vanished into thin air in the prolonged aftermath of the Second World War. Against such a tumultuous historical and philosophical backdrop, how is the idea of sociological so rigid in India? This summons enquiries in which the various chapters in this book provide aid, if not conclusive answers.

Time and space, to reiterate, determine the nature of a discipline. This applies to sociology in the context of India too. Social anthropology, in its various avatars in the wake of colonial encounters in India, becomes a background in which sociology in India takes its disciplinary shape fraught with historical and socio-political conditions. Beginning with the call for nationalistic refashioning (indigenising) of an otherwise 'Western' discipline, and an appeal to participate in the nation-building programme in post-independent India—the long trajectory of sociology's becoming in India offers several junctures at which a variety of notions of sociological emerge. But they do not remain linear, simple and ready-for-disciplinary propaganda. Some neologisms may befit this case, such as disciplinary fundamentalism, sociological intolerance, anthropological bigotry etc. These varied notions of sociological helped the discipline to become visible in India's institutional, public and political life (fairly debated by Indian sociologists). But it also had disabling impact on the discipline, or on the professional practitioners of the discipline. Due to these rigid notions of what makes a work sociological, a particular way of seeing became prevalent in India, which was more inclined to take concepts and perspectives, preferences and prejudices for granted. As a result, there was lack of comprehension of the anomalies, of disciplinary rigidity. Hence, sociology in India seemed to have created (rather identified) some of the key 'devils' which many sociologists would not want to die. Keeping the devil alive corresponded with the unquestioned way of seeing. This book seeks to show the devil in the gatekeeping, rigidly defined disciplinary boundaries and intellectual division of labour in the mode of knowledge production in sociology in India. While these issues genuinely warranted attention in sociology and social anthropology in India, they did become too hegemonic to let one think 'out of the box'. Towards the end of this book, there is discussion on the steady standardisation of sociology in India. A standardised way of seeing prevailed in which there was little room for methodological pluralism. Paradoxically, this was in spite of the pioneers of sociology in India who had set the sociological framework for methodologically nuanced understanding of India society. A fixed and rigid understanding of what constitutes sociology in India became the hegemonic methodological devil. While sociologists today identify a devil in painstaking detail, they don't seem to want it to die. Death of the devil will pose an identity crisis to the professionals of sociology. This is where the book reverts to polemics and shows the rigidity of sociology in a particular, predominant, way of seeing. This way of seeing in sociology refuses to play with the idea of reflexivity, even though it may indulge itself in fashionable talks and random mentions.

Sandwiched between the two sets of polemics, the book follows the method of systematic and close reading, of the plethora of available literatures. The discursive framework of the book allows straddling between sociology in India and beyond in order to fathom various notions of sociological. This is, however, within a clearly stated authorial scheme in which the key question, seemingly an innocent one, is to learn—what really sociological means!

Premise of Proposition

The premise upon which the issue of being sociological is critically evaluated in this book draws from various insightful propositions available in sociological literatures. This is indeed eclectic reading of selected materials in accordance with the imperative of arriving at the key idea of being sociological. Keeping this central concern in mind while perusing such books, we get a glimpse of a critique of dominant tendencies, trends and tricks that are involved in being sociological. However, in the same breath, through the perusal, readers may also seek to go beyond and highlight what more could the idea of being sociological mean.

To begin with, there is a trope of crisis in the discipline that hogs attention. Closer home, in India, the enumeration of crises in doing sociology has multiplied strands of thought.[10] To make this debate conducive for this book, it must be read in relation with the idea of being sociological. Crises in sociology are about problematic of *being* sociological. It is possible to evince that there are two registers of crises. One is voiced from a gerontological perspective, such as that of T.N. Madan who laments the lack of attempts to rescue pioneers of sociology and social anthropology from 'disciplinary amnesia'.[11] The point is that the pioneers' contributions are yet to be adequately discussed and understood in contemporary sociology in India. The sociological legacies from history may provide insights for advancement in contemporary practices. And the other is the lament by sociologists about a contemporary crisis in sociology and anthropology in India. The crisis pertains to the decline in the vaguely defined and debatable categories such 'quality' and 'standards'. The lament is about the contemporary sociological practices that is not up to the expected rigour. Words such as quality, standard and rigour appear to be taken-for-granted categories through which the scholars judge the status of the disciplinary practices. Among many others, A.R. Vasavi responded to the crisis and proposed that sociology in India is 'fragmented and diluted, unable to forge an identity of its own, respond to changing times, and generate new schools of theory, methods and perspectives' (2011, 402). Ironically, however, Vasavi coupled her diagnosis with the clarion call of 'pluralizing sociology' in India. To do so will essentially entail a critical debate on the taken-for-granted categories—quality, standard and rigour. Are the two registers of lament interrelated? The question requires sociologists and anthropologists to conduct more reflexive, critical exploration, to which the book returns in the latter chapters.

Moreover, it is also important to place a couple of other issues pertaining to being sociological in India, arising from the history of sociology and thereof conventional practices. One is the perennial preoccupation with and confinement to national territory, though with a red herring, namely, the dichotomy of national and international.[12] A regional framework of sociology and social anthropology which could encourage research on novel thematic issues pertaining to the region, the underexplored socio-cultural contexts, as a whole is almost out of existence. The logic of gatekeeping, governing the nature and scope of the discipline, has been historically present in sociology and social anthropology in India. It has not only cartographically confined professional sociological teaching and research but also strictly defined the thematic areas that are deemed worth sociological scrutiny. One can easily get a sense of the expectations one has to serve while being sociological in the context of India. In an interesting footnote in the published conference proceedings of the International Sociological Association, Partha Nath Mukherji noted:

> In the early sixties when T. K. Oommen and myself (without knowing each other) had selected to work for our PhD on the same gramdan (literally, village gift) *sarvodaya* (literally, welfare – for – all) movements inspired by Gandhian ideology at widely different places, both of us were subject to well-meaning, condescending, good-humored banter by some of our masters in Indian Sociology. Quite clearly, we were doing something interesting, but was it sociology was the question.[13]

It is an abiding tendency amongst sociologists and social anthropologists to raise objections or pass ridicule on new areas of enquiry under the shield of the vague notion of what is sociological and what is not. Moreover, one of the reasons, among several others, behind the lack of encouragement for intellectual adventures undertaking due risk, could be the binaries underpinning discursive frameworks. The binaries are of local and global, without heeding the trans-local or the regional. Furthermore, the binaries refer to the national and the international, without heeding the transnational, the South Asian. This surfaces bluntly, for example, in T.K. Oommen's advocacy for 'internationalization of Sociology' (1991). While it reckons with the delimiting impact of the national rootedness of the discipline, and appeals for creating a non-Western notion of internationalisation, it seldom engages with the regional. Oommen, joining the ilk of nationalist sociologists, only eclectically uses instances from various nation states in the region, and hardly delves into the intricate details of the 'region' or regional sociology. Hetukar Jha (2005, 397) articulated the necessity of sociology in India taking a more serious regional turn, which perhaps was drowned in the dominant din of metropolitan sociologists. Exceptionally, Sujata Patel (2010, 7) proposed a skeletal idea of three-tier configuration of diverse sociological traditions—national, regional and global. This proposition enables for a more nuanced rethinking of disciplinary history, practices, themes of research and intersections of various traditions. In short, Patel enables us to comprehend the role of sociology beyond conventional binaries[14] and thereby opens new possibilities for 'many sociologies' within as well as without national contexts.

The trope of crisis in sociological self-reflection surfaced elsewhere, precisely in the West, much before sociologists in India began talking about it with the turn of millennium in the 2000s. Placed in a different context, of Western sociology, nonetheless, it contributed more than mere crisis mongering. It is one thing to identify a crisis as a monolith; it is yet another thing to find the means to address these. What we see in the existing disciplinary histories from the region is the absence of the latter. Hence, Alvin Gouldner and his propositions still hold relevance in this part of the world as well. A critical and sought-after thinker in the 1970s, Gouldner evoked the idea of crisis to pave the way for novel possibilities for a 'new sociology' that he invariably deemed to be 'sociology of sociology' and 'reflexive sociology'. What he had in mind was sociology with radicalism, thus enabling it to be self-reflective. It was an elaborate discussion on sociology's ability to take a look at itself, and likewise the ability of sociologists to critically encounter the self-reflection in the analytical mirror. In this wake,

> the sociologists' task today is not only to see people as they see themselves, nor to see themselves as others see them; it is also to see themselves as they see other people. What it needs is a new and heightened self-awareness among sociologists, which would lead them to ask the same kind of questions about themselves as they do about taxicab drivers or doctors, and to answer them in the same ways. (1970, 25)

Gouldner could underline a peculiarity in being sociological. This was owed to methodological dualism based on 'feared vulnerability of the scholar's self' (496). Being sociological is determined by, to begin with, this fear that one's personal passions, including emotions such as disgust, pity, anger, outrage, etc., will interrupt the public performances of being a sociologist. Second, methodological dualism, the evident way of coping with the fear of vulnerability, characterises being sociological. In implication, this dualism is about a perpetual dilemma: to be sociological or not, to be a professional sociologist or a person of passion, to be or not to be, and so on so forth. This dualism is reflected in most sociological preoccupations. Gouldner observes,

> Methodological Dualism entails a fantasy of the sociologist's God-like invisibility and of his Olympian power to influence – or not influence – those around him, as he pleases. In contrast, the Methodological Monism of a Reflexive Sociology believes that sociologists are really only mortal, that they inevitably change others and are changed by them; and that knowing and changing are distinguishable but not separable processes. (497)[15]

This complicates the imagination of being sociological. On one hand, it is about operating with methodological dualism in order to shy away from what one could be, that is, a vulnerable ego. And on the other hand, it ought to be about pursuing methodological monism in which the gap between the seeker of knowledge and subject is perpetually bridged. Gouldner's critical comprehension and persuasion in the 1970s had a precursor in the decade of 1960s, in the sociology of C. Wright Mills, whose classical work opened up a great deal of possibilities of rethinking sociology. Gitlin (2000, 229) referred to him as a 'guiding knight of radicalism' for many in the 1960s, one who offered many ruptures in the conventional way of seeing in the sociological practices. The word imagination became an intimately nuanced companion in the sociology of Mills unlike its relative absence in the classical sociology. A key was the relation between biographical and historical, personal and public, that characterised the idea of sociological imagination. And it is premised upon a radical critique of the prevalent modes of 'being sociological', particularly with reference to the American scenario relevant in our part of the hemisphere too. What was it about being sociological that troubled Mills? Being sociological meant subscribing to what the field of sociology solicited. It meant, Mills observed, following 'a set of bureaucratic techniques which inhibit social inquiry by methodological pretensions, which congest such work by obscurantist conceptions, or which trivialise it by concern with minor problems unconnected with publicly relevant issues' (1959, 20).

Along these lines, Mills sounds a crisis in social studies due to the inhibitions, obscurities and trivialities that dominate what social scientists do. Interestingly enough, Mills is not a crisis monger, which many could be elsewhere.[16] He sets a mission to rescue us from what he calls 'pale sociology'.[17] The best manifesto of the mission is in the appendix of the book, *The Sociological Imagination*, titled 'On Intellectual Craftsmanship'.

It presents to us a list of wishful thinking, or a way to succeed in materialising the promises of sociology. The idea of being sociological is directly discussed in relation with intellectual craftsmanship adopted by sociologists in particular and social scientists in general. Being sociological, through a craft, involves a relation between scholarship and personal lives of the scholars. It emphasises the category of experience. Mills delivered a relevant, insightful proposition:

> Scholarship is a choice of how to live as well as a choice of career; whether he knows it or not, the intellectual workman forms his own self as he works toward the perfection of his craft; to realise his own potentialities, and any opportunities that come his way, he constructs a character which has as its core the qualities of the good workman. (2000, 196)

To make the proposition more convenient for readers, Mills explained the imperative further. It demands that sociologists use their life experience in their intellectual work. The craftsmanship entails a relationship between the personhood of the sociologists and the object of enquiry. This too refers to what it could mean to be sociological, wherein individual experience of the scholar qua sociologist comes in the shaping of scholarship, the produce. To give more concrete body to his proposition, Mills discussed the imperative of a personal diary, a private journal, to capture 'fringe thoughts' stemming from the experiences of everyday life, 'snatches of conversations overheard on the street, or for that matter, dreams'.[18] To be sociological, it is crucial to treasure the smallest of experiences, which could be written down, systematically connected with various strands of thoughts in the private writings. It indeed requires 'self-reflective habit', not necessarily through presentations at conferences or prestigious fellowships at highly ranked universities. It certainly does not come from the habit of writing a finished piece, which can garner funding from various agencies. About such practices, Mills has a sense of derision mixed with acceptance of inevitable. As he says:

> it is bound in some degree to be salesmanship, and, given prevailing expectations, very likely to result in painstaking pretensions; the project is likely to be 'presented', rounded out in some arbitrary manner long before it ought to be; it is often a contrived thing, aimed at getting the money for ulterior purposes, however valuable, as well as for the research presented.[19]

While Mills is suggesting the ways forward, he tends to elucidate the prevalent too. It is possible, on the one hand, to adopt a self-reflective habit and write to capture experiences that could pave the way towards advancement. On the other, however, there is a mode of being sociological, unreflective about the writing preferences, as teaching programmes. The community of peers would begin to preserve disciplinary status quo, including the list of themes that ought to be researched into and areas be taught in teaching programs. Against such a practice, Mills expected a free intellectual community and association of scholars without subservience to the monolithic array of problems. He observed

> Three kinds of interludes—on problem, methods, theory—ought to come out of the work of social scientists, and lead into it again; they should be shaped by work-in-progress and to some extent guide that work. It is for such interludes that a professional association finds its intellectual reason for being.[20]

Are there such formal, professional associations to promote works in progress that could depart from the familiar list of thematic of enquiries in research work or teaching programmes? How much of our work dwells upon our personal experiences that summon a radical departure from the comfortable notions of being sociological? In other words, how much risk is undertaken, in the three areas of interludes that Mills identified above—in a chosen research problem, method, and theories? Our known ways of being sociological makes us merely technicians. And sociological imagination, an indispensable feature of being sociological, requires us to be more artist than technician. As Mills put it:

> The sociological imagination, I remind you, in considerable part consists of the capacity to shift from one perspective to another, and in the process to build up an adequate view of a total society and of its components. It is this imagination, of course, that sets off the social scientists from the mere technician.[21]

Unlike a technician's skill, the sociological imagination entails a playfulness of the mind as well as a fierce drive to make sense of the world. A technician is too precisely trained in what is already known. The sociological imagination enables one to play with the scholar's own vague images and notions. It is through such forms and notions that original ideas emerge. Clearly, then, the experiences of a sociologist assume greater significance. It translates the idea of being sociological into being a playful artist, ever hungry for words, phrases, hammering on concepts, acknowledging new problems and responding to the imperative of methodological innovations.[22] In this context, it makes sense to revisit another classical work, Robert Nisbet's *Sociology*, arguably, an art form.[23]

Nisbet's intervention is a logical accompaniment of the above-discussed 'crisis in Western sociology'. It seems equally relevant in the context of South Asia. Bolstering a case for 'sociology as an art form', Nisbet suggested:

> How alike are the sociologist and artist's efforts to endow subject matter with what Herbert Read, the art historian and critic, has called 'the illusion of motion'. No mean esthetic skill is involved in Marx's depiction of capitalism as a structure in motion, in Tocqueville's rendering of equality as a dynamic process, or Weber's of rationalization. (1976, 7–8)

Nisbet put together Tocqueville, Marx, Weber and the other sociologists along with Burke, Blake, Carlyle, Balzac underlining the aesthetic impetus in their thought systems. There is an essential unity of art and science, no matter how eclipsed it may seem in the wake of politics that separates the two. Presenting a prophylaxis against scientism, to emphasise the unity of science and art, Nisbet suggests:

> when Kepler wrote, 'the roads by which men arrive at their insights into celestial matters seem to me almost as worthy of wonder as those matters themselves', it would never have occurred to him that there was any significant difference between what he, the theologian, the philosopher, and the artist were engaged in. (4–5)

In his work, Nisbet enlisted a number of common thematic ideas in social sciences in the nineteenth century, such as community, masses, power, development, progress, conflict, egalitarianism, anomie, alienation and disorganisation. He also suggested that there are identical themes in the world of art—painting, literature, even music. Social scientists have benefitted from their engagement with works of art and in comprehending thematic realities. To make it more explicit, Nisbet surmised:

> Scientists Marx, Weber, Durkheim, and Simmel were without question. But they were also artists, and had they not been artists, had they contented themselves with demonstrating solely what had been arrived at through aseptic problem design, through meticulous verification, and through constructions of theory which pass muster in a graduate course in methodology of sociology today, the entire world of thought would be much poorer. (7)

Turning geopolitically inwards, the sociological inclination towards art was not absent in sociology in South Asia, though its influence has been historically muted and marginalised. It is relevant to briefly allude to the extensive deliberations of Radhakamal Mukerjee,[24] one of the pioneering thinkers setting the temperament of sociology in India. It is curious to note that Mukerjee, mostly noted for presenting a sociological challenge to the predominance of positivism of economics, wrote a number of well-known essays on the issue of art and its relation to society, civilisation, religion and polity. One of the essays, titled 'The Meaning and Evolution of Art in Society' (1945), published in the *American Sociological Review*, was accompanied by an editorial note:

> The Editors think that American sociologists will be interested in the contemporary thinking of an eminent Indian sociologist in the eventful year of 1945. (496)

It was evident that the world at large was curious about an Indian sociologist's venture into the domain of art. Perhaps, it reflected the uncanny potentials and width of being sociological in India during the early days. And that attention perhaps came with the realisation that Western sociology hardly made serious engagement with art, then. Indeed, it was only a couple of decades later that the 'crisis in western sociology' referred to above become pronounced. However, before it was pronounced, Mukerjee in India had articulated:

> Art is at once a social product and an established means of social control.... Modern sociologists should now vindicate the importance of this fertile field—the study of art forms as the unchecked efflorescence and clarified utterance of culture, as its principal measure, directive force as well as means of control. (496–497)

Let's now take a heuristic jump cut to the contemporary, and ask: 'then what happened?' Could sociology in India persist with its engagement with arts? Or for that matter, could sociologists persist with the ability to bring forth novel issues and ways of seeing in sociology? Rather than attempting to answer such difficult questions, it is easier to quickly mention a curious development on the contemporary discursive trope in India. Many years after Gouldner's announcement of crisis in Western sociology, some sociologists in India began to pronounce their own 'crises'.[25] This notion of crises was mostly characterised by the motif of 'lament' on the allegedly deplorable condition of teaching, research and writing in sociology in India. This was more succinctly underlined in Vasavi's proposition that sociology in India is 'fragmented and diluted, unable to forge an identity of its own, respond to changing times, and generate new schools of theory, methods and perspectives' (2011, 402). Did the announcement of such crises lead to a call for a 'new sociology', as happened when Gouldner made a similar proclamation? Or did it augur any other optimistic consequence of the realisation of the crises? Perhaps the answer lies in the course of time that is yet to come rather in the times that have passed. But then, there is a curious observation to share, which unfortunately speaks of an ongoing separation of art and sociology in India. Take, for example, some attempts by sociologists to recount the stories of pioneers in this field. Madan (2003, 15) has called it, while reproducing selected works of Radhakamal Mukerjee, an attempt to rescue pioneers from 'disciplinary amnesia'. Curiously enough, however, it hardly takes note of Mukerjee's sustained engagement with the artefacts of cultural articulations. Does it mean there has been a strategy to keep the engagements with the arts and other civilisational entities by some pioneers away from the sociological framework when recounting the contributions of these pioneers? This requires further investigation that is beyond the purview of the subject of this book. Suffice to say that it underlines the narrowing down of sociology in the name of professionalisation that diminishes a creative engagement with the methodological concerns and the idea of sociological.

To deduce from the foregoing, we tend to vacillate between the legitimacy of self-experiential–methodological orientation and the cancellation of self in our imagination of being sociological. This spells out what kind of thematic issues, research questions and methodological orientation could make us sociological. We notice the imperative of engaging with the category of experience on one hand, and a strong doubt about experiences on the other. The dilemma persists when we return to the positivist development in classical sociology. And the post-positivist sociological debates on the ways of seeing are indeed an array of responses to this dilemma, as subsequent chapters in this book discuss. If sociology in India suffers this methodological dilemma, it is not without reason and background. But the lamentable part is that there is seldom an effort to move towards a post-dilemma development in sociological discussion on methodology. And this calls for a strong polemic enabling the delivery of a dramatic soliloquy—to be sociological or not to be. To be extraordinary or ordinary while doing sociology. To adopt this or that way of seeing in order to be sociological. And so on so forth. Beyond delimiting dilemmas, there is a creative ambivalence.

The Way Ahead: Ambivalence about Being Sociological

The intellectual history of sociology and social anthropology in India shows a curious case of ambivalence towards the idea of being sociological. As soon as the teaching and learning, research and writing, are rid of this creative ambivalence, the growth of the disciplinary scholarship hits a vantage point from where it becomes nearly impossible to ask what it means to be sociological. Sociological pursuits in India enables a debate on the quest of the local with an eye at the universal, an opportunity to unearth socio-cultural and political particularities while seeking to make sense of the generalisable principles of the modern meta-narratives. The quest of indigenisation of social sciences, starting with the debate in the historically significant journal *Contributions to Indian Sociology*,[26] continues perhaps even now as we seek for understanding the discipline in regional framework of South Asia.[27]

This ambivalent attitude[28] provided creative possibilities in doing sociology. It corresponded with an ambivalent relationship between tradition and modernity, body of thoughts rooted in contexts and body of theories emerging from contexts far away. It was a relationship of ambivalence, to be precise, between traditions in India and the field of modern enquiries called sociology and social anthropology. At the cusp of such ambivalence, a master thinker such as D.P. Mukerji engaged with ifs and buts of sociological–methodological inclination to 'scientific method'. He ruminated:

> A pure science has been built up by intellect, by eschewing the concrete in the shape of practices and traditions, ethics, history, and lastly, the subjective attitude. But all these are living factors, stern realities, and facts as much as the so-called scientific facts. They rebel, not alone for being eliminated, but also for being tyrannized over in turn by intellect, which serves its function by reducing everything to a mechanism—the like producing the like. (2004, 12)

The selectivity of scientific reason leaves behind philosophy and religion, causing an opposition of humanities and sciences. The two wings of university buildings accommodate these opposite disciplines, though the courses of study may have the same objective. This is a situation of despair that summons, as Mukerji suggested, a synthesis of objective and subjective in order to make sense of social relations. A rationalist perspective may discard not-so-rationalist, subjectivist and relativist accounts of the social realities. And yet the partial truths of the lesser social scientists may have better appeal, as Mukerji noted:

> A scientific historian marshalling an array of facts cannot produce a book half so enjoyable as that of a nationalist historian however unscientifically partial he may be. For his vision of his country as a person and his identification with it is clearer and closer, and as such his history becomes readable. A gardener in his garden is a more delightful man than the botanist in his laboratory, he will sing, but the other will not. (43)

The critical engagement with the science question in sociology thus began quite early in India. This was about the idea of sociological, which delved upon the scientific methodological temperament while being sufficiently sceptical about it. Wrestling the disciplinary hegemony of economics, in order to develop a theory of institution and values, Radhakamal Mukerjee underlined a methodological imperative for sociology. It was about the relationship of science and philosophy in a sociological way of seeing so that it can apprehend a significant aspect of society. This significant aspect is, as Mukerjee underlined, 'the subjective and invisible one, which is usually taken for granted, and which underlies all human relationships, namely values, ideals, and norms that define, maintain, and regulate the visible social structure and interaction, give them cohesion and stability so that they cross the boundaries of time and space' (2003, 122).

If there is a scientific way of seeing in sociology, there ought to be normative, socio-psychological and philosophical ways too. Radhakamal Mukerjee envisaged sociology venturing into the 'ensemble of instincts and impulses' that can divulge the cultural values integral to economic institutions and behaviour. There are many such instances of methodological interrogations, systematic as well as polemical, in the annals of sociology that solicit our attention in order to debate the possibilities with methodological orientation. Maintaining a spirit, conducive for sociological as well as generic intellectual progress, D.P. Mukerji advocated 'derivative minds', 'eccentricities', and 'non-expertise' in the intellectual pursuits of university academia. This advocacy is indeed helpful in anticipating a qualitatively different kind of sociological-qua-intellectual quest. Mukerji says:

> It appears that some eccentricities will have to be cultivated, some non-expertise and non-uniformities fostered, some dangerous thoughts to be taught, a few reckless adventures undertaken, and some syntheses of knowledge attempted. The university should be the arena of a few of these forays into the unknown. At present, unfortunately, they are not. (2003, 209)

The sociologists in India debated on the peculiarity of being sociological, with the issue, 'For a Sociology of India' in the 1950s.[29] The debate pivoted on the complementarity of Indology and sociology and social anthropology in India. It meant to acknowledge and endeavour to develop the lexicon of the local–contextual–textual cognitive categories to be employed in sociological studies in the country. But it was also about making the ethnographic practices more nuanced following the methodological proposition owed to the tradition engendered by *L'Année Sociologique*, the journal founded by Emile Durkheim in 1896 along with Marcel Mauss. Nevertheless, the central question—whether there can be sociology of India with the contextual cognitive categories—triggered intellectual unrest[30] and an iota of sarcasm.[31] The dust may, or may not, have settled but one ought to recall this instance in order to make note of the methodological adventures in the making of sociological in India, a country where mythology and history undercut each other rather neatly. The intellectual fermentations, reflected in debates and discourses,[32] was, however, fraught with academic narcissism and the dominance of an elite minority. Dhanagre (2014, 9) noted the scholastic presence of sociology programmes, and in the same breath, lamented the absence of a strong epistemic community that could work on legacy of the pioneers of sociology and rigour in teaching–learning as well as in research and writing. Likewise, in a significant Foreword to a collection of the writings of Dhanagre, Partha Nath Mukherji[33] wondered why there could never be a culture of critical debate among the celebrated scholars of sociology in India. For example, there was one such exceptional debate between Ramkrishna Mukherjee and M.N. Srinivas on the issue of method in postcolonial India. Ramkrishna Mukherjee was a proponent of Marxist methodology and M.N. Srinivas advocated structural functionalism. Both opponents in the debate, however, viewed methodology, theories and concepts as tools in the service of development. Such examples are few and far between. He observed with due wit and sarcasm:

> Indian sociologists have not been able to measure up with the mature culture of debates and discourses that have stimulated and enriched social science knowledge production in the West. Both Srinivas and Ramkrishna shy away from even addressing each other directly. It is a far cry, for instance, from the confrontation between Karl Popper and Theodor Adorno. (2014, xx)

While this is so amongst sociologists, there is an exceptional instance of conversation between Gopal Guru and Sundar Sarukkai (2012, 2019) unravelling the intricacies of sensorial experience of the social in everyday life that makes one optimistic. This strengthens the reasons to be ambivalent about being sociological so that one could benefit from the debates that bring about a coming together of philosophical and sociological, epistemological and ontological inter alia.

This brief realisation calls for a more textually informed reasoning with the possibilities in the field of methodology. The book seeks to do so through eight chapters, which have been divided into metaphorical subsections, namely, dawn, forenoon and afternoon, dusk. By so doing the book attempts to make a modest attempt to retrieve the creative ambivalence, in sociology in particular and social sciences in general. The metaphorical entitling of subsections means nothing more than enticing readers to go beyond the text, beyond ideas as well. This book, to reiterate a stylistic point mentioned at the outset, presents some of the most significant selections of materials that constitute methodological discussions. Chapters 2 and 3 unravel scientific epistemology inclusive of methods laced with philosophical deliberations, followed by the idea of 'sociology before sociology' that reveals the importance of precursors. The idea is to modestly show a genealogy of way of seeing in classical sociology known as positivism, imbued with inherent ambivalence. There is a good deal of solace in the ambivalent notion of sociological in classical sociological thinking in Chapter 4. However, critical debates on the nature and scope of science, followed by disputes with positivism, in Chapter 5, leads the way to epistemological departures. Toying with an idea of post-positivism in Chapter 6, the book attempts to take the bull by the horn, and complicate the notion of experience, which already had a trajectory as elucidated in the previous chapters since the advent of scientific epistemology and its various cognates in social sciences. Experience appears in various hues in the discursive trajectory emanating from the history and philosophy of science. Reconnecting the preceding chapters, Chapter 6 features a discussion that brings in ways of seeing in sociology through the lens of gender and subaltern, Dalit and caste. Chapter 7 aims to aid in understanding the complexity of experience, the challenges of alleged relativism, and possible resolves in reflexivity. A return to the issue of reflexivity becomes imperative in order to offer the ways of sorting out intrigue-ridden ways of seeing in sociology. The intrigue of experience that bemused philosophers and bothered sociologists in India divulges in a polemic in Chapter 8. The tone of lament, though dramatically foregrounded, is not at the price of the promises. Chapter 9 is an anxious epilogue, narrating a phenomenological experience of doing sociology, in which personal–emotional and public–professional concerns meet.

In various chapters, the book enjoins upon the readership a responsibility to think of the contextual peculiarity while dealing with pure textual materials. After all, it is about ways of seeing in sociology, and seeing is as subjectively individual as objectively general. Needless to say, there are serious limitations which will leave the readership wanting more analytical debates. For example, there was a consciously felt need, which is put to rest, to deal with the complications of being sociological in dealing with sensory performative practices. It was also necessary to do a systematic analysis of the resources, which various philosophers including B.K. Matilal or J.N. Mohanty engaged with. And there is a corpus of literature on thoughts emanating from the religious canons and treatises, including Islamic and Buddhist thoughts that merit attention in the methodological explorations in sociology. Such resources may add to the exercise of developing more nuances in ways of being sociological in the region of South Asia. There are a number of possibilities left open for future explorations. It is also done, in the spirit of a teacher, to allow the readers to go beyond this, that or any other book.

References

Banks, M. *Visual Methods in Social Research*. London: Sage, 2001.

Banks, M., and Howard Morphy (eds). *Rethinking Visual Anthropology*. New Haven: Yale University Press, 1997.

Banks, M., and J. Ruby (eds). *Made to be Seen: Perspectives on the History of Visual Anthropology*. Chicago: Chicago University Press, 2011.

Berger, John. *Ways of Seeing*. London: British Broadcasting Corporation and Penguin Books, 1972.

Bottomore, T.B. 'Sociology in India', *British Journal of Sociology* 13 (1962): 98–106.

Burawoy, Michael. *Public Sociology*. Cambridge: Polity Press, 2021.

Das, Veena. 'Sociological Research in India—The State of Crisis', *Economic and Political Weekly* 28, no. 23 (1993): 1159–1161.

Denzin, Norman K. 'Presidential Address on "Sociological Imagination Revisited"', *The Sociological Quarterly* 31, no. 1 (1990): 1–22.

Deshpande, Satish. 'Crisis in Sociology: A Tired Discipline', *Economic and Political Weekly* 29, no. 10 (1994): 575–576.

Dhanagre, D.N. *The Writings of D. N. Dhanagre: The Missing Tradition: Debates and Discourses in Indian Sociology*. Delhi: Orient Blackswan, 2014.

Gitlin, Todd. 'Afterword'. In *The Sociological Imagination*, edited by C.W. Mills, 229–40. New York: Oxford University Press, 2000.

Gouldner, A. *The Coming Crisis in Western Sociology*. New York: Basic Books, 1970.

Guru, Gopal, and Sundar Sarukkai. *The Cracked Mirror: An Indian Debate on Experience and Theory*. New Delhi: Oxford University Press, 2012.

———. *Experience, Caste, and the Everyday Social*. New Delhi: Oxford University Press, 2019.

Jha, Hetukar. 'Indian Sociology in Crisis: The Need for Regional Orientation', *Sociological Bulletin* 54, no. 3 (2005): 396–411.

Madan, T.N. (ed.). *Sociology at the University of Lucknow: The First Half Century, 1921–1975*. New Delhi: Oxford University Press, 2003.

———. *Sociological Traditions: Methods and Perspectives in the Sociology of India*. Delhi: Sage, 2011.

Mills, C.W. *The Sociological Imagination*. New York: Oxford University Press, 2000 (1959).

Mukerjee, R. 'The Meaning and Evolution of Art in Society', *American Sociological Review* 10, no. 4 (1945): 496–503.

———. 'Sociology as Science and as Philosophy'. In *Sociology at the University of Lucknow: The First Half Century, 1921–1975*, edited by T.N. Madan, 121–141. New Delhi: Oxford University Press, 2003.

Mukerji, D.P. 'The Intellectuals in India'. In *Sociology at the University of Lucknow: The First Half Century, 1921–1975*, edited by T.N. Madan, 197–211. New Delhi: Oxford University Press, 2003.

———. *Personality and the Social Sciences*. Delhi: Rupa & Co., 2004.

Mukherji, Partha Nath, and Chandan Sengupta (eds). *Indigeneity and Universality in Social Science: A South Asian Response*. Delhi: Sage, 2004.

Mukherji, Partha Nath. 'Foreword'. In *The Writings of D. N. Dhanagre: The Missing Tradition: Debates and Discourses in Indian Sociology*, edited by D.N. Dhangare, xi–xx. Delhi: Orient Blackswan, 2014.

Nisbet, R. *Sociology as an Art Form*. London: Oxford University Press, 1976.

Obeyesekere, Gananath. 'The Great Tradition and the Little in the Perspective of Sinhalese Buddhism', *Journal of Asian Studies* 22, no. 2 (1963): 139–153. Available at doi: https://doi.org/10.2307/2050008.

Patel, S. 'Beyond Binaries: A Case for Self-Reflexive Sociologies', *Current Sociology* 54, no. 3 (2006): 381–395. Available at https://doi.org/10.1177/0011392106063187.

———. (ed.). *The ISA Handbook of Diverse Sociological Traditions*. London: Sage, 2010.

———. 'Toward Internationalism: Beyond Colonial and Nationalist Sociologies'. In *Theories about and Strategies against Hegemonic Social Sciences*, edited by M. Kuhn and S. Yazawa, 119–132. Tokyo: Center for Global Studies, Seijo University, 2013.

Pathak, Avijit. *Indian Modernity: Contradiction, Paradoxes and Possibilities*. Delhi: Akaar, 2015.

Pathak, Dev Nath (ed.). *Intersections in Sociology, Art and Art History: A Conversation with Parul Dave-Mukherji*. Delhi: Aakar and Department of Sociology, South Asian University, 2016.

———. *Another South Asia!* Delhi: Primus, 2018.

———. *In Defence of the Ordinary: Everyday Awakenings*. Delhi: Bloomsbury, 2021.

Pathak, Dev Nath (ed.). *Seeing South Asia: Visuals Beyond Borders*. Delhi: Routledge, 2022.

———. 'Being and Becoming (of/with) Burawoy: An Anxious Apprehension of Public Sociology in South Asia', *International Sociology Reviews* 37, no. 5 (2022): 557–568. Available at ps://doi.org/10.1177/02685809221138018.

Raju, Raghuram. *Philosophy and India: Ancestors, Outsiders, and Predecessors.* Delhi: Oxford University Press, 2013.

Thakur, Manish. *The Quest for Indian Sociology: Radhakamal Mukerjee and Our Times*. Shimla: Indian Institute of Advanced Studies, 2015.

Vasavi, A.R. 'Pluralising the Sociology of India'. In *Contributions to Indian Sociology* 45, no. 3 (2011): 399–426.

Wright, E.O. *Envisioning Real Utopias*. London: Verso, 2010.

———. *Stardust to Stardust: Reflections on Living and Dying*. Chicago: Haymarket Books, 2020.

2

PERSISTENT PRECURSORS: A PHILOSOPHICAL-SCIENTIFIC BACKDROP

The modern philosophy of science, and consequent scientific epistemology, had an explicit relationship with faith, with Christianity. An authority that was a bridge between physics and metaphysics, pertains to modern science. The authority of science and scientific rationality was to guide and regulate various stakeholders. This chapter presents a discussion on the Enlightenment philosophy, through the works of the philosophers known as encyclopaedists that nourished science and scientific rationality. Known as a significant movement in the history of modern philosophy, the Enlightenment was a turf on which propositions about the relation of experience and knowledge unfolded. What version of experience was upheld, and whose experience was it? What to know and how were among some of the central questions. Which knowledge is credible and which is not in the scientific epistemology was abiding too. Some of these questions are at the core of the idea of sociological that has been flagged in the previous chapter. The ways of seeing in sociology essentially emanate from scientific epistemology. We will return to these questions in the latter chapters to understand how a particular variety of being sociological acquired centre stage in relation to the philosophical nuggets owed to the Enlightenment age. How positivism, one of the most dominant methodological ways of seeing, was articulated in engagement with the philosophical notions of the Enlightenment. This chapter, however, shall unspool the philosophical background to being sociological, a methodological way of seeing. The attempt is to show how the age of Enlightenment interacted with a variety of historical factors and thus shaped scientific epistemology, though not without an inherent intrigue.

Articulated in various modes, this intrigue finds an echo in a poem by a grandmother for a grandchild who was destined to become an eminent rational philosopher.

> O science metaphysical,
> And very, very quizzical,
> You only make this maze of life the mazier;
> For boasting to illuminate

Such riddles as Will and Fate
You muddle them to hazier and hazier …
You know no more than I
What is laughter, tear or sigh,
Or love, or hate, or anger or compassion;
Metaphysics then adieu,
Without you, I can do
And I think you'll very soon be out of fashion.[1]

Lady Russell, also known as Lady John Russell and Countess Russell, was the wife of John Russell, the prime minister of the United Kingdom, during the reign of Queen Victoria. An occasional poet, grandmother and guardian of Bertrand Russell, she penned this intriguing poem, an exposition fraught with argument and counter-argument, in 1897. Perhaps, the apprehension and accomplishments of modern science articulated in this simple poem sums up what is going to unfold in this chapter. This poem reveals the dilemma about the strides of modern science—whether one can or cannot celebrate the scientific. This dilemma acquires intellectual longevity in the critical engagement with the philosophical-scientific trajectory of thoughts among the precursors for a sociological way of seeing in the twentieth-century social sciences too. We shall get to read more about the precursors and their dilemmas in the latter part of the chapter. Suffice it to say, in the beginning, the philosophical thoughts underlined a triumph as it led, or so is claimed, the Platonic cavemen to the light of truth. Just as it was for Plato, the cavemen gradually broke free from the chains of ignorance and turned to the light, the men of science sought freedom and rationality. However, knowledge was further classified in science. As rational as it could be, Bertrand Russell was not unaware of it. Hence, he winsomely proposed with child-like simplicity:

> There are two sorts of knowledge: knowledge of things, and knowledge of truths. We shall be concerned exclusively with knowledge of things … though it would be harsh to assume that human beings ever, in fact, have acquaintance with things without at the same time knowing some truth about them. (2003, 191)

That itself meant that things of scientific reasoning usually separated from the knowledge of truth are perhaps not so separable. We know about something since we are acquainted; but in the same vein, we also want to know the truth about it, something that is more than mere acquaintance. This meant that I knew my body since I was adequately familiar with it by now, but I am irresistibly curious about something about my body that is beyond the known. Science comes with a discourse on epistemology, methods and techniques inter alia. It comes with an attitude, common sense and worldview as well. While scientific practices and outcomes would be deemed, as Russell says, knowledge of things, it is hard to separate from it the elements which may arise from the knowledge of truth, epistemological discourses. Much later, there appeared a dominant view that science is an epistemological perspective independent of human belief. This was scientific realism, a bone of contention amongst the historians and sociologists, about which Nagel (1987, 8) critically said, it's the view from nowhere! Such a scientific realism ignores the humane and social foundation of science. There have been manifold efforts to locate the scientific view *somewhere*, as well as *elsewhere*. *Somewhere* alludes to the contexts where modern science rises through systematic philosophical reflections, development of procedures, and theories. And *elsewhere* underlines all those domains which appear spurious from the vantage point of scientific realism that results in Nagel's phrase—a view from nowhere. Someone like Putnam (1987, 1990) laboured to convince us about the various layers of *elsewhere* that render science as a contextual and relational endeavour. Scientific realism puts human actors as seekers of knowledge in the centre; however, it does not allow us to see the relationship between the knower and the object of knowledge. It is a kind of scientific-qua-metaphysical realism that reduces causation into a dehumanised phenomenon. Ironically, the seeker of knowledge, a human, is in the centre while the human relationships with knowledge are marginalised. The causation in scientific realism was a more logical and philosophical formulation than a humanised instance. Putnam underlines the human relational aspects of causation to serve us twofold aspects of the truth, the logical causation of things and the experience of humans. This is Putnam's internalism, as it spells out the internal character of the epistemic object and the inherent process of scientific view. One aspect pertains to fact, the epistemic, while the other to conventionality, the seemingly non-epistemic. Both could come together in a scientific view, making the knowledge contextual and relational. This enables us to think of scientific epistemology from *elsewhere*, as the contextual science, to which this chapter returns in the latter part. In the following pages, we shall notice a historical dimension of science's *elsewhere* before we plunge into what could be termed scientific epistemology.

Following Russel then, it becomes significant to note the role of the knowledge of thing and knowledge of truth in science. It hence becomes imperative to read a large pool of contributions from across the globe, including Aryabhatta, Copernicus, Galileo, Kepler, Newton, J.C. Bose, Ramanujan, Einstein as well as the very recent Hawking.

This is curious that the names from across historical epochs have been pronounced in a single sentence. For, most of the time, the history of modern science tends to show the advent of science with what has been famously known as the 'Copernican Revolution', though with a pinch of salt.[2] The Copernican Revolution refers to the shift in astronomy from the Christian geocentric way of seeing the universe in which Earth was the centre. The Polish astronomer Nicolaus Copernicus propounded a heliocentric model in which the sun was central. This was marked as a revolutionary moment in scientific thinking in the sixteenth century. No wonder, the historian of science Thomas Kuhn forcefully showed that the Copernican Revolution brought about a watershed moment in the history of science. But he also underlined that Ptolemaic astronomy was mature enough to ensure progress in science.[3] This was with a rider, as Kuhn noticed, Ptolemaic astronomy dwelt upon a philosophical premise fraught with 'blinders' and 'entanglement', and hence could not decentre the earth (1957, 86–90). Despite the importance of the Copernican Revolution, one cannot perhaps dismiss the role of pre-Copernican contributions. For example, even though Aristotle, the Greek philosopher in the fourth century BC, did not establish a tradition of biology, there is a strong argument to suggest that Aristotelian biology was adequately scientific. Aristotle is hitherto hailed as the father of biology due to his contribution to the biological knowledge of the origin of species and mammals. Likewise, how can one ignore another Greek mathematician Archimedes for his immensely valuable contribution to mathematics, which was recognised as science by the late sixteenth century? His calculation in 250 BC of the value of 'pi', the ratio of a circle's circumference and its diameter, is hitherto used in mathematics. Besides, his theory of hydrostatics, the loss of the body's weight immersed in liquid, is still a common lesson in physics. Such examples from the pre-Copernican history of science lead us to take the categorical celebration of the Copernican Revolution with due scepticism. Instead, there is a thesis to support that medieval philosophy was a precondition for modern science. Moreover, many of the scientific problems emerged from the philosophy and common sense of the time. However, it was typically in modern science that,

> procedures for resolving those problems were new, and the intellectual tools they constructed to facilitate those procedures were drawn not from philosophy but from astronomy and law. No medieval philosopher had a view of natural science as making progress, and no medieval natural philosopher was engaged in research, if we understand that to mean the gathering of relevant new information. (Wootton 2016, 575)

One cannot, however, entirely dismiss the discursive, philosophical backdrop of modern science even though one distinguishes it from the predecessors' traditions of knowing in the pre-Copernican time. This will surface when we discuss some of the individual philosophers in the latter part of this essay. The decentring activity assumed different hues when modern science arrived in South Asia, with its stress on methods, procedures, and collection of 'relevant information' in research.

Al-Biruni's *Tarikh-i-Hind*, which dates back to the first millennium AD, is read as the earliest account of the scientific and technical acumen available in India. In continuity with the ancient scientific temperament, there appears to be modern science in colonial India, where romantic inclinations did not disappear. A critical reading of modern sciences in India, indigenous in origin and nature, gives a sense of romantic and scientific inclinations intertwined (Raina 2003, 16). But modern science in the colonies of the empire comes with a power play between the coloniser and the colonised. For in the strides of modern science many local epistemologies of scientific significance, indigenous to the colonised, were brushed aside as non-scientific. During the British rule, colonial science arrived in India with a mission to educate the natives, of benighted heathen, about the inadequacy of precolonial quests of science.[4] The objective was to prove that the knowledge of the natives was flawed and it was in need of adequate, qua modern, scientific training. This was an intellectual power game between the colonised and the coloniser in which the modern science of the coloniser was superior. Kumar's (1995) archival materials elucidated that colonial science, akin to colonialism, was a set of institutions or structures, an economic as well as a cultural intervention. This interventionist science was geared to perform what was encoded elsewhere. For example, 'In Britain itself there had occurred a gradual shift from science-as-a vocation to science-as-enterprise' (16). The Industrial Revolution founded an entrepreneurial, result-oriented ideology of science. This implied a production base emerging from scientific and technological development. But on the other hand, it also meant an intricate relationship between science and the state, very vivid in the context of colonial science. In the colonies, a notion of state scientist emerged, one which had to perform a complex role of serving the colonial state as well as science. 'This state claimed superiority in terms of structure, power, race, etc. Science claimed superiority in terms of knowledge and inter alia helped the colonial state dismiss "other" epistemologies. Both needed each other and became mutually dependent' (15).

Despite the debates revolving around considering precolonial epistemologies in various parts of South Asia as scientific, there is a consensus about the quests in ancient and medieval South Asia that were of a scientific nature.[5] This could be distinguished from post seventeenth-century modern science by considering it as 'proto-science and technology' (Gunawardana 1993, 178). Proto-science and technology included a wide array of explorations and development—from the spectacular works of Savai Jai Singh's exploration in astronomy and Tipu Sultan's rocket propellant mechanism to the ordinary methods of preparing soil, grafting, harvesting techniques, iron smelting, practical systems of ploughing developed by the peasants, including the *phad* system inter alia. These were all to do with the needs of royalty and subjects, guided by an enmeshed version of theory and practice, religious and material, cultural and economic imperatives. They thus did not engender an exclusive body of sophisticated theory and philosophy, which could be considered over and above everything else. Whereas modern science began with a conscious idea of philosophy, as a philosophically informed vocation, before it succumbed to the state and acquired enterprising tendencies.[6] This is candidly stated by sociologist Max Weber, who connected the scientific with the socio-economic spirit of capitalism; 'calculations, even with decimals, and algebra have been carried on in India, where the decimal system was invented. But it was only made use of by developing capitalism in the West, while in India it led to no modern arithmetic or book-keeping' (1968, 24).

But then, what Weber observed was in the backdrop of modern history that had depicted India in various hues. Raina aptly sums up the curious history of science in colonial South Asia:

> And as Eurocentric theory began to consolidate its hold in the history of science towards the end of the eighteenth century, India was painted as a civilisation that had entered a state of decline from a phase of scientific creativity.[7]

The loss of ancient wisdom, Raina further elaborates, provided legitimacy to the colonial civilising mission through modern science. This was an instance of scientific imperialism, with the lofty goals of illuminating the regions of darkness and superstition in the colony. In such a historical wake there emerged a class of modern educated Indians that sought legitimacy for their scientific enterprise. This class of Indians dwelt upon the orientalist knowledge and epistemic understanding of the universality of science.

What was that scientific epistemology that became the singular trajectory in colonial science? Which science emerged to be a premise upon which all other variants of sciences, including what was termed proto-science, were trivialised and trashed? While the basic feature of proto-science was an inherent ordinariness, due to its direct relationship with socio-cultural, religious and practical requirements, what was the inclination of post seventeenth-century modern science? Let's explore these questions after a brief overview of what made modern scientific epistemology.

Science and Its Ways of Seeing: Philosophical Propositions

Science happens *somewhere*, and then it begins to obsessively clamour for the status of *nowhere*. This is perhaps the moral of the following discussion in which the attempt is to unearth this epistemological dilemma. Universally, the advent of modern science is a point of departure for epistemological reasoning in modern philosophy. Even though it is complicated to suggest as to where exactly science begins, one can perhaps agree with Russell:

> The first serious eruption of science was the publication of the Copernican theory in 1543, but the theory did not become influential until it was taken up and improved by Kepler and Galileo in the seventeenth century. Then began the long fight between science and dogma, in which traditionalists fought a losing battle against new knowledge.[8] (2003, 454)

The four names—Copernicus, Kepler, Galileo and Newton—are the backdrop of the new knowledge, namely, modern science. New knowledge also had its share of fights between ecclesiastical authorities, the Church, and the proponents of science. Scientific discoveries and concomitant discourses disturbed the status quo, the social and religious order of Christianity. Despite this, it is interesting to remember that there was a particular affinity between new science and Christianity. Needless to say, it was an intriguing relation between scientists and religiosity given the ennobled secularism of modern science. The so-called 'secular-ness' of modern science was critiqued in Merton's thesis that Puritanism fostered science (1938, 1973).[9]

Moreover, the discourses emanating from new knowledge were more inclined to encourage freedom of the individual, of agency in subjectivity, and even anarchy.[10] Or, in a more congratulatory term, as Immanuel Kant put it, this was a fight against 'self-incurred immaturity'. The latter was an allusion to the traditional dependence of humans on the powerful authorities of the Church. Allegedly, such dependence had fostered an inability to ask questions as independent thinkers and the intellectual progress suffered. Answering the question, as to what is Enlightenment, Kant, delivered a clarion call for the Enlightenment movement, *Sepere Aude*! Have courage to use your own understanding!'[11]

To reiterate, the seeds of this were in Nicolaus Copernicus' rebuttal of the geocentric proposition that the earth was at the centre of the universe while the sun had a diurnal rotation as well as an annual revolution about the earth. Interestingly enough, the key work of Copernicus, which elaborated heliocentric theory, *De Revolutionibus Orbium Coelestium*, was published much later, in 1543, the year of his death. A devout Polish ecclesiastic of unimpeachable orthodoxy, Copernicus had dedicated this to the Pope, which enabled it to escape the official Catholic condemnation until the time of Galileo. Though there were problems in the precision of mathematical calculations and lack of empirical verification, this theory dethroned the earth and thereby upset the Christian theology.[12] The heliocentric theory, however, could not get widely disseminated until Johannes Kepler, a Protestant astronomer inclined to Pythagoreanism.[13] He added details of the elliptical mobility of planetary (heavenly) bodies, including the earth. Consistent with Kepler, and accepting his findings, Galileo Galilei developed a theory of dynamics. Using the concepts of acceleration and change in velocity, he showed the circular movement of a body towards the centre of a circle. Moreover, Galileo's Law of Inertia aided in explaining the reason why the rotating earth does not slip away. He also explored Milky Way and its stars, the satellites of Jupiter inter alia. What matters most, once again, is the discursive implications of the scientific advances that Galileo made. As Russell said:

> Galileo, as everyone knows, was condemned by the Inquisition, first privately in 1616, and then publicly in 1633, on which latter occasion he recanted, and promised never again to maintain that the earth rotates or revolves … But it failed to prevent men of science from adopting the heliocentric theory, and did considerable damage to the Church by its stupidity. (2003, 492)

The trail of science, to be followed by the philosophers in the succeeding centuries, was duly set. The ultimate addition was Isaac Newton, upon whom the abundance of praise has been showered from all quarters. His celebration begins with his much-celebrated *Principia Mathematica* in 1687. John Locke called him the incomparable Mr Newton, Edmund Halley deemed Newton closest to God, Hume praised him as the greatest and rarest genius ever and Leibniz went to the extent of suggesting that Newton's mathematical contribution was equal to all achievements in science. Newton had become an example, a yardstick, to judge the uprightness of others. In fact, when Kant had to pay a compliment to Condorcet for his precision of moral reasoning, Kant called him the Newton of the moral world. No wonder Alexander Pope voiced it as an epitaph:

> Nature and nature's laws lay hid in night
> God said, Let Newton be! And all was light.[14]

Belonging to a Puritan family, Newton's orientation in science, mathematics and philosophy emerged from his readings of Aristotle and Descartes among others. Likewise, he was known to have had cordial association with the empiricist philosophers Locke and Leibniz too. Such familiarity and engagement with philosophers enabled Newton to acquire a space in the philosophical discourse of his time. He developed calculus in mathematics, the law of gravity in physical science, and contributed to optics, mechanics, astronomy, experimental chemistry, alchemy and theology. His philosophical acumen showed in the *Principia*, and his stature continued to outgrow erstwhile standards. His body of work along with the pervasive admiration by philosophers gave birth to the phenomenon termed as Newtonianism. As a value-orientation and ideological position, in Newtonianism,

> the term "Newtonian" refers to several different intellectual strands unfolding in the eighteenth century, some of them tied more closely to Voltaire, Pemberton, and Maclaurin—or for that matter to those who saw themselves as extending his work, such as Clairaut, Euler, d'Alembert, Lagrange, and Laplace—than to Newton himself.[15]

New knowledge, also known as new science, had taken birth. It had started dethroning traditional authorities and decentring central dogmas. A discourse, of a largely philosophical nature ensued alongside discoveries and inventions, and the development of methods and techniques applicable in science. Among some of the earliest philosophers laying out the modern groundwork for the scientific way of seeing are Francis Bacon and Rene Descartes. For Lord Bacon, as he was respectfully addressed, the *Novum Organum*, or true suggestions for the interpretation of nature, is a special ability of the seeker of knowledge. Such ability is aptly and simply expressed through aphorisms that Bacon uses to outline the characteristics of the knower and knowledge. The very first aphorism says it all: 'man, as the minister and interpreter of nature, does and understands as much as his observations on the order of nature, either with regard to things or the mind, permit him, and neither knows nor is capable of more' (1844, 9). The foreclosure is vivid and the conclusiveness clinical.

There is no redemption for man who may aspire to know more than the available observation. Bacon discredits all other sources of information. The correlation of knowledge and power, that is, those who know shall dominate nature, is very clear on the very first page of the treatise, in the third aphorism. The aphorism reveals that anything that either propagates ignorance or unobservable experiences is 'vulgar notion', more hurtful than useful in the quest of truth. The ideal pursuit is when one constructs axioms based on the senses (particularly sensory experiences) and then 'ascends' continually till one arrives at the most general axioms. This is the Baconian inductive logic that starts from the particular to reach the general in a hierarchical arrangement of axioms. But human minds resort to laziness and operate with vulgar notions; Bacon called them idols of the mind and the phantasmagoria. Usages such as vulgar notions, the idols of mind and the phantasmagoria allude to the presuppositions, prejudices and perspectives with which humans usually perceive their world. They are vulgar in Baconian scheme since they obscure an independent and scientifically objective understanding. By page seventeen of the treatise, Bacon is ready to describe the characteristics of the phantoms which one ought to be fighting in order to be an eligible member of the scientific community—or a seeker of truth. His Aphorism 39 states: 'four species of idols beset human minds: to which (for distinction's sake) we have assigned names: calling the first idols of the tribe; the second idols of the den; the third idols of the market; the fourth idols of the theatre' (17). As one can sense, all these idols are iconic expression of human existence, of being in the world, an ontological terrain that is held suspicious by Bacon. The world that we belong to is a source of imperfection as far as, ironically enough, understanding the nature of this world is concerned. There is a description about each category of idols and the impactful positions they may have in the cognitive–intellectual reasoning of humans. But essentially, Bacon is convinced that people must wage a crusade against them in order to know them.

A similar crusade is visible in Rene Descartes. Since the trope is of the advent of scientific epistemology, Rene Descartes' meditations assume significance. The founder of modern philosophy had good grounding in mathematics, as he invented the initial version of coordinate geometry. He was profoundly aware of the developments in physical astronomy. Seeking the independence of the mind, Descartes indulged in an 'ironical act', a suggestive precursor to his famous meditations that were compiled in *Discourse on Method* (1637) and *Meditation* (1642). To cope with the Bavarian winter in 1619, Descartes got into a stove and meditated all day. Russell quipped, 'Socrates used to meditate all day in the snow, but Descartes' mind worked only when he was warm' (Russell 2003, 512).

And what was it that Descartes accomplished through his meditations?

A method of, and justification for, doubting. His six meditations, qua theses, are crucial. The first forces us to believe that we can doubt all, particularly material, things. The second one propounds that a free mind can distinguish the intellectual (pertaining to the mind) from the sensational (pertaining to the body). The third thesis states that the idea of God can have only God as its cause (just like an idea of a perfect machine originates in the mind of its maker). According to the fourth one, everything we clearly and distinctively perceive is true; and everything true also reveals what constitutes falsity. As per the fifth thesis, the certainty of geometrical demonstrations depends on the knowledge of God. And the last and sixth one, which sets on the methodological debate, is about the distinction of intellect and imagination, and the mind and the body. Even though the mind and the body are conjoined, and we perceive them as a single entity, Descartes proposed a separation.

Such a separation serves the purpose of maintaining methodological purity in scientific epistemology, which will turn out to be an apple of discord as we progress in this chapter.

The Cartesian justification and substantiation of the separation had an epistemological objective. This was meant to suggest that 'reason or good sense' is commonly and equally inherent in all humans. This good sense is distinguishable from bodily sensations (bad sense). Anyone can, if willing, doubt and distinguish good sense from all other sensations. Dwelling upon the mathematical idea of the *incontrovertible,* Descartes persuades us to find indubitable; this would also mean to 'reject as completely false everything in which I could detect the least doubt, in order to see if anything thereafter remained in my belief that was completely indubitable' (2006, 28). Imagination need not lead to what things are; it is an active work of 'I' that does. The idea of 'I am thinking therefore I exist', leads to the traumatic realisation that, 'if I had merely ceased thinking, I would have no reason to believe that I existed, even if everything else I had ever imagined has been true' (28–29). 'I' as a thinking thing can doubt, understand, conceive, affirm, deny, will, imagine and feel.[16]

The truth or falsity of my imagination requires me to be actively engaged in thinking. And in turn, the existence of I resides in thinking. So distinct from the rest of the body is this 'I' that 'it would not stop being everything it is, even if the body were not to exist' (29). This is what sculpts the 'I' as such 'a perfect being', independent of the 'sensuous body' and 'corporeal things in the realm of the sensory', and thereof feelings. This 'I' resonates with another perfect being such as God, akin to the incontrovertible such as the idea of a triangle or equidistance of the sphere from its centre.

The Cartesian philosophy thus accomplishes a mind–body dualism, originally a formulation by Plato in the light of Christian theological ideas, as an essential disposition of the seeker of knowledge in the realm of science. There have been significant critical debates on Cartesian dualism, one of the most systematic and earliest being by Gilbert Ryle (2009 [1949]). The latter deemed the mind to be a philosophical illusion created in Descartes' philosophy. However, this dualism works for Descartes distinguishing three kinds of ideas: innate ideas, foreign ideas that come from without and ideas invented by an individual. Except the innate ideas, Descartes deems other two dubious and continues to put a premium on 'I', allowing a lapse to subjectivism. One could underline many inconsistencies in such an emphasis on dualism but what matters for this discussion are the extraordinary characteristics of the knower, to be an 'I' that is a thinking thing, and thus be able to steer clear of anything that can emerge from any other sources.

Much of Cartesian formulations constituted the premise upon which the philosophical empiricism of science could be erected. Descartes' influence notwithstanding, John Locke, an important Enlightenment encyclopaedist, departed from the Cartesian thesis of innate ideas, the a priori, that can be traced back to Greek scholasticism. This critical departure from the idea of a priori was crucial for Locke in order to develop empiricism as scientific methodology in his treatise titled *An Essay Concerning Human Understanding*. In this regard, steering clear of syllogistic reasoning, Locke propounded an idea of reason. Russell paraphrases Locke when he says, 'God has not been so sparing to men to make them barely two-legged creatures, and left it to Aristotle to make them rational' (2003, 554). For Locke, reason is dual: it includes enquiry that leads to knowledge with certainty and the investigation of probable propositions that are parts of human wisdom as well practice. Such probable propositions we tend to figure out embedded in our practices, and we are not able to prove their logical certainty. The probable nature of a proposition dwells upon one's own experience or that of others. In short, reason enables people to get a variety of experiences through which one gets to 'ideas'. Ideas are derived from two sources—sensation (involving the sense organs) and perception (involving the mind, as internal sense). With a bit of inconsistency in formulation, Locke further adds that there are three kinds of knowledge of real existence. One is intuitive knowledge of our own existence, the second is demonstrative knowledge of God's existence and the third is sensitive knowledge of things that come from the senses. Intuitive knowledge is accessible through our experiences that our reason can aid in getting at. Demonstrative knowledge, also known to be knowledge accessed through reason, presupposes agreement or disagreement between two or more ideas. And likewise, reason can enable us to arrive at knowledge that arises from our senses.

All our knowledge is thus an acquisition of these ideas, with dual reasoning, as though inscriptions on tabula rasa, a blank slate. None of our knowledge, following Locke's empiricism, antedates experience. In short, no empirical knowledge is a priori to experience. This was a bold innovation refuting philosophical positions from Plato down to Descartes and Leibniz, which had separated knowledge from sensation, perception and experience. However, Locke could not settle a paradox: if sensation has a cause, why shall it be dependent on experience for understanding? It gives rise to scepticism about an inherently essentialist notion of experience which underpins Locke's formulations. Locke's experientialist empiricism, as it were, does not satisfy when one asks a simple question informed by scepticism: one knows the cause and effect that is involved in romantic relationships. It may well neigh be explained by simply holding hormones responsible. Yet, every lover and beloved longs to write a detailed, even melodramatic, story about the experience of love. Is this notion of an experiential narrative different from what Locke's empiricism offers us? Yes, it is, in the sense that the detailed narration of experience that may be a common tendency of people in everyday life, it may not be so common for scientists who seek to explain their experiments. They would be keen to be content with causal explanation about the experience of experimenting. This causal explanation of a scientist's 'experienced' experiment need not have the detailed narrative, that could, for the sake of imagination, explain how the scientist came to think of the experiment under discussion, or his experience when the experiment was underway: Was there a sense of trepidation? Did the scientist' personal qua emotional being play any role in the experience of the experiment? Such details are methodically left aside in a scientist's explanation. And this is what constitutes Locke's experiential explanation in the last analysis. But for a sceptic like David Hume, there is always something more to the causal explanation. There is a large domain of uncertainty that calls for what we can call juicy stories in the scheme of explanation. With Hume, we begin to understand that a child witnessing the steady rise of an early morning crimson sun in the eastern horizon is an invitation for a different experiential narrative that includes the causal explanation only as a basic technical requirement. We witness an old tree, standing rooted with many spreading branches and we can instantly indulge in amateur poetry or sketching. This is a qualitatively different domain of experiential knowledge fraught with subjective uncertainty that concerns a sceptic such as Hume.

This is a line of curiosity that enabled Hume to propose a sceptical stance: we don't perceive own brain, yet, we have an idea of it. Hume was interested in uncertain knowledge that could emerge from empirical data by inferences and yet could not be sufficiently demonstrative. He suggested that only in algebra and arithmetic could there be reasoning with certainly. This certainty begins to thin as we enter geometry. For, the truth claims of the axioms entails taken-for-granted assumptions held as truth. In geometry, we prove a theorem providing evidence through calculations whereas an axiom remains an unquestioned sacred entity. Based on this, Hume distinguishes the non-mathematical human experiences in which uncertainty in the empirical information is intact. Thus, most of our ideas, related to space and time or identity, dwell upon impressions, whereas causation allows us to draw inferences from one occurrence or another. It boils down to a bottom line: we can only know cause and effect from our experiences with certainty. Everything else is a game of impressions based on experiences of causes and effects. In other words, what appears to us as a necessary connection among objects is really only a connection among the ideas of those objects. Our mind, influenced by customs or sets of inherited notions, works with the connections of the ideas of the objects. Unlike the certainty of cause and effect, human experiences are fraught with uncertainty due to the predominant role of individual impressions and perceptions. As a strong proponent of scepticism in modern philosophy, Hume added uncertainty to the certainty promised in scientific epistemology, even though the role of reason remains crucial. And this is aptly summarised when he suggests, as Russell noted, that 'there is no such thing as a rational philosophy: if we believe that fire warms, or water refreshes, this is only because it costs us too much pains to think otherwise' (cited in Russell 2003, 611).[17]

The dilemma, whether knowledge is a priori or an accumulation of experiences, thus remained unresolved. At best, it took a turn when unresolved problems of the mind were left for a romantic resolve offered by the heart. The late eighteenth century witnessed the regime of 'heart-based philosophy' (this figures prominently in the next chapter), as it were, in which the name of Jean-Jacques Rousseau is prominent. German idealism, with an affinity with the Romantic movement,[18] has an urge for intellectual advances. Names of Hegel, Fichte, Shelling and Kant is prominent in German idealism. However, Kant is of crucial significance with his philosophically nuanced synthesis of the stances of his predecessors to find a possible answer to the dilemma of a priori and posteriori knowledge. Educated in Leibniz's philosophy, steeped in Hume and Rousseau, there is an evident systematisation of the positions to the credit of Kant, a diligent philosophy professor, unlike many of the predecessors who were not tied by any educational institution. Therefore, perhaps, he had to read Rousseau's *Emile* several times, for the intellectual clarity as an academic. He overcame the aesthetic style of the text and fathomed the propositions with due diligence. Ironically, he was himself not without remarkable stylistic issues, which Russell (2003) recognised as Miltonic sublimity alluding the poetic aesthetics of the famous English poet John Milton. It is well known that Kant was drawn to Milton's poetry. Kant's stylistic inclinations reflected in a wide array of writings on bewildering range of themes from earthquakes to aesthetics, from geography to science, from mathematics to philosophy. However, his most important work, *The Critique of Pure Reason* (1781) is noted for cardinal significance in the discussion on scientific epistemology. Starting with a proposition that restores experience, rescuing it from romantic and sceptic doubts, Kant says, 'Experience is without doubt the first product that our understanding brings forth as it works on the raw material of sensible sensations' (1998, 127). Though experience is important, as evident, Kant does not dismiss the 'sensible sensations', and getting into the details he proposes something that reconciles different positions in the debates on scientific knowledge.

Kant proposes knowledge to be bound by experience, a posteriori, as well as be independent a priori cognitions. Hence a part of it could be inferred from experience, while there is an equally large part that is beyond the scheme of experience. Likewise, Kant operates with the scheme of propositions/judgements that could be divided into two, Analytic and Synthetic. In an analytic proposition, also known for affirmative nature, the predicate is part of the subject. An example is 'a tall man is a man' or 'an equilateral triangle is a triangle'. Such propositions (judgement of clarification) operate with the law of contradiction, and hence an opposite articulation, such as an equilateral triangle is not a triangle, will be self-contradictory. Analytic propositions thus have a win-win effect in a discourse, be it in science or the socio-cultural world. One need not ask for more evidences in order to accept an analytic proposition. On the other hand, the synthetic propositions, also known as judgement of amplification, are known only through experience. Merely conceptual analyses cannot lead to such a proposition that solicits cross-references to various sources. For example, 'Tuesday was a wet day' immediately reflects an experiential background. If shared with testimonials, there is little doubt about the wetness of the day. Likewise, when recorded in history with adequate testimonials, such experiences become milestones; say for example, 'Napolean was a great general'. In Kant's words:

> If I say: "All bodies are extended", then this is an analytic judgement. For I do not need to go outside the concept that I combine with the word "body".... On the contrary if I say: "All bodies are heavy", then the predicate is something entirely different from that which I think is the mere concept of a body in general. The addition of such a predicate thus yields a synthetic judgement. (1998, 130)

It is clear from the examples that analytic judgements don't *amplify* our cognition. Such judgments set out, and make more intelligible, concepts, which we already have. This aids, for sure, in clarifying, whereas synthetic judgements give more than the concept of the subject for our cognition. Synthetic judgements entail the role of experience, and thereby, reasoning with the additional concepts which are not present in the statement of the judgement. Facts of history and empirical details in geography and science are in the category of synthetic propositions. These are empirical propositions emerging from and backed by observational data. This appears to be fine, until Kant put forth for discussion a tricky idea, a possibility of a *synthetic a priori judgement*, the intertwined opposites as it were. A speculative a priori judgement could make us seek for causes, other sets of concepts, that would be possible through experience. Knowledge without such mixing, purely a priori, calls for pure cognition qua pure reason, in which principles of cognition are a priori, a given.

> An organum of pure reason would be a sum total of those principles in accordance with which all pure *a priori* cognitions can be acquired and actually brought about.... I call all cognition **transcendental** that occupied not so much the objects but rather with our a priori concept of objects in general. A system of such concepts would be called transcendental philosophy. (132–133, emphasis in original)

Unlike the pure and speculative reason of transcendental philosophy, there is a practical domain fraught with motives, related to feelings, which belongs to the empirical sources of cognition. This involves doctrine of methods, of practical reason, which enables us to investigate our domains of experiences. Roughly, this is the domain of experiences dominated by perceptions empirically connected with the material world, which, according to Kant, is, the phenomenon. This is not dependent on the accidental occurrence, chance events, but has a pattern and calculable frequency. The phenomenon, such as sound and sight, appears as an a priori in the sense that it does not always require experience to vouch for it. Yet it is always available for further enquiry based on sensory perceptions. On the other hand, distinguishable from the phenomenon, Kant describes noumena as things-in-themselves, fraught with accidental occurrences and subjective sensations, which are grasped with pure intuitions. God, soul and the cosmos are some of the examples of noumena, which one can conceive but hard to perceive. A mystic's realm of experience is fraught with noumena, whereas a scientific knowledge is the sensory perceptions of things available in the world of phenomenon. Needless to say, it is seldom possible to be sure about understanding noumena, say for example, a mystic's experience or a madman's fantasy.

Despite recognising the role of a priori- and intuition-based observations, Kant also highlights its limits.

> Mathematics gives us a splendid example of how far we can go with a priori cognition independently of experience.... Likewise, Plato abandoned the world of the senses because it posed so many hindrances for the understanding and dared to go beyond it on the wings of the ideas, in the empty space of pure understanding. (1998, 129)

And hence, it is advisable that scientific enquiries should, in any domain of understanding, operate with reason and analyses of the concepts of the objects in the external world. There is a sense of a double edge in Kantian conclusion;[19] on one hand it suggests that experience must conform to categories and on the other, categories ought to conform to experience too. This is particularly so in scientific epistemology where fundamental axioms are synthetic a priori in nature.

What is the objective of this discursive development, philosophically relating science to the idea of progress? Kant aptly summed it up in a lecture answering the question what is enlightenment, which was incidentally also title of the lecture: 'The freedom to make public use of one's reason in all matters'.[20] This freedom is from all authorities that demand obedience, conformity, docile agency and overall 'self-incurred immaturity'. Kant went on enlisting such forces that are responsible for sustaining the immaturity of humanity. It could be religion and religious institutions, the state, a revolution and its leadership, bureaucracy, the army, and so on. They all forcefully state, 'Don't argue'.

> The officer says: Don't argue, get on parade!
> The Tax-official: Don't argue, pay!
> The clergyman: Don't argue, believe!
>
> (Only one ruler in the world says: Argue as much as you like and about whatever you like, but obey!).[21]

That last is a reference to Frederick the Great, the King of Prussia, who set his subjects free to argue in the eighteenth century. This was an allusion to the imperative of intellectual freedom from authority. An authority is eventually privileged, so each of these—a clergyman, an officer, a tax official or a scholar—shall be able to apply reason, be rational and thus be free to make a choice. Each is an equally endowed citizen with the freedom to think. And as spelled earlier, freedom to think charts a journey determined by philosophy of science, scientific epistemology and methodological empiricism. Each mind is thus a thing of extraordinary calibre despite the Cartesian apprehension of challenges arising from one's own body and external influences. Pointing out the limits of the philosophically envisaged freedom could further complicate this. For, unlike Kant's formulation, freedom, reason and moral law are not so neatly separable. And a priori does not defy historicity. On a critical note, Das Gupta (2019) has underlined Kant's anti-historicist stance by underlining the lack of empirical references to human desires and needs. Such neat division of the knowable and not knowable is not valid even in the wake of the new developments in physics, such as the advent of quantum mechanics, let alone science in general. The idea that theory-based causal explanations amount to scientific epistemology is challenged in the face of the fact that behaviour of a single electron does not fully guarantee an exact prediction of the behaviour of all electrons. Quantum mechanics does not abide by causal determination. Hence, we notice that there are particles following causal laws alongside the waves which can be only interpreted as probability clouds. Kant's reliance on the Newtonian paradigm, an a priori virtue of causality, does not allow him to see the human involvement in science. And that 'the historicity of science will show that science is not beyond the control and influences of history. In fact, science being a creation of man is subjected to various sociological and historical conditions' (Das Gupta 2019, 53). Thus, we notice that science is manmade rather than god made, and hence the ability to experience, know and explain is manmade too. The *somewhere*, declared *nowhere*, thus finds *elsewhere*. The latter is the human world with inherent historical and social complexities.

Post-Enlightenment Science

The post in post-Enlightenment is not an allusion to anti-foundational thinking, a departure from the foundation created by the Enlightenment philosophes. We return to the idea of a radical departure from the epistemological foundations in the latter chapters in this book. For the time being, 'post-Enlightenment' is a ceremonial celebration of the different voices in the philosophy of science.

Ernst Cassirer, the German philosopher, presents a reality check coupled with a congratulatory note, showing that the Enlightenment mostly worked on the intellectual heritage of the past. He summarises the philosophical achievement of the age, saying:

> Enlightenment philosophy simply fell heir to the heritage of those centuries; it ordered, sifted, developed, and clarified this heritage rather than contributed and gave currency to new and original ideas. Yet in spite of this dependence with respect to content, the Enlightenment produced a completely original form of philosophic thought. (1951, vi–vii)

In this complex outcome, 'a new methodological order' dominates eighteenth-century thought. 'The attempt to solve the central problem of philosophic method involves recourse to Newton's "Rules of Philosophizing" rather than to Descartes' "Discourse on Method". For Newton's method is not that of pure deduction, but that of analysis' (Cassier 1951, 7). Reason thereby is not an inheritance from metaphysics; it becomes an acquisition with methodological rigour, and thus Newton was ennobled to methodological supremacy known as Newtonianism.

But then, much later when the world was facing the Second World War, the discontents of the Enlightenment became sharper. Max Horkheimer and Theodor Adorno spearheaded yet another discourse on the ramifications of the Enlightenment in an essay titled 'Dialectic of Enlightenment: Philosophical Fragments', first published in 1944. This was followed by the book, *Eclipse of Reason* in which Horkheimer continued to show the problems of reason that was erected as the hallmark of being scientific. Horkheimer (1931) had already articulated the imperative to develop social philosophy in his address, sharpening a critique of positivism and empiricism of, particularly, the Vienna Circle.[22] Adorno's essay was a more philosophically, and historically too, systematic attack on self-congratulatory claims of the proponents of the Enlightenment. It upsets the set with an allegation that, 'Enlightenment is totalitarian' (2002, 4). Such a totalitarian epistemological regime dismantled all other authorities to create a singular one, which determines right and wrong, the calculable and the incalculable, the mythical and the real. In the scheme of Enlightenment, technology is the essence of knowledge, exploitation is a means of progress. In short, 'Enlightenment's program was the disenchantment of the world. It wanted to dispel myths, to overthrow fantasy with knowledge' (1). But it ended up with another set of myth and fantasy that masquerade as science.

The earlier mentioned was not only a juicy polemic that emerged from the Frankfurt School. The collapse of the world order that history witnessed during and in the aftermath of the Second World War enabled critical minds to rethink not only the moral philosophy but also scientific premises of progress. This rethinking questioned the normative conditioning and consequences of science, philosophy and the Enlightenment. The normativity of science was well established by a crucial figure in sociology of science, Robert Merton.[23] He did not disrupt the epistemic privilege of science in his sociology but aided in placing it at the intersections of religion, politics and social institutions. He repeats a 'Max Weber act for science',[24] and suggests that the rise of science in seventeenth-century England was preconditioned by Pietism. Merton's (1968) dissertation elaborated a social structure in which science unfolds. For example, scientists operate with hierarchy, which is best explicated in 'the Matthew Effect in Science'.[25] Furthermore, science is higher in validity than social science, not only due to truth claims but also because of higher 'codification'. This meant that scientists operate with more consensus (higher codification) and less disagreements unlike social scientists. This reflects in the statistical data of science journals such as *The Physical Review*, which tend to accept 80 per cent of the submitted contributions, whereas a journal such as the *American Sociological Review* accepts only about 10 per cent. This reflects on the consensus-driven worldview of the community of scientists. Though there could be many flaws in such propositions, Merton's sociology of science aids in understanding that science is not free from value orientation. And that is why he happens to be a proponent of an order-oriented science which could engender general, universal principles. In this regard, he points out two aspects of science:

> first, the cultural context in any given nation of society may predispose scientists to focus on certain problems, to be sensitive to some and not other problems on the frontiers of science.... But this is basically different from the second issue; the criteria of validity of claims to scientific knowledge are not matters of national taste and culture. Sooner or later, competing claims to validity are settled by the universalistic criteria. (1973, 271)

Some of the other voices on the promises and objective of the Enlightenment era emerged from South Asia too. Recently, anthropologist Gananath Obeyesekere articulated it with due ambivalence. Considering himself a product of two kinds of Enlightenment, the European and the Buddhist, he noted, 'one cannot live *without* Reason and one cannot live *with* it either, at least in its exclusionary sense Enlightenment or Euro-rational sense' (2012, 4). There was a more flexible sense of reason, particularly in Descartes' meditation, as long as it allowed the intuitive knowledge of cogito, the pure intellect discussed in the preceding pages of this chapter. However, with the collapse of Cartesian thought in the wake of radical Enlightenment, the meaning of 'enlightenment' underwent changes. According to Obeyesekere, 'the Enlightenment we know is not a single movement. It has its own ups and downs, but, whether in its early mild or later moderate and radical forms, one thing is clear: the persistence of Reason as the pathways to knowledge, leading to what Peter Gay calls its "rationalist myopia"' (3). A poignant form of experience such as *vision* became an avoidable absurdity, arational urge, and unworthy of investigation. Due to such a vexed nature of the Enlightenment, Obeyesekere opts for the term 'awakening' to refer to the enlightenment of Buddha. He thereby endeavours to show that the Buddhist version of enlightenment engenders a body of rationality which is not hostile to visions. In short, a response from South Asia to the promises and objective of enlightenment seeks to show contextual, socio-religious and civilisational components in the rationality that may arise from Buddhist epistemology. This is, however, another side of the story that 'the Euro-rationality has become the dominant way of thought in modern intellectual and scientific disciplines and inevitably associated with irreversible social and economic "progress"' (Obeyesekere 2012, 364). The scientific epistemology pertaining to the age of the Enlightenment has replaced various works of logic, for example, the epistemology of the Buddhist logicians like Dignaga and Dharmakirti. In the same vein under the dominance of the Western science, an experience such as vision became medicalised and termed hysteria. But then, it is difficult to conclude that we, in South Asia, have entered the historical epoch characterised by disenchantment. Instead, we live in the experiential domain ruled by the dialectic of enchantment and disenchantment as we negotiate between the two notions of enlightenment mentioned above.

Rethinking enlightenment is compelling in the domain of philosophy. Roy Bhaskar (2002), for example, seeks for an ontological shift to propose another idea of enlightenment, against the Enlightenment. Reading sources such as medieval poet from the West Asia, Jalaluddin Rumi's *Masnavi*, and ancient texts from South Asia such as the 'Upanishads' and Buddhist teachings enabled Bhaskar to propose a philosophy of meta-reality where an individual seeker of knowledge could come together with the world of duality. Unlike the separation of the self and the world, that empiricist science advocated in the heyday of eighteenth-century Enlightenment, Bhaskar underlines another possibility, as he notes:

> there is no opposition between an individual's self-realization, or enlightenment and universal self-realization, they mutually entail each other. The Buddhist ideal of the Bodhisattva is just an expression of the logic of that. There can be ultimately no individual Buddha-hood without universal Buddha-hood and conversely there can be no universal utopian secular society without individual Buddha-hood, in that sense, individual Buddha-hood. (2002, 53)

One can furthermore explore various philosophically potent metaphysical strands of thoughts from across epochs in South Asia that can offer another way of thinking about enlightenment. The ancient philosopher sage Adi Shankara emphasised on a notion of *aham brahmasmi* (the absolute in me) as the bottom line of his philosophy of *adwaita* (non-dualism). This trope of non-duality could be perhaps conducive for developing a body of ways of seeing. Non-duality finds another popular expression in the poetry of saint poet Kabir[26] in the fifteenth century too. Likewise, the *qawwali* singers in various parts of South Asia sing special numbers in praise of the Sufi saint Mansoor who reached the ecstasy of devotional love and claimed *anal haq*[27] (I am truth) and was condemned to death. The tradition of such proclamations continued in the devotional poetry even in twentieth-century India.

In this wake, this is important to join Zygmunt Bauman (2000, 6) in posing a relevant question: 'Sociological Enlightenment—for whom, about what?' It leads us to realise the control of the *les philosophes*, the cultural–intellectual elites who controlled the project of Enlightenment in eighteenth century. Thereof philosophy, and science, deemed nature to be a numb entity to which they could inscribe meanings. In so doing, they marginalised the lay people as the scientists and philosophers, discussed in this chapter, adopted what Bauman called the 'self-referentiality of scientific narrative' (2000, 73). It was primarily a reference to the supremacy of the Enlightenment's scientific narrative in front of which everything else was spurious.

Back in India, there was a surge of critical discussions on the hegemonic characteristics of modern science. The scientific epistemology in the colonies, critically discussed earlier in this chapter, was tied to a civilisational mission. The epistemology and colonial rule served the objectives of those who assumed the significance of 'intimate enemies'. Reading Ashis Nandy's psychoanalysis of the colonised psyche of India during the period of colonial rule aids in understanding the internalisation of the values of the colonial oppressors by the native

Indians educated in modern scientific epistemology. One comes to realise that the rise of science and thereof notion of progress was not an artifice of the colonisers alone; it entailed the pursuits of natives too in some sense, who sought to replace the 'sahibs' (the British masters rulers). On the other hand, the Nehruvian dream of an Indian nation with a scientific temper moved on to become a technocratic regime of the Indian nation state. The scientific utopias that history may have offered began to transform into a techno-managerial ideology to coerce and control, and, in short, rule an imagined unruly India. This continues to manifest in the science and technology policies even in contemporary India. A number of state scientists participate in the formulation of these policies and emphasise core ideas such as self-reliance, nation building, development and so on. Such a policy perspective seldom takes note of the movements in which the real progress of science lies, let alone the constructive worlds of the scientists who operationalise various kinds of development in science and technology. Sekhsaria's (2019) study of the scientific–technological innovation in the laboratory of C.V. Dharmadhikari, a former professor at the University of Pune, elaborates the collaborative exercise in which various service providers from the world at large join. It is high time one realises the importance of the citizen in formulating a science and technology policy, the constructive relationship of scientists with the world at large and the basic idea that the meaning of science is contingent on the meaning of society.

Thus, it is natural that some of the forerunners of social sciences, and sociology in particular, tend to engage, respond and negotiate with the new methodology as well as the inherited philosophical propositions. And this tends to be the case even with the trinity in classical sociology—Emile Durkheim, Max Weber and Karl Marx. We deliberate on this in the Chapters 3 and 4. What is important to note is that the interface of the history, philosophy and sociology of science resurfaces with yet another discussion when a dispute, known as the positivism dispute in German sociology, breaks out. The dispute provided a debate amongst philosophers and historians of science and sociologists exploring a post-positivist way of seeing and is covered in Chapter 5. This was when philosophers, historians and sociologists locked horns over the nature of science.

This chapter has set the stage to cast light on the classical sociologists' response to the outcomes of scientific epistemology in the late nineteenth and early twentieth centuries. The paradigm of positivism, one of the most predominant methodologies, a way of seeing in classical sociology, emerges in the backdrop of this chapter and the next. For, there was something more to the story of Enlightenment that shall be told before turning to formal sociology. The story about counter-currents of the eighteenth-century Enlightenment is important for understanding the gradual transformation of the philosophical into social, the abstract into concrete. The next chapter, suggestively titled 'Sociology before Sociology', shall focus on the precursors and predecessors of the formal sociology. Both, this chapter on the scientific epistemology of the Enlightenment and the next chapter on the counter-currents are essential background for the emergence of the formal sociological ways of seeing.

References

Alvares, C. *Homo Faber: Technology and Culture in India, China and the West, 1500 to the Present Day*. Netherlands: Springer, 1979.

Baber, Zaheer. *The Science of Empire: Scientific Knowledge, Civilization and Colonial Rule in India*. Albany: State University of New York Press, 1996.

Bacon, Francis. *Novum Organum*. London: William Pickering, 1844.

Basalla, G. 'The Spread of Western Science', *Science* 156 (1967): 611–622.

Bauman, Zygmunt. 'Sociological Enlightenment—For Whom, about What?', *Theory, Culture, and Society* 17, no. 2 (2000): 71–82.

Bhaskar, Roy. *Reflections on Meta-reality, A Philosophy for the Present: Transcendence, Emancipation and Everyday Life*. Delhi: Sage, 2002.

Bierstedt, Robert. 'Sociological Thought in the Eighteenth Century'. In *A History of Sociological Analysis*, edited by Tom Bottomore and Robert Nisbet, 3–39. London: Heinemann, 1978.

Bottomore, Tom. *The Frankfurt School*. London: Routledge, 1989.

Cassirer, Ernst. *The Philosophy of Enlightenment*. Princeton, New Jersey: Princeton University Press, 1951.

Chattopadhyay, Debiprasad. *History of Science and Technology in Ancient India: The Beginnings*. Calcutta: Firma K.L. Mukhopadhyaya, 1986.

Cole, Stephen. 'Merton's Contribution to the Sociology of Science', *Social Studies of Science* 34, no. 6 (2004): 829–844.

Das Gupta, Amitabha. *Meaning, Agency and the Making of a Social World*. New Delhi: Routledge, 2019.

Descartes, Rene. *A Discourse on the Method of Correctly Conducting One's Reason and Seeking Truth in the Sciences*, trans. with an Introduction and Notes by Ian Maclean. London: Oxford University Press, 2006.

———. *Meditations on First Philosophy: With Selections from the Objections and Replies*, trans. with and Introduction and Notes by Michael Moriarty. London: Oxford University Press, 2006.

Dharampal. *Indian Science and technology in the Eighteenth Century: Some Contemporary European Accounts*. Mapusa, Goa: Other India Press, 1971.

Engell, James. *The Creative Imagination: Enlightenment to Romanticism*. Cambridge, Massachusetts: Harvard University Press, 1981.

Gunawardana, R.A.L.H. 1993. 'Proto-Science, and Technology in Pre-colonial South Asia'. In *Cultural Interaction in South Asia in Historical Perspective*, edited by S.A.I. Tirmizi, 178–208. New Delhi: Hamdard Institute of Historical Research, 1993.

Habib, I., and D. Raina. 'Copernicus, Columbus and the Role of Science in Nineteenth-Century India', *Social Scientist* 17, no. 3/4 (1989): 51–66.

Horkheimer, M. *Between Philosophy and Social Science: Selected Early Writings*. Cambridge, MA: MIT Press, 1993 (1931).

Horkheimer, M., and Adorno, T. *Dialectic of Enlightenment*. Stanford, California: Stanford University Press, 2002.

Kant, I. *Critique of Pure Reason*. Cambridge: Cambridge University Press, 1998.

———. 'What is Enlightenment', http://www.columbia.edu/acis/ets/CCREAD/etscc/kant.html (accessed 20 September 2023).

Kuhn, Thomas. *The Copernican Revolution: Planetary Astronomy in the Development of Western Thought*. Cambridge, MA: Harvard University Press, 1957.

———. *The Structure of Scientific Revolutions*. Chicago: University of Chicago Press, 1962.

Kumar, Deepak. *Science and the Raj: A Study of British India*. New Delhi: Oxford University Press, 1995.

Merton, Robert K. 'Science, Society and Technology in Seventeenth Century England'. In *OSIRIS: Studies on the History and Philosophy of Science and on the History of Leaning and Culture*, edited by George Sarton, 362–632. Bruges: The St Catherine Press, 1938.

———. 'The Matthew Effect in Science: The Reward and Communication Systems of Science are Considered', *Science* 159, no. 3810 (1968): 56–63.

———. 'The Normative Structure of Science'. In *The Sociology of Science: Theoretical and Empirical Investigations*, edited by Robert K. Merton and N.W. Storer, 267–278. Chicago: Chicago University Press, 1973.

Nagel, T. *The View from Nowhere*. New York: Oxford University Press, 1987.

Nandy, Ashis (ed.). *Science, Hegemony and Violence: A Requiem for Modernity*. New Delhi: Oxford University Press, 1990.

Obeyesekere, Gananath. *The Awakened Ones: Phenomenology of Visionary Experience*. New York: Columbia University Press, 2012.

Putnam, H. *The Many Faces of Realism*. LaSalle, Illinois: Open Court, 1987.

———. *Realism with a Human Face*. Cambridge, MA: Harvard University Press, 1990.

Rahman, M.A. 'Basheer—The Sufi', *Indian Literature* 53, no. 1(249) (2009): 79–87.

Raina, Dhruv. *Images and Contexts: The Historiography of Science and Modernity in India*. New Delhi: Oxford University Press, 2003.

Ray, P.C. *History of Hindu Chemistry* (II). Calcutta: The Bengal Chemical and Pharmaceutical Works Limited, 1909.

Richardson, Alan. 'Robert K. Merton and Philosophy of Science', *Social Studies of Science* 34, no. 6 (2004): 855–858.

Russell, Bertrand. *The Basic Writings of Bertrand Russell*, edited by Robert E. Egner and Lester E. Denonn. London and New York: Routledge, 2003.

Ryle, G. *The Concept of Mind*. New York: Routledge, 2009 (1949).

Sekhsaria, Pankaj. *Instrumental Lives: An Intimate Biogrpahy of Indian Laboratory*. New Delhi: Routledge, 2019.

Smith, George, 'Isaac Newton', *The Stanford Encyclopedia of Philosophy*, 2008, https://plato.stanford.edu/archives/fall2008/entries/newton/ (accessed 20 August 2024).

Vaudeville, Charlotte, and Harry B. Partin. 'Kabīr and Interior Religion', *History of Religions* 3, no. 2 (1964): 191–201.

Weber, Max. *The Protestant Ethic and The Spirit of Capitalism*, trans. by Talcott Parsons. London: Unwin University Books, 1968.

Wootton, David. *The Invention of Science: A New History of Scientific Revolution*. London: Penguin, 2016.

Part 2

FORENOON AND AFTERNOON

3

PREDECESSORS AND PRECURSORS: A CASE OF SOCIOLOGY BEFORE SOCIOLOGY

Ideologies and utopias that we find in modern social sciences in the age typically known as 'classical' during the late nineteenth and early twentieth centuries, originated among its predecessors in the eighteenth century. The predecessors' works, the focus of this chapter, aid in understanding the advent of ambiguities and ambivalence in the nature of sociology. This is arguably the time in history, from the eighteenth to the early nineteenth centuries, in which a kind of sociology before the beginning of the formal discipline of sociology unfolded. The chapter suggestively terms it a 'sociology' before the 'sociology', to flag the theoretical dispositions inclined to what became a predominant way of seeing in sociology, that is, positivism. The latter originates from some of the key precursors, discussed further down in this chapter. Suffice it to say, this was a methodological paradigm that animated the sociologists' way of seeing in the age when the sociological classics emerged.

This chapter provides a bridge between the previous and the subsequent chapters in this book. The chapter leads us to see that there were significant thinkers presenting counter-currents to the Enlightenment age that dominated the eighteenth century. These thinkers sought to set the milestones before the advent of the age of sociological classics. These thinkers, precursors and predecessors, were responding to the Enlightenment epistemology with an attention to social institutions. Before the chapter proceeds, it is pertinent to raise a little curiosity, a somewhat polemical reflection on the emergence of the sociological trinity. This shall enable us to identify many other thinkers who aid in understanding, and debating, the notion of sociological. Hence, we are not seeking a linear return to the sociological trinity in the subsequent chapter; instead, it is a critical and creatively mischievous return to them by the virtue of a modest realisation of the existence of sociology before a sociological way of seeing began to take conclusive shape.

Seemingly, precursors and predecessors are inevitable entities in modern sciences. Nothing starts ex nihilo—nothing emerges out of a vacuum. This lesson is an outcome of the discussion in this chapter that will attempt to put together some of the key precursors and predecessors, which were in the background of the sociological classics of the twentieth century. For, there is always a background of an author's departures from the explorations that happened in the past. The students who start studying sociology in college experience it more acutely as they are perturbed by the preordained burden, the background loaded with the contributions of precursors and predecessors. So many threads are entangled, that most of our efforts are about disentangling them. Thanks to some of the predecessors who have done that, it makes it easier to talk about the familiar raconteurs and move ahead to tell our own stories as students and teachers. After all, sociology is all about stories, followed by more stories, and stories about stories, as one of the most remarkable minds of our times, Zygmunt Bauman (2000, 74) believed. And what are these stories, followed by more stories, and stories about stories? They are about the relationship of sociology with modernity, the intricate embrace of sociology and science, and paradoxically,[1] sociology's ability to offer critiques and departures from both, modernity and science of one kind, to arrive *elsewhere*.[2] We are continuing with the notion of *elsewhere* from the previous chapter. It's the domain of interrogation, where everything settled is subject to mischievous unsettling. If it affects scientific epistemology, so does it impact the sociological way of seeing. This makes the story of sociology interesting, the idea of being sociological, quizzical, and the ways of seeing in sociology profoundly complex.

To begin with, it is imperative to make note of the predecessors who inherited the spirit of the Enlightenment before the beginning of the age of the sociological classics. Given the importance of these precursors and predecessors of formal sociology, the discursive fulcrum in this chapter, it appears imperative to indulge in a series of rhetorical questions about the so-called founding figures, alias, father(s) of sociology, and their contributions. These questions, often appearing as jokes made in a classroom, amuse teachers and students. The question is if there is a father of sociology, which father do we refer to, social or biological? After all, the biological father is responsible for the birth of a child, and a social father nurtures and socialises the child. We also hear another question: Is sociology a child of one father or many? For, a discipline's birth is not a one-time event, instead it emerges and takes shape through a historical process. Amid such questions, we hear from our students another probing point: Who is the mother who arguably plays second fiddle in the melodramatic birth of this baby called sociology? All such witty questions come in handy to break the ice in our classroom discussions on sociology. Meanwhile, all of them could be translated into deeper probing questions regarding the parentage and inherent patriarchy behind the conception of the founding fathers of sociology. However, for the time being, it would suffice to say that many predecessors seem to have contributed to the contours that led to the becoming of sociology. And by the same stretch, this also leads us to understand the becoming of sociological, our key curiosity.

Sociology, as an heir of eighteenth-century philosophy, was more inclined to celebrate Isaac Newton instead of René Descartes, the foundational figure of modern philosophy and scientific epistemology. Even though René Descartes was important for his philosophical deliberation, Newton became an icon due to his scientific methods. To reiterate a point from the previous chapter, as a scientist with more sophisticated methods and the ability to deliver generalisable laws, Newton had progressed ahead of Copernicus, Kepler and Galileo. He developed a more flawless way of seeing when it came to science. The Newtonian way of seeing, as indicated in the previous chapter, seals off the philosophical debate on the nature and scope of scientific epistemology. This was one of the key arguments that Cassirer established in a treatise on the Enlightenment philosophy. Hence, this is not surprising that methodologically, Newton became the new god for many who took to look at the social world. But then the discursive spirit, frames of references and value orientation that interrupted the scientific ways of looking at social reality was fraught with the syntheses, amalgamation of science and values, of old theses and new directions. As the previous chapter showed, the most prominent of such syntheses emerged from the Encyclopaedists, the philosophers upholding the clarion call of the Enlightenment. These syntheses of various kinds, including that of Immanuel Kant (in Chapter 2), engaged and departed from the Cartesian, Baconian and Lockean ideas while taking note of the supremacy of Newtonian accomplishment. This recapitulation from the previous chapter helps to situate the complex background to which many of the predecessors had to respond. The names of Montesquieu and Jean-Jacques Rousseau, Louis de Bonald and Joseph de Maistre as bearers of conservative and romantic interventions shall figure prominently in the discussion in this chapter. Their ways of seeing along with that of Saint-Simon and August Comte, as visionaries of sociology in this chapter, shall set the stage for the full-swing discussion on classical sociology in the subsequent chapter.

The fact that a combination of Montesquieu and Rousseau, and Bonald and Maistre, were critically responding to the Enlightenment is suggestive of the complicated character of European modernity. If there was a strong presence of Enlightenment rationality in European modernity, it also had the conservative and the romantic strands. The previous chapter focused on the scientific epistemology of the Enlightenment, without getting into the counter-currents, i.e., the conservatives and the romantics. Sociology, as this chapter and the subsequent one shall elucidate, shapes up in this complex framework. In other words, it was not a simple Enlightenment framework in which only one kind of scientific way of seeing prevailed. For, it was with the conservatives, as Gunnar Myrdal (1962, 17) among others pointed out, that realism in the way of seeing the social world dawned upon sociology. Speculative deliberation on the natural order shifted to realistic deliberation on actual, concrete social structures and institutions. However, before turning to conservatism in the following section, it is worth looking at other predecessors of sociology.

It is necessary to say a few words about the scheme of omission and commission of names and bodies of scholarship in the following parts of this chapter. Following a cue from Nisbet (1967, 5), often thinkers are discussed as dramatis personae, hinting at the dramatic importance of the thinkers in the history of thoughts. Or, as a second tendency, the system/body of thought, alluding to a school or ism, is the criteria to discuss thinkers. As this book is geared towards a central question, vis-à-vis the way of seeing in sociology, the parameters of discussion and analyses are simpler. There is a selective presentation of those thoughts and ideas that address the central question of the book. Therefore, this chapter painstakingly avoids getting carried away by the dramatis personae as well as the enchanting body of thoughts that each thinker presents. Lastly, there is no pretence of representing all, or many, of the thinkers and philosophers who may be worth a mention otherwise. This is determined by those who informed about a quasi-sociology before sociology formally came into being. This chapter creatively meanders through jumps in time and trajectories of thoughts, with the central question about the way of seeing atop the searchlight.

Forerunners' Run: Extra Miles from the Foundation?

Interestingly, Emile Durkheim acknowledged Montesquieu and Rousseau as sociology's *précurseur*,[3] meaning forerunners. Though not acknowledged as the founding father figures in the sociology textbooks, Durkheim hailed the two as important predecessors of sociology. Montesquieu and Rousseau were keen to unravel the finer components responsible for the maintenance of order in society, and their philosophy was thus directly responding to some of the more crucial social concerns.[4] Montesquieu's *Spirit of the Laws*[5] was a systematic study of unearthing, classifying and interpreting the social types empirically seen in society. Some of the social types that he elaborated were monarchical, despotic and republican. Each of these social types entails an elaborate system that supports it. Montesquieu emphasised that these social types possess a unique 'principle' or 'inner force', according to which each type functions. If the principle for the societal type, for example, despotism, is fear, for monarchy it is an honour and for democracy it is a virtue. Laws are in accordance with the principle of the type that it seeks to govern. Montesquieu's study was guided by the objective of exploring 'what is' rather than 'what ought to be', in society.

Hailed as 'ambivalent Cartesian',[6] Montesquieu's theory exhibits an explicit commitment to Cartesian rationalism without accepting the conclusive ideas thereof. Hence, while on one hand, Montesquieu *meditated* upon various ideas in a fairly Cartesian manner of doubting to arrive at the indubitable, he was also keen to gather his impressions of the world without rejecting them as external distractions. On this, he made a critical departure from the Cartesian dualism of body and mind. While he maintained a rational outlook in his propositions, he believed in the possibility of a rational science of the concrete social world of humans rather than abstract notions of philosophers. Berlin (1980, 141) duly notes that Montesquieu upheld Cartesian methods without applying them in his own observations. The way of seeing that enables Montesquieu to present a prognostic explanation of society through its types is akin to that of a physician. Berlin observes:

> A physician does not, after all, usually ask himself what precisely it is that good health consists in.... Similarly, Montesquieu assumed that the idea of political and moral health is too familiar to need analysis, that when it is present this is quite patent, and that to be rational is to recognise it for what it is, to know the symptoms, to know how to cure the relevant diseases and how to maintain the organism. (1980, 142–143)

As a way of seeing, his quest for social types relied more on an intellectual understanding of what principle underlies the types rather than merely a morphological discovery of the empirical forms. And through the details of these socio-political types, Montesquieu predisposed sociological ways of seeing interrelated institutions. In other words, one ought to be seeing through the social institutions, the patterns of interactions, and most importantly the general principles that govern the social and the political. Moreover, Montesquieu hinted at the importance of adopting the perspective of others, the views of the outsiders of an institution rather than only dwelling upon the experiences of the insiders. The idea of comparative perspective thereby takes a methodological form. With such an orientation, Montesquieu contributed a discussion on 'spirit', as a force derived from general principles of institutions, relations and interactions. While doing so, his works anticipated the ideas of division of labour, its role in determining the characteristics of social relations and the concomitant idea of social solidarity, reverberant in Durkheim's sociology. His theoretical contribution is of immense value as it aids in understanding how society can uphold itself in the wake of explicit utilitarianism interfering with human relations. Given the methodological focus, the knowledge about institutions that Montesquieu delivered, with due theoretical sophistication, is out of the purview of this discussion. It is, however, worth reiterating that some of the components of the methodological apparatus that come to the fore in classical sociology, were interspersed in Montesquieu's contributions. If one can know the human world and its inherent properties, a science of such a world is possible. Montesquieu had faith in science, and an optimism about the role of modernity while also being fairly sceptical about it, unlike the other Encyclopaedists of the Enlightenment. This was scepticism about the high hopes of human perfection, the transition from traditional to rational, and suspicion about Enlightenment ideals. There was a sense of 'natural conservatism'[7] in Montesquieu's outlook that distinguished his way of seeing from that of his contemporaries. The best way to comprehend this, as a crucial component in Montesquieu's way of seeing, is to understand how he wrote about something as impersonal as laws:

> Laws, in their most general signification, are the necessary relations arising from the nature of things. In this sense all beings have their laws: the Deity his laws, the material world its laws, the intelligences superior to man their laws, the beasts their laws, man his laws.[8]

Guided by facts rather than abstract principles attained as a priori from the realms of philosophical reasoning, Montesquieu did not reject the significance of religions, traditions and social institutions. Moreover, he maintained a semblance of relativism about the cause and effects without subscribing to his compatriots, the Encyclopaedists, for whom a clear logical causal explanation was an end result in scientific enquiry. Steering clear of any such prior epistemological determination, Montesquieu was like a curious child seeking to see the probable causes of equally probable consequences. This is most explicit when he ruminated on the transition from the laws of nature to positive laws. With the knowledge of their existence, humans understand the need to preserve themselves against any existential threat. They develop knowledge of the laws of nature and accordingly ensure a safe life. However,

> As soon as man enters into a state of society he loses the sense of his weakness; equality ceases, and then commences the state of war.... The individuals likewise of each society become sensible of their force; hence the principal advantages of this society they endeavour to convert to their own emolument, which constitutes a state of war between individuals.[9]

No wonder Durkheim is quoted to have written, 'it is Montesquieu who first laid down the fundamental principles of social science. Not that he stated them in explicit terms. He speculated very little about the conditions of the science he inaugurated'.[10]

Like Montesquieu, Rousseau's contribution was geared to build on the idea of order in a social world where individuals have free will and the freedom to make choices. Walking the bridge between Enlightenment rationalism and romantic utopianism, he sought to show the possibility of perfection in humans. His understanding was that the age of modern science had brought about a chasm between the social and natural behaviour of humanity. Rousseau's romantic way of seeing provides him with a view of the divide between the social and natural. He advocates that social men and natural men can reconcile for a better society. For that to happen, Rousseau emphasised the imperative of restoring the sciences and the arts, which could contribute to the purification, rather than the alleged corruption, of morality wrought by a misleading science and distorted arts.[11] For, departing from the rationalist shortsightedness,[12] natural men are not as savage as we might think and social men are not as utilitarian as the socio-political and economic perspectives show. Thus, Rousseau rejected the Hobbesian idea of the natural state as a war of each against all. As evident, naturalist romanticism becomes a way of seeing in Rousseau's negotiation as well as a departure from the plain rationalism of the Enlightenment, enabling him to see more than what was shown and seen in the epoch dominated by scientific empiricism. His way of seeing thus encapsulated sentimentalism and intellectualism, truth and lies, facts and fables, as he emphasised mythology, ordinary citizens and a practice-oriented outlook. This is well elucidated in the two volumes of *Discourses*[13] that show that Rousseau sees things differently. A classic announcement of this is in the *Discourse on Science and Art*: 'If our sciences are vain in the objects they set for themselves, they are even more dangerous in the effects they produce'.[14] However, while doing so, Rousseau maintained his commitment to truth, with the principle *vitam impendere vero*, which is Latin for 'to risk one's life for truth'.[15] The paradoxical epistemological position[16] thus shows through the discussions interspersed in various works of Rousseau, including *Emile*, a treatise on education.

The evil, Rousseau believed, was not in the natural state of being. Instead, man becomes a warrior only after he becomes a citizen. Despite this, Rousseau was more hopeful with the citizens than with the philosophers. Their practical knowledge, imbued with natural perceptions, was a better source of understanding them and their world. And it was the citizens' ignorance of the abstract rationalism that Rousseau employed as a stance against the Enlightenment. He defended this ignorance,[17] and in this wake, the only way to bring about a semblance of order was through a realisation:

> You need me, for I am rich and you are poor. Let us therefore make a contract with one another. I will do you honor to permit you to serve me under the condition that you give me what little you still have left for the trouble I shall take in commanding you.[18]

And thus, against the background elucidated above, Rousseau's discussion on social contract makes sense. In arriving at these destinations in terms of theorising and proposing, there is a clear methodological orientation. It pertains to an objective evaluation of the prejudices that occupies the social world as well as its interpreters. For example, Rousseau critically evaluated Hobbes' thesis as well as the social and natural world. In doing so, the methodological orientation of Rousseau dwelt upon some of the axiomatic ideas pertaining to the Enlightenment, his self-evaluated prejudice, that natural is corrupted by social. This was in tandem with, on one hand, Locke's empiricism, that knowledge is by and large a posteriori proposition. One experiences, and thus one knows, and acts, in the social world. But then, on the other hand, Rousseau's axiom underpinned another implication, and that is about the state of nature. The natural state also entails knowledge, propositions and actions. This is available for our understanding, empirically too. The natural nurtures our ability of intuition, meditation and a more liberating kind of existence for both, citizens and seekers of knowledge. In a nutshell, Rousseau's methodological proposition can be dubbed as an evaluative empiricism. Perhaps this serves us well to make sense of the human world, which is rife with intersections of the natural and the social. Rousseau did not present a replica of scientific empiricism, which could pretend value neutrality. His departure from the Enlightenment notions of knowing was on the basis of what he learnt from Socrates. Rousseau refashioned some of the Socratic ideals in an endeavour to develop a unique way of seeing. 'Rousseau's Socrates',[19] as it were, persuades us to start with the Socratic premise—

know that we do not know. According to Rousseau, it was better to be ignorant than complacent and arrogant with pseudo-knowledge. He located an abundance of pseudo-knowledge amongst the proponents of the Enlightenment, and hence a concomitant doubt about the Enlightenment way of seeing. Philosophers were thus not reliable characters in his scheme of knowing. If there is any virtue, it is in 'the sublime science of simple souls'; it is with the citizens who could still afford to be ignorant and acknowledge being so. The Enlightenment philosophers created a worldview rife with opinions and dazzling illusions rather than the application of reason. The tyrannical authority of science undermined the domain from where virtues, morals and sanity in the state of freedom could emerge. 'Civil freedom is a condition that depends not so much on the mind as on the heart'[20] for Rousseau. The regime of the mind has dented the art, artists and their practices. Rousseau's lament was explicit, and perhaps relevant even today, as he noted:

> Every artist wishes to be applauded. The praises of his contemporaries are the most precious part of his reward. What will he do to obtain that praise … where one of the sexes dares to approve only what corresponds to the pusillanimity of the other and people let masterpieces of dramatic poetry fall by the wayside and repelled by works of wonderful harmony.[21]

Rousseau's lament about the state of sciences and arts, under the regime of rationalism vis-à-vis the Enlightenment, was coupled with the way forward that he saw and showed. It was to return to the natural and the sublime within the framework of science and arts, the social and the political, the philosophical and the moral. And on a curious note, it was also about requisite candour in pursuit of truth that enabled Rousseau to see the significance of lies. Rousseau prompts us to see the relationship of truth and lies, and its usefulness in general happiness and the enjoyment of rights. Though he did not answer some of the puzzles that arose from this interrelationship; he was more interested in underlining that truth was embodied, belonging to the subjective experience of the humans. It is in the realm of such embodied experience that truth and lie, fact and fiction, had an interrelationship. This is where he was distinguishable from Kant, as he did not operate with the categorical divide of the metaphysical and the physical. Having emphasised the importance of truth, he turned to lies, which are as useful for general happiness and rights as truth. As Rousseau said, 'Magnanimous lie! Is there a truth so beautiful that it could be preferred to you?'[22] And he continued in this vein in his self-reflective account in *Rêveries*:

> How many embarrassing discussions would be easily avoided by saying to oneself: Let us always be truthful at the risk of anything that can happen by it … distinguish the cases where truth is rigorously due, from those where one can withhold it without injustice and disguise it without lying: for I found that such cases really existed.[23]

It is not impossible to gauge the departures Rousseau makes from his contemporaries in offering a way of seeing, duly complex and suggestive of a new approach to the human world. In this, he emphasised some of the socio-cultural components and characters that usually played second fiddle in the larger meta-narrative of the Enlightenment. It is therefore not surprising that Durkheim, with his share of disagreements, held him as one of the precursors to sociological way of seeing.

The romantic and conservative tendencies that informs the background of the nineteenth century and the inception of the sociological way of seeing, presented a curious relationship with the Enlightenment thoughts. A critical discussion on 'how does one know' occupied empiricists and sceptics in the seventeenth century and the Enlightenment encyclopaedists of the eighteenth century. This has been alluded to previously while discussing David Hume and Immanuel Kant. They had pointed out the inevitable roles and presence of tradition, imagination, feeling and religion in the human world, which were somewhat irrational forces according to the rationalist scheme of the Enlightenment and Newtonian world of science. Continuing along this line of thought, the categories of community, family, society and nation were beginning to appear as important loci of human engagements in conservative thinking. There was a sense of radicalism implicit in the conservative ideas of the late eighteenth century, particularly after the French Revolution. The romantic and conservative thoughts,[24] thus, were also sceptical about the revolutionary processes in uprooting such important loci. Many names come to the fore in this regard, such as Edmund Burke, Louis de Bonald, Joseph de Maistre, Hugues Felicité de Lamennais, Francois Rene de Chateaubriand in France; Justus Möser, Adam Miller, Friedrich Carl von Savigny, Georg Wilhelm Friedrich Hegel in Germany; Johannes von Müller and Karl Ludwig von Haller in Switzerland; and Juan Donso Cortés and Jaime Luciano Balmes in Spain. They have been deemed radical 'prophets of the past',[25] though their reasoning provides much headway towards the future.

Conservatism upheld a particular methodological style, to borrow the idea from Mannheim (1953, 7). In the conservative methodology, the Cartesian determination of rationality or the empiricism of the Age of Reason are combated with empirical observation of everything seen in the social world. It allowed historicism to replace the deductive procedure of eighteenth-century philosophers. The conservatives thus saw a real man unlike their predecessors, who saw abstract man. The conservative's man, in other words, was not a philosopher's envisioned man. It was the way man is—natural and social at once, and potentially more than what philosophers get to see. It is a historically concrete man, such as a Frenchman or an Englishman, peasant, aristocrat, churchman, businessman, soldier or statesman. These historical entities have equally tangible institutions and customs. By putting the real, concrete and historical in the centre of analysis, one can suggest that the conservative brought about a sociological turn in philosophical ruminations that was richer with the works of the likes of Montesquieu and Rousseau. Moreover, the conservatives delivered a conceptual turf inclined to the typology of the traditionalist and the modernist. This was in the conservative scheme of contrasting the *ancien régime* with medieval roots and the twin forces of revolutionary democracy with the industrial movement. This found innumerable expressions across the early history of social sciences and sociology particularly. Nisbet points out, 'there are various ways of stating the typology: in Sir Henry Maine, "status" vs "contract"; in Tocqueville "aristocratic" vs "democratic"; in Marx, "feudal" vs "capitalist"; in Toennes, *Gemeinschaft* vs *Gesellschaft*; in Weber, "traditional" vs "rational-bureaucratic"; in Simmel, "rural" vs "urban"; and so on' (1978, 81). These typologies engendered more concepts that are in currency till date.[26]

In this regard, it is imperative to recall Edmund Burke's *Reflections on the Revolution in France*, a work that not only presented a lucid critique of a highly celebrated revolution in the history of modern politics, but also laying out the contours of more socially sensitive propositions. This work delivers a pointed rebuttal to the rationalist position on the French Revolution. Giving due space to community, Burke showed that individuals are erroneously perceived as wielding abstract rights. If there is a community, there will be a past encapsulating tradition, customs and institutions of the predecessors. Such a past will have continuity in the present. No revolution has the moral right to destroy it in order to deliver abstract notions. And likewise, the state cannot be a contract made by a few individuals. Instead, it ought to be an organic unity, inclusive of national community. Burke proposed that the state

> is a partnership in all science; a partnership in all art; a partnership in every virtue, and in all perfection. As the ends of such a partnership cannot be obtained in many generations, it becomes a partnership not only between those who are living, but between those who are dead and those are to be born.[27]

The brief reading of Burke's conservatism, reverberant in Hegel's philosophical conceptions, aids in realising that the precursor to the sociological way of seeing inherited grains of conservatism. While Burke offers a glimpse of the methodological stand through his discussion on what constitute the world of socio-political and moral realities, the way of seeing becomes more explicit in Hegel. Reason is not an entity that ought to be thought of as a means to an end or an abstract tool in the hand of a few enlightened philosophers. Instead, it exists in the realm of reality, because the rational and the real are intertwined. Thereby, Hegel arrived at the notion of cosmic force, the Idea, the Spirit, the Absolute, even God. It is through these notions that the relationship of the natural and the social comes to the fore for philosophical recognition in the Hegelian scheme. One should not dismiss Hegel because he offered 'surprising conclusions'.[28] The surprising conclusion was the Hegelian celebration of the Prussian state as an ultimate manifestation of the Spirit. It, however, makes sense in the Hegelian framework of conservatism. But then, there was a promising paradox in Hegel's conservatism. The Hegelian scheme of reasoning locates reason and rationality in the realm of reality. There is an acute awareness of socio-political dynamics and dialectical development in society. This paradox in Hegel is perhaps sufficient to steer clear of the Hegelian inclination towards the Prussian state, a monarchy. Hegel held this monarchy as an absolute spirit and manifestation of the 'Cosmic reason' in order to please the rulers of Prussia.

In contemporary parlance, conservatism may be deemed to be a pejorative word. In the age of progress, who would like to be called a conservative? At best, we employ this word only to identify a political position associated with a political party or backward thinking. Back in the eighteenth century, conservatism was a respectable body of philosophical ruminations. It offered a perspective about the intricacies of the social and the political, the traditional and the modern, communitarian and the national. Some of these concerns remained central in sociological ruminations later in the twentieth century. In addition to Edmund Burke, one must also note two more conservative thinkers, diehard traditionalists who glorified the lost medieval order—Bonald and Maistre. They revived the terms that had been marginalised in the eighteenth-century celebration of the values of modernity—reason, rationality, individualism, secularism and freedom. The usages of terms such as divine providence, original sin, final causes and infallible church were central in the conservative scheme of reasoning. By discrediting the immediate past in order to go further back in history, the conservatives tended to add a different sense of historicism in their deliberations. Moreover, both the conservative thinkers explicitly referred to an anthropological turn in otherwise philosophical discourse that dominated the eras before and after the French Revolution. Both spoke through polemics, which assailed most of the rationalist proponents of the seventeenth and eighteenth centuries, including Montesquieu and Rousseau. It must have indeed been fairly radical to shrug off the legacy of two centuries in the wake of the socio-political churnings in France.

First and foremost, Bonald aimed to diminish the role of the individual in the creation of works of art and literature by showing them as socio-cultural artefacts. By doing so, he addressed Montesquieu and Rousseau's approach of putting aside socio-moral conditioning and the role of the collective in the creation of knowledge. Maistre attacked Rousseau for the dichotomised understanding of man, as social and natural, as though there was nothing in common between the two. Likewise, Bonald rejected the idea of natural man and natural right, in order to emphasise that all men are social and so are men's rights. If they are not natural, they are not the abstract weapons of the Enlightenment philosophers either. The social man with social rights existent in definite and concrete social relationships could not be made a passive tool in the revolutionary agenda of the handful of philosophers. Maistre gave premium to the family as a prototype of society, with an argument that sexual differentiation pertained to the divine purpose behind the order on the earth. In Maistre's conservative scheme, a lawgiver like Moses, the Hebrew prophet from approximately the thirteenth century BC and an important figure in the Bible, was far more important than the Enlightenment encyclopaedists. For, an ancient lawgiver emphasised on the moral underpinnings of the physical/social unity.

Evidently, Bonald sharpened a way of seeing for future sociology that would emphasise the scheme of social in the making of men and their institutions. Bonald also deemed ideas to be innate in men. However, this stance does not align him with Cartesian philosophy, because innate ideas are socially communicated. The word and language become crucial instruments of truth, an idea that figured prominently in the sociology of Emile Durkheim. Language, following the Old Testament, emerged prior to society. And furthermore, family, the church and state authority preserved God and tradition, which, over generations, has been passed on to mankind. The language, and everything about the divine articulated in a language, pertains to the Providence, the almighty. Hence, the attempt by humans to derive the meaning of their life through language cannot be arbitrary and relative to their interpretations. We learn and use them, the language and the meanings, not in seclusion. Out quest of meanings through the language is in relationship with one another as well as with the divine. A supporter of Restoration, of the status quo of the medieval social order, Bonald was envisioning a reconstruction of a post-Revolution, post-Reformation French society. This envisioning aimed at restoring the church and the feudal social system. This was an important response to the conservative understanding of the bourgeoisie-led industrial revolution. It was allegedly in the interest of the bourgeoisie to undermine sacred social units, namely, human relations, social institutions and cultural practices.

Such a background had influenced Henri de Saint-Simon, the late eighteenth-century French thinker and social reformer known for sowing the seeds for the discipline of sociology. He had a liberal approach towards understanding the anomalies of industrial society. But, the solution that he offered were duly connected with the conservative proposition. For example, Saint-Simon's emphasis on the Christian socialism, that is, a religious order for equality and brotherhood of men, revealed the amalgamation of both, the scientific rationality and the conservative inclinations. Also, to reiterate, Bonald's propositions discussed above were anticipation of the sociology of Emile Durkheim that unfolded more concretely in the nineteenth century. Durkheim marshalled the conservative insights into his discussion on the idea of organic solidarity in the industrial society. Moreover, if God was the expression of society for Bonald, for Durkheim, it was the opposite: society was an expression of God.

Both Bonald and Maistre departed from Burke in casting aspersions on the ideas of Reformation; particularly Maistre, who was keen to show function of institutions, held the Reformation for the evil in society. They singled out Protestantism, capitalism and science as the key movers of disturbances in social order. On the whole, conservative thought had shifted attention from the free individual to the group, from social change to stability. It added a new perspective for reasoning in social contexts.[29]

Founding Figures: To Posit a Vision and an Ism

Some of the well-known founding figures of sociology attempted to posit a vision in the backdrop of the above discussion. The vision was not free from ideologies and utopias, as these founding figures had to straddle many zones of thoughts. These thinkers carried forward the ways of seeing of the precursors and began to develop the vision for a formal sociology. There is an uncanny combination of vision and ideological moorings that played an important role in shaping up a domain of enquiry in early sociology.

This section seeks to place Saint-Simon and August Comte together for variety of reasons. One explicit reason is the evident proximity of ideas of the two insofar as the way of seeing is concerned. Zeitlin observed that in the works of Saint-Simon, 'virtually all of Comte's ideas originated and which he so ungraciously plagiarized' (1968, 57). If one could discredit thinkers of the twentieth century on the charge of plagiarism, many of the so-called founding figures will be ejected from the scheme of classical sociology, perhaps. Overlapping of ideas without due acknowledgement for the origin of the same was not yet a legal concern. The following is an attempt to present a narrative putting together the Saint-Simon and his seeming protégé.[30]

Henri de Saint-Simon shared the conservative critique of the revolutionary philosophical proposition and the French Revolution, even though he had participated in the American Revolution as an artillery captain at Yorktown in America. In his own words, 'I did not wish to take part in it [the French revolution], because, on one hand, I was convinced that the *Ancien Regime* could not be prolonged, and, on the other, I had an aversion to destruction.'[31] There was an inherent utopianism[32] which inspired Saint-Simon's science and socialism, positive politics and internationalism.

What he did not seem to share with the conservatives, however, was the uncritical submission to a particular kind of order that belonged to medieval history, or the ancient regime. That did not mean that he remained passive during the revolution. He relinquished his aristocratic title and presided the meetings of the socialist commune; he was felicitated with the certificate of good citizen and actively participated in radical circles even though his romantic and conservative inclination was explicit. And hence, despite all this, he remained committed to the idea of reconstructing an order in otherwise a disorderly society post revolution. Therefore, Saint-Simon's approach was perhaps the first-ever embodiment of an intellectual ambivalence that characterises modern, formal sociology. He accepted the merit of conservative arguments in favour of social order but also expressed continuity with eighteenth-century rationalism in his deliberation on ideas such as positivism, industrialism, internationalism and need of a new religion. Moreover, his take on socialism, though more of utopian nature, was expressive of his interest in dealing with the anomalies of the new world order that was being enforced by capitalism. In this reconstruction, if the notion of order was important, so was the role of science. He envisaged that a new elite, with a scientific spirit and international orientation in industrial society, would replace the educated elite of the Middle Ages as science would be new religion. The international order in the Middle Ages was possible due to the church, an international organisation. While one cannot go back, one can explore similar alternatives in modern times, with science and positive philosophy binding nations across the world. This was at the core of Saint-Simon's promulgation on positivism, which tried to synthesise the learnings from the seventeenth and eighteenth centuries. This version of positivism played an important role in sociology in the nineteenth century, which is the focus of the next chapter.

Akin to Newtonian physics, positivism was to aid in the science of the human–social world. Only positivism, akin to the religious doctrine of the past, could engender a set of common truths that would bind humans in mutual trust and respect. Saint-Simon proposed this on the basis of his comprehension of social groups across human history. Instead of imagining irresolvable friction, he perceived a possibility of coexistence of plural social structures. He expected property owners and others to join in collaboration towards meeting the ideal of a socialism, which was premised upon scientific truths. It is evident that Saint-Simon tried to refashion science with a strong sense of positive thinking. He imagined even politics to be informed by science, and thereby he assumed that political questions would be essentially scientific in nature. It is no wonder then that Durkheim credited Saint-Simon for the origin and evolution of positivism, as he observed, Saint-Simon was

> the first to conceive that between the formal generalities of metaphysical philosophy and the narrow specialisation of the particular sciences, there was a place for a new enterprise, whose pattern he supplied and himself attempted. Therefore, it is to him that one must, in full justice, award the honour currently given to Comte. (1958, 104)

Even the stages of intellectual growth and the emergence of positive philosophy that Comte claimed as his contribution were elucidated by Saint-Simon. However, on several fronts, one can critique Saint-Simon, such as in his enthusiastic proposition of socialism in which there was no critical dismantling of the private property even though it was antithetical to socialist principles. His ultimate faith in scientific generalisable truths for society was equally problematic. Be that as it may, the idea of positivism took a tangible shape in Saint-Simon's discussion, paving the way for a new science to emerge, which, in the course of time, came to be called sociology.

Almost every beginner of sociology knows that the term, sociology is preceded by social physics, in Comte's discussion. However, prior to the coinage and currency of the term, Comte had to establish himself as a philosopher repudiating some of his predecessors and negotiating with many in the process of developing a positive philosophy. The latter was already sufficiently anticipated by Saint-Simon.[33] Comte, too, stressed on the negative intentions and implications of the Enlightenment and the Revolution. The Enlightenment philosophers were, as per Comte, metaphysicians who broke away from the old order of the theological stage and paved the way for something more positive. The imperative was to use the ground prepared during the Enlightenment and work on the positive stage. As evident, this formulation entailed three stages, theological, metaphysical and positive, which Comte proclaimed to have verified through experience. Giddens notes that Comte,

> claimed to have achieved personal verification of the law of the three stages in his periods of insanity, which he had experienced, he claimed, as regression back though from positivism to metaphysics to theology on the level of his personality, in his recovery retracing these stages forward again. (1978, 241)

As dramatically narcissistic as it may sound, this is how Comte sought to repudiate even Hegelian dialectic. In the post-French Revolution age, he noted the rise of social anarchy due to the collapse of social institutions. As a remedy to the deplorable anarchy, he presented his social physics that would bring about a replacement for the old order that had outlived its utility. Every stage in Comte's evolutionary scheme had its dogma. On this point, there is a critique of the Enlightenment encyclopaedists as well as the French Revolution. Comte noted that the progressive metaphysicians, that is, the Enlightenment encyclopaedists, created another set of dogmas, departing from theological stage. Such progressive dogmas were also reverberant in the French Revolution. These dogmas, some of them being equality, sovereignty and liberty, were key characteristics of the eighteenth century. Only specialised vision enables one to see through such dogmas, if one is adequately scientific. Hence, as Comte led us to believe, laypersons were not to be trusted in the positive philosophy. This is similar to how astronomers, physicists and chemists don't need interference of the non-experts in their respective scientific domains of enquiry. This is, however, with recognition that in the hierarchy of sciences, the science of human world, that is, sociology, will be deemed the youngest. The distinction of this particular branch of science toward which Comte was inclined began to take an exclusive character in the finitude and conclusion of positive philosophy. It revealed the centrality of positive scientific method, the quality of truth and the importance of trained expertise in Comte's sociology. These methods were clones of scientific methods, subordinating imagination to observation and reason to facts. And it was through such practices that a seeker of knowledge about the social world could fathom the relation of parts with the whole. Comte prophetically ruminated:

> By including social science in the scientific hierarchy, the positive spirit admits to success in this study only well-prepared and disciplined minds so trained in the preceding departments of knowledge as to be fit for the complex problems of the last. The long and difficult preliminary elaboration must disgust and deter vulgar and ill-prepared mind, and subdue the most rebellious.[34]

This is a version of positivism in the works of Saint-Simon and August Comte, methodologically more tangible in Durkheim's functionalist sociology in the late nineteenth century. This positivism is, however, different from the philosophical positivism of the Vienna Circle.[35] The circle, comprising mathematicians, physicists, philosophers and scientists, began to function in the first quarter of the twentieth century. Self-proclaimed progenitors of new enlightenment, the circle was, according to one of the raconteurs Herbert Feigl, carrying forward the spirit of Hume and Comte with a more developed logical tool.[36] It sought to reconfigure empiricism, dismissing the Kantian idea of synthetic a priori, and mostly stressed on hypothetic-deductive logic. The Vienna Circle's early form of logical empiricism, interchangeably known as logical positivism or neo-positivism, advanced to contemporary analytical philosophy that still attracts philosophers. The formative stage witnessed the active role of the Austrian physicist and philosopher Ernst Mach, mathematician Hans Hahn, philosophers Otto Neurath and Rudolf Carnap among others. Though not members, Bertrand Russell and Ludwig Wittgenstein were also involved in the philosophical churnings of the circle.

Giddens underlined similarities in Comte's and Mach's treatment of positivism insofar as the methods of scientific observation, logical deduction and the position of scientific knowledge in industrial society were concerned. They both seem to have shared a departure from metaphysics, inclined to rebuilding the social world with a scientific lexicography. While there was no scope for a reflexive subject in Comte's positive philosophy, Mach's logical positivism even rejected the role of theories in making truth claims. This happened to be a mainstay of the Vienna Circle positivism—no mediation of theories and concepts in the empirical facts. But Mach set the scene for more robust development of logical tools, which could steer clear of meaningless statements, unlikely to sustain testability and verification. Carnap shifted from the radicalism of logical positivism to a relatively liberal, though not deviating from, the positive philosophy of Mach that had rendered the metaphysics as doctrines without cognitive meaning. Carnap's liberalism was characterised by his stress on the idea of rebuilding knowledge and the scientific theories. Carnap alleged the logical positivists reduced scientific theories into mere protocol statements, an irrevocable recipe of actions in the scientific practices. When science becomes a protocol, 'correspondence rules' are the real litmus test. The correspondence rules, alternatively known as correspondence theory, are meant to emphasise the direct correlation between the observation and statement of truth. Carnap underlined the possibility of creative elements, thoughts and perceptions, playing an important role in between observation and statement. In short, it was to underline that observation statements could not be entirely theory-free. This was Carnap's epistemological liberalism in which the mathematical relationship between observation and a statement of truth was transformed into an artistic relationship fraught with mediating theories and insights. One can therefore deem Carnap's intervention as a significant countercurrent within the Vienna Circle. This furthermore led to accepting that predictions too could be a deductive–nomological explanation about the future. That drew a parallel between the positivism of early sociology and that of the Circle. Also, it emerged that *verstehen*, which Hempel referred to as the method of empathic understanding, could be a method for engendering hypothesis.[37] Needless to say, this found a resonance in the sociology of Max Weber. The direct relationship of the scientific positivism of the Vienna Circle and sociology becomes more palpable with Otto Neurath, who deemed sociology as a part of the division of labour in the totality of unified science. Linking behaviourism with positivism, Neurath's thoughts furthered the exploration of methodology. In this light, it is worth mentioning that Ernest Nagel's *The Structure of Science* served great deal in discussing science and sociology. And Hans Zetterberg's *On Theory and Verification in Sociology* was considered important in linking the takeaway from the Circle in discussion on sociological methods.

If one has to make a simple summary about what positivism stands for, it could be worth recalling the five fundamental 'tenets of positivism'.[38] First, positivism puts forth unity of scientific method or scientism, enforcing methodological monism. The latter means that the method of natural science is universal for all other sciences. Second, positivism thrives on naturalism or phenomenalism, also known as methodological naturalism. This means that the subject matter of all sciences shall be deemed to have a similar objective. This furthermore entails three levels—reductionism (each unit can be reduced into a single entity for study), the correspondence theory of truth (that the finding shall correspond with reality) and phenomenalism or objectivism (since nature is objectified and external to science, it shall be neutrally observed). The third tenet of positivism is putting empiricism as a key methodology that requires one to investigate through sense organs. Empiricism here relies on the logical methods of inductivism (for verifying the observation and causal explanation) and deductive logic for deriving a hypothesis from general laws. Fourth, positivism stands for value neutrality as an ethical and methodological commitment. This is deemed imperative since scientific knowledge distinguishes fact and value. The fifth and last tenet of positivism renders science as a domain of instrumental knowledge, eventually facilitating technically useful knowledge.

It won't be an excessive reading between the lines to suggest that positivism and sociology are conjoined twins. Yet the conjoined twins seem to have a non-linear relationship according to the methodological scheme of nineteenth-century sociologists. Both seem to be happening at once in the minds, and letters, of some of the thinkers who claimed to have laid the theoretical grounds for doing sociology in the later centuries. As we will notice in the following chapter, there is a consistent and critical engagement with positivist postulates in the classical sociology of the trinity. However, it is difficult to declare a categorically linear relationship between sociology and positivism. It will come across sharply in the next chapter that the relationship was fraught with the methodological ways of seeing of each sociologist. Yet, we cannot deny the preoccupation with positivism which has been so strong that sociology can be declared some kind of positivistic enterprise with some riders. No matter how many gallons of ink may have been spent on writing against positivism in the so-called 'post-positivist'[39] sociology, the conjoined twins are alive and kicking in teaching, research and writings. Many sociologists won't deviate from positivism. Such a deviation entails an apprehension that the discipline of sociology will have an existential crisis.

In the deliberations of the forerunners in this chapter, the fundamental imagination of how to be oriented in a particular way of seeing the social world clearly comes through. In this wake, revisiting the trinity in classical sociology is an interesting enterprise. It is, however, fraught with a major question. Who shall be discussed first? Logic would recommend a chronological appearance, and thus it shall be a discussion on Marx and the way of seeing that emanates from Marx's writings. For example, Giddens'[40] bestseller commentary puts them in the following order: Marx, Durkheim and Weber. However, as history shows, it is with Emile Durkheim that a feasible model of positivism appears, though it is tightly knit with a functionalist framework. And therefore it is appropriate to start with Durkheim. In the next chapter the attempt is not to recapitulate the entire body of work of a thinker. It is primarily centred on the question of how do they tend to be sociological. Even though this question does not surface as such in Marx, the methodological discussion shall acquire the centre stage. With a turn to Weber, the complications of sociological ways of seeing shall begin to surface. On the whole, the next chapter presents a view of how the Enlightenment epistemology discussed in the previous chapter, and its countercurrents, the precursors discussed in this chapter, come to find a place in the age of sociological classics.

References

Alexander, Jeffery C. 'Beyond the Epistemological Dilemma: General Theory in a Postpositivist Mode', *Sociological Forum* 5, no. 4 (December 1990): 531–544.

Bauman, Zygmunt. 'Sociological Enlightenment—For Whom, About What?', *Theory, Culture, and Society* 17, no. 2 (2000): 71–82.

Berlin, Isaiah. 'Montesquieu', In *Against the Current: Essays in the History of Ideas, by Isaiah Berlin*, edited by Henry Hardy, 130–161. New York: Viking, 1980.

Durkheim, Emile. *Socialism and Saint Simon*. London: Routledge and Kegan Paul, 1958.

———. *Montesquieu and Rousseau*. Ann Arbor: The University of Michigan Press, 1960.

Giddens, Anthony. 'Positivism and Its Critics'. In *A History of Sociological Analysis*, edited by Tom Bottomore and Robert Nisbet, 237–287. London: Heinemann, 1978.

———. *Capitalism and Modern Social Theory: An Analysis of the Writings of Marx, Durkheim and Max Weber*. Delhi: Cambridge University Press, 2009.

Gourevitch, Victor. 'Rousseau on the Arts and Sciences', *The Journal of Philosophy* 69, no. 20 (1972): 737–754.

Jones, Robert Alun. 'Ambivalent Cartesians: Durkheim, Montesquieu and Method', *American Journal of Sociology* 100, no. 1 (1994): 1–39.

Mannheim, Karl. 'Conservative Thought'. In *Essays on Sociology and Social Psychology*, edited by Paul Kecskemeti, 74–164. New York: Oxford University Press, 1953.

Marshall, Terence E. 'Rousseau and Enlightenment', *Political Theory* 6, no. 4 (1978): 421–455.

Montesquieu, Charles de. *The Spirit of Law*. London: G. Bell & Sons Ltd, 1752. https://www.marxists.org/reference/subject/philosophy/works/fr/montesqu.htm (accessed 12 September 2021).

Mukherji, Partha Nath (ed.). *Methodology in Social Research: Dilemmas and Perspectives*. Delhi: Sage, 2000.

Myrdal, Gunnar. *An American Dilemma* (vol. 2), 1047. New York: Harper and Row, 1962.

Nisbet, R. 'Conservatism and Sociology', *American Journal of Sociology* 58 (1952): 167–175.

———. *The Sociological Tradition*. London: Heinemann, 1967.

———. 'Conservatism'. In *A History of Sociological Analysis*, edited by Tom Bottomore and Robert Nisbet, 80–118. London: Heinemann, 1978.

Orwin, Clifford. 'Rousseau's Socratism', *The Journal of Politics* 60, no. 1 (1998): 174–187.

Pathak, Avijit. 'Teaching/Learning Sociology: A Critical Engagement with Modernity', *Sociological Bulletin* 53, no. 1 (2004): 31–48. https://doi.org/10.1177/0038022920040102.

———. *Indian Modernity*. Delhi: Aakar, 2015.

Saint-Simon, Henri. *Henri Saint-Simon (1760–1825): Selected Writings on Science, Industry, and Social Organization*, edited by Keith Taylor. New York: Holmes and Meier, 1975.

Zeitlin, Irving M. *Ideology and the Development of Sociological Theory*. New Jersey: Prentice-Hall Inc, 1968.

4

RETURN TO THE TRINITY: SOCIOLOGICAL IN MARX, WEBER AND DURKHEIM

An excerpt from the Mahabharata's very first section, the 'Adi Parv', illustrates some very critical insights on the way of seeing. This excerpt will be an abiding feature in this chapter that will discuss ways of seeing emanating from the classical sociological trinity: Marx, Weber and Durkheim. The discussion shall underline the presence of a particular motif that underpins the methodological components of classical sociology in the late nineteenth and early twentieth centuries. To understand this motif and how it characterizes the methodological way of seeing in classical sociology, we turn to the following episode, the 'Adi Parv' in the epic Mahabharata.

In the prelude, a job-seeking teacher of archery named Dronacharya, a Kshatriya guru was employed by Bhishma, the guardian of the kingdom of Hastinapur and the grandfather of the Pandavas and the Kauravas, cousins and princely scions of the kingdom. One of the Pandavas, Arjun, who was dear to his teacher Dronacharya, realised that practice is more important than (in)sight while eating his dinner in complete darkness. He thus began to practice archery during pitch-dark nights. Impressed by his determination, Dronacharya promised him the best of knowledge and training so that no one would be equal to the supremacy of Arjun's knowledge in *dhanurvidya* (archery). It was this very promise that was a reason why Dronacharya denied his lessons to another promising young archer, Eklavya, a member of the tribe that lived in the jungle. He was purportedly rejected on the basis that his birth made him an ineligible student to Dronacharya. Not one to give up, Eklavya learnt archery in hiding. On discovering this, and the prodigious skills displayed by Eklavya, Dronacharya, remembering the promise he made to Arjun to train him to be the best archer in the world, manipulated Eklavya into cutting off his thumb as *guru-dakshina*. Post this incident, Dronacharya arranged for a special test for all his students. He had an artificial wooden bird perched on the branch and hidden among the dense foliage of the tree. The guru then summoned all his disciples to ask them a similar question meant to test their concentration. Everybody failed to provide the answer

Dronacharya wanted and retreated without firing an arrow. Arjun was the only one who could answer correctly.

The Guru asked: 'Do you see the tree, the bird, as well as me?'

Arjun confidently responded: 'My venerable teacher, I see nothing but the bird's eye.'

To test the examinee further, Dronacharya asked him another question: 'Tell me how the bird looks in shape and size.'

Arjun replied: 'I know nothing of how it looks; I see nothing but the bird's eye.'

Ecstatic, Dronacharya told him to release the arrow and Arjun successfully shot the eye of the bird.[1]

This tale presents the crux of the formulaic way of being sociological in which those who follow the given order of things, the status quo of society, are eligible trainees and those who don't, like Eklavya, become outsiders. Not that all eligible trainees tend to make it to the last goalpost, in this case, the bird's eye. Nor is it that all seemingly ineligible candidates are any less competent, such as Eklavya. Besides, the tale centralises a notion, the Arjun-motif, a single-minded and uncritical pursuit of a given methodology and goal. The motif's strength is manifest in the fact that Arjun can practise archery even in the night, almost blindfolded. Not a critical reflection, but a surrender to the methodology that characterises the Arjun-motif. This motif will be underlined in the predominant ways of seeing established in classical sociology. What does it really mean? This chapter unfolds the sociological ways of seeing of the three key sociological thinkers resonating with the Arjun-motif. The question then is who can be seen as the appropriate trainee in a sociological way of seeing and who cannot.

Most of the teachings and learnings about the thinkers and the courses on classical sociological theories are geared to the epistemological destinations of the thinkers, the theories and concepts. This chapter seeks to see the thinkers' ways of seeing revealed in the theoretical destinations they arrived at rather than merely reproducing theories and concepts. It shall enable us to understand the thinkers' engagement with the ideas that pertain to the scientific epistemology owed to the Enlightenment, and the counter-currents owed to the precursors and predecessors discussed in Chapters 2 and 3, respectively. Their ways of seeing are a negotiation, contestation and reformulation of the insights from the scientific epistemology of the Enlightenment and the conservative and romantic insights. Suffice it to say that the way of seeing in the age of sociological classics in the late nineteenth and early twentieth century meant seeing 'things' like a 'thing' and not like yet another human in the vicinity. It is somewhat akin to Arjun seeing only the eye of the bird. Like Arjun, the scholars who aspire to do sociology must steer clear of the broader vision of the world. Instead, they ought to be single-minded, focused and steadfast on the imperatives of being sociological, as has been discussed in detail in this chapter. Essentially, the sociological way of seeing demands to join the trinity in the 'fight against phantoms', a common idea to all members of the trinity, despite the difference in their respective theoretical objectives. And as it would seem, the fight against phantoms becomes an essential characteristic of any aspiring sociologist.

At the outset, it is wise to share a puzzle that often surfaces when it comes to the trinity. The preceding chapter echoes the apprehension of the puzzle: who shall be deemed the trinity in the classical sociology of the late nineteenth and early twentieth century? To reiterate, it dealt with the omission and commission of the thinkers in the scheme of discussing classical sociology.[2] Why is it always Karl Marx, Emile Durkheim and Max Weber when one speaks about the trinity in sociology? Why not Ferdinand Tönnies, Georg Simmel and Wilfred Pareto? Or Herbert Spencer, Saint-Simon and Georg Simmel? In short, why not some or other permutations and combinations of the thinkers' names which are heard in classical sociology more often than not?

Connell (1997, 511), a sociologist known for an elaborate discussion on masculinity, raised a curious question with regard to the inclusion and exclusion of theorists in the axis of the classics. The centrality of three men and their theories, making a trinity was due to historical reasons. The three thinkers provided theoretical moorings to engage with the historical condition of the nineteenth century characterised by the changes in polity, economy and society. Their bodies of work served the immediate requirement of sociology in an industrialised society. The canons of the classics became identity-defining for the discipline. Notwithstanding, there has been an interest in exploring other thinkers of equally eminent contributions. One can debate on the issue but this chapter leaves this fundamental apprehension unresolved. Besides, this is not the only puzzle that preoccupies us. There is another equally important and daunting one, which also has been left unresolved. This is about the advent of a disciplinary boundary. Are the three thinkers in the trinity strictly confined to the disciplinary boundaries of sociology? What about other disciplines where these thinkers may figure in discussions with more or less the same prominence? Is naming the trinity an act of disciplinary socialisation, where theoretical gods are invoked, reaffirmed and critically eulogised? These are a few discomforting questions that haunt a discussion that is supposed to be about a relatively modern body of thought, seemingly secular and claimed to be rational. The fact of the matter is that all three in the trinity seem to be intellectually promiscuous enough to feed themselves on a variety of sources, which could be now identified with different disciplines. The so-called intellectual promiscuity of the three is indeed enticing and adds enchanting values to the discussion they present in their respective bodies of work. Even though students of philosophy may not be reading the philosophically potent works of Emile Durkheim, no one can perhaps deny his philosophical overtures.[3] Born in a Jewish family, Durkheim did not become a rabbi like his father and yet maintained a deep interest in moral philosophy abutting Christianity. Committed to secular modernity and scientific temperament, he became a teacher of philosophy in a state secondary school, and, subsequently influenced by psychology, went on to study philosophy and became a lecturer in social philosophy in France.

Likewise, it is imperative to remember the varied interests of, and in, Karl Marx. Read across the disciplines, who could forget a young poetic Marx who wrote an impassioned lyrical and spiritually elevating letter to his father upon arriving in Berlin in 1837? The letters seem to anticipate the making of an encyclopaedic Marx. The then nineteen-year-old complained about the lack of poetry and sentiments in the unnaturalness of the study of law in Germany. Interested in philosophy and poetry, Marx was studying law while also regularly frequenting the poets' club active at the time and sought to find a philosophical bridge between what he painfully found as separated twins—art and science, philosophy and law. A student reading Marx ought to be aware of a possible link between the young Marx and the one deemed more scientific. But reading Marx is terribly preconditioned by various manipulations and divides, agendas and vested interests, rather than what early Indian sociologist D.P. Mukerji had proposed, Marxology, which is reading Marxian literature without any iota of ideological indoctrination and implementing Marxian insights in making sense of social reality.

At worst, various disciplines would divide Marx into young and mature, romantic and scientific.[4] Accordingly, Marx' works are characterised by certain kinds of adjectives. For example, some academics called the works of young Marx naïve, sentimentalist, and romantic. Such adjectives for a young Marx's works are often used by those in academics more inclined to the works of a mature, scientific and historically substantiated Marx. Indeed, this division refers to a politics of preference entailed in the selection of Marxian texts. A believer in Marxism is seldom at ease with the romantic inclinations of a young Marx. Such a believer has an orthodox model of Marxism dominating the choice of Marx' works. As a result, any discussion on Marx, suffice to say, cannot satisfy a Marxist. Furthermore, there is a diversity of Marxism that corresponds with diverse Marxist political activism such as Leninism, Trotskyism, Libertarian Marxism, Maoism etc. That makes the discussion of Marx' works even more challenging. For, one never knows what kind of Marxist is among the audience. And besides, when theorists are elevated to pedestals and treated like sacred entities, there is a taken for granted intolerance towards any creative deviance or schematic erring.

A more or less similar trajectory emerges when one seeks to place Max Weber as a classical sociologist, in spite of the fact that Weberian theorisation on bureaucracy, authority and class may find resonance in the studies on politics, law, governance and administration. Enmeshed in the German tradition of ideas, Weber is as much a political economist and sociologist as his works are available for insightful readings. A Marxist reader may selectively read Weber in order to show the limitations of his historical approach in comparison with Marx's historical materialism. But it is difficult to dismiss Weber's poignant perspective and counterintuitive arguments. Once again, Weber's personal and biographic details, his upbringing in Puritan morality of an orthodox Calvinist family, his deep interest in economic history and his brief stint as a jurisprudence professor make for the chequered intellectual development.

Therefore, it becomes a challenge to justify, for many enmeshed reasons, the sociological trinity.

Be that as it may, this chapter commits an intellectual risk of perpetuating the familiar names as part of the trinity, ignoring the reaffirmation of the disciplinary boundary that is implicit in the act of discussing the trinity of classical sociology. However, as pointed out, the intention is to underline that the cross-disciplinary nourishment of such thinkers leads to discussions that are conducive to many disciplines in social science. Hence, their ways of seeing consist in the peculiarity of epistemic deliberations, negotiation as well as a departure from the predecessors and a proposition to think of a qualitatively different science of society. In so doing, the classical sociology of the trinity succumbs to the Arjun-motif flagged at the onset, to which the chapter returns eventually.

The Trinity Revisited

As a 'less propagandist'[5] among many from his generation, Emile Durkheim derived methodological impetus from the founding figures such as Saint-Simon and August Comte, as well as from some of the less discussed thinkers from France and Germany. For example, Durkheim's predilection for organic analogy, which he employed to describe the relationship of social with biological, was a takeaway from Albert Schäffle.[6] He also borrowed from him the idea of the collective conscience—the common belief, values and behaviour in a society. Moreover, Durkheim absorbed the German economic theory set by the likes of Adolph Wagner and Gustav Schmoller, which was a departure from the individualistic utilitarianism of orthodox economic theory. Similarly, one can underline the links between Durkheim's stress on the social function of religion with Wilhelm Wundt's discussion on social cohesion arising from religious life. Needless to say, alongside these readings, Durkheim engaged with other predecessors of his to shape a way of seeing in sociology that entails moralistic sociologising for all practical and methodological purposes. We noted in the previous chapter that Durkheim deemed Montesquieu and Rousseau to be the precursors of sociology. Throughout Durkheim's sociology, including classics such as *The Division of Labour, The Elementary Forms of Religious Life,* even *Suicide,* which is about applying *The Rules of Sociological Method* and arriving at typologies, one can read Durkheim's moral concern. This was in tandem with his primary training in educational philosophy as a young Lycée teacher and the subsequent development in his university life. His *Moral Education* is a testimonial of his ways of seeing and being sociological.

And what is the way of seeing in the sociology of Emile Durkheim?

It is, following *The Rules,* to see, interpret, understand and explain 'social facts as things' (Durkheim 1982, 60). Any student of sociology knows about social fact and its three characteristics that render it as a detached, self-sufficient and general 'thing'. The point is how one really gets to such a 'thing'. Since the imagined destination is a thing, the voyagers have to train themselves to become 'things' too. To become so, one has to get rid of *notiones vulgares* or *praenotiones*, that is, a priori notions, against which the philosopher Francis Bacon waged a battle, calling them *idols of minds.* Durkheim does not seem to disagree with Bacon as he says,

> It is these *idola* which, resembling ghost-like creatures, distort the true appearance of things, but which we nevertheless mistake for the things themselves. It is because this imagined world offers no resistance that the mind, feeling completely unchecked, gives rein to limitless ambitions, believing it possible to construct—or rather reconstruct—the world through its own power and according to its wishes. (62)

Durkheim (1998) was so professionally inclined that in the hundreds of letters he wrote to his nephew Marcel Mauss between 1893 and 1917, he seldom sounded like an uncle. Rather than any avuncular charm, volumes of words in his letters comprise tall demands from his nephew about the importance of carving out an exclusive nature of the discipline of sociology. The letters reveal a great deal about the Durkheimian way of seeing in sociology, about what sociology ought to be doing. An image of an intellectually uptight, poker-faced uncle delivering sermons about the upkeep of sociological pursuits is what one gets out of these letters, dramatically divorced from the emotions one anticipates in avuncular kinship. These letters, however, also eventually aided in understanding the establishment and rise of *Année Sociologique* as the 'Training Ground for Sociology'.[7] Other than being a consistent forum for the development of sociology, *Année Sociologique* also became a major formal academic journal founded by Durkheim and Mauss in 1896.

Durkheim finds support from Comte and Spencer, Locke and Condillac, in the methodological fight against the phantom qua presupposition of the mind. This is not so easy, because sustained disciplining in the methodological way of seeing is a prerequisite. Towards the act of discarding all the preconceptions, Durkheim invokes Descartes' method of doubt that can enable one to 'think like thing'.[8] However, Durkheim's prescience is in his words:

> what makes emancipation from such notions peculiarly difficult in sociology is that sentiment so often intervenes. We enthuse over political and religious beliefs and moral practices very differently from what we do over the objects of the physical world. Consequently this emotional quality is transmitted to the way in which we conceive and explain our beliefs … feeling is an object for scientific study, not the criterion of scientific truth. (1982, 73–74)

This is, however, to be accomplished through a way of seeing that, as a consequence or precondition distinguishes sociologists from the rest. To begin with, sociologists must define things as objectively as possible by dwelling upon sense perceptions, and observable data, rather than a priori conceptions. But sense perception and experience can be subjective. Science thus expects us to be rid of observable data too personal to us. Likewise, 'when the sociologist undertakes to investigate any order of social facts he must strive to consider them from a viewpoint where they present themselves in isolation from their individual manifestations' (82–83). While this disciplining is important and resonant with Durkheim's eighteenth-century predecessors, there is another side of his discussion on *The Rules*. This is expressed in a methodological responsibility that Durkheim entrusts sociologists with. As he noted, 'The principal purpose of any science of life, whether individual or social, is in the end to define and explain the normal state and distinguish it from the abnormal' (104). Thus, *The Rules* created the possibility for sociologists to be moral agents of an imagined ideal world. One should hence also think, as Giddens did, that Durkheim 'was not primarily concerned with "the problem of order", but with the problem of "the changing nature of order" in the context of a definite conception of social development' (2009, ix). And towards this, Durkheim set the following rules to be observed while interpreting and analysing social facts, which are,

> *(1) A social fact is normal for a given social type, viewed at a given phase of its development, when it occurs in the average society of that species considered at the corresponding phase of its evolution.*
> *(2) The results of the preceding method can be verified by demonstrating that the general character of the phenomenon is related to the general conditions of collective life in the social type under consideration.* (1982, 97; emphasis in original)

In addition to the two rules quoted here, there is a third rule to reinforce the second, the need for verification. From the stated rules, it is evident that Durkheim's way of seeing is preconditioned by the material that is being seen. He agreed with his teacher Emile Boutroux that a discipline may be called science if it has a definite field to explore.[9] 'Things' and reality rather than mere ideas constitute this field. These 'things' play an important role in determining the way one should approach, see, and fathom them. After setting the rules, Durkheim embarked on an interesting discussion about crime, deviance and pathology in a society, to mark out that such seemingly abnormal characteristics could be reflective of a social normal. While excessiveness could be pathological, crime could be normal if it occurs in the *average society*. And as if presenting a precious nugget of wisdom, Durkheim remarked, 'nothing is good indefinitely and without limits' (1982, 101). Thereby, he revealed that even in the apparently scientific readings of any phenomenon, there is this side that is fraught with certain philosophically sophisticated assumptions. He cited the example of Socrates who was tried under the Athenian law. However, the independence of thought, which was then Socrates' crime, was useful for his country as well as humanity as a whole. The crime and punishment, in the case of Socrates, paved the way for a new morality and a new faith. Likewise, the deeds of the heretics compelled the need for liberal thinking in society.

With the normal and the abnormal of social facts of a given species, Durkheim emphasised the need for a classification of the species, the morphology of society that constitutes a major part of his works. It leads towards the most important, and last, act in the performance of being sociological. While morphology, with details about the normal and the abnormal of social facts, is fine, it is not all about explaining any social phenomenon. And with a discussion on the explanatory act, Durkheim almost came full circle on an aspired way of seeing in sociology. What is the explanatory act in Durkheim's way of seeing? In his words, 'when one undertakes to explain a social phenomenon the efficient cause which produced it and the function it fulfils must be investigated separately (123). Here function does not stand for a 'goal' or an 'end', nor does it allude to 'intention'. Intention is too subjective and goal/end connotes a utilitarian motive. Such instant interpretations are not worth consideration in the Durkheimian way of seeing. The function of a social fact is the correspondence between it and the general needs of the social organism. While the exploration of cause could still belong to the very basic kind of scientific investigation, Durkheim's notion of function turned out to be a sociological mysticism at work, amounting to what has been known as sociologism.[10] This was indeed to carry forward the unfinished task Saint-Simon had set, towards founding a new religious ideology, a New Christianity, which propelled Durkheim to develop a science of morality for a modern industrial society engaging with the Kantian question of 'categorical imperative'.[11] While doing so, he was mindful of the significance of the numerals as well as lucid descriptive prose, and the combination of numbers and narration rendered his works into rich readings. Even in a work like *Suicide*, where he worked with statistical figures to come up with a tangible idea of 'average' in determining typologies, he was not divorced from moralistic narration. This is most outstanding in *The Elementary Forms of Religious Life,* which is by and large based on discussing symbols as manifestations of 'collective sentiments' and 'collective representation'. To sum it up, Durkheim presented a curiously unique version of positivism as his way of seeing in functionalist sociology. There appears 'quantitative and qualitative analyses as an integrated whole'[12] without any disjunction between positivism and interpretive sociology in this way of seeing. This was evidently a perfect implementation of positive philosophy in sociology that executed scientific epistemology of the past to offer constructive, positive, possibilities of society in the present and the future.

Marx, too, like the founders of positivism in sociology, grappled with the negative orientation of the Enlightenment. Before outlining the Marxian way of seeing, it is worth a quick reflection on the 'close, uneasy, contentions relationship between Marxism and Sociology'.[13] The closeness is due to the similarity in the contours of classical, positivistic, sociology as envisaged by Saint-Simon, August Comte, and before them, the significant Encyclopaedists of the Enlightenment. It is about a positive reconstruction of the social with the aid of a new science. Marxism expresses a similar concern though the epistemological position differs from many sociologists, and the objectives and plan of action in Marxism are geared towards a more active struggle towards transformation. This closeness makes it necessary for sociologists to place Marx as one of the important thinkers in sociology and his way of seeing thus occupied a central role among sociologists and social anthropologists. On the other hand, there was unease between the sociological and Marxism due to the variant historical conditions. Sociology responds to the historical imperative of rebuilding a social order to curtail anarchy and anomalies; this entailed a way of seeing in which the radical epistemological propositions from the Enlightenment as well as its counter-currents were accommodated; whereas Marxism is inclined to a radical way of seeing the anomalies of the industrial society in which the given social order has to be eventually uprooted and replaced by a communist order. Even though Marxism is a full body of theory, it shows little sympathy for the conservative bedrock that is crucial in sociology at large. In Marxist, the social-cultural realities, called superstructure–epiphenomenal, are secondary in comparison with the economic core of the society. This is known as economic determinism in the Marxian way of seeing. However, the superstructure–epiphenomenal is inevitably important in the rest of sociology. Rather than segregating the social, cultural and economic, the broader sociological framework puts them as interrelated components of a dynamic society. This paradoxical relationship between sociology and Marxism notwithstanding becomes a rich premise for sociologists to devise a sociological–Marxian body of thought as it were. This peculiarity will always be recalled since the Marxian way of seeing complements the sociological methodology in the ultimate analysis as tacitly present in the following discussion. Having noted the unease, it is desirable not to seek to show a direct correlation between the Marxian way of seeing and positivism, though there are arguments in favour as well against such a possible correlation.[14] The first thing to understand is the significance that the Marxian way of seeing holds in sociology.

To begin with, Marx hails the revolutionary spirit of eighteenth-century philosophy calling it a 'universal ferment into which the "powers of the past" are swept.... It was a revolution beside which the French Revolution was child's play, a world struggle beside which the struggles of the Diadochi appear insignificant' (2010, 33). *Diadochi*, literally meaning residue, is a term used in chemistry to refer to the residue left after distillation. In the historical sense, *diadochi* also refers to the rival successors of the Greek emperor Alexander the Great who aspired to claim the Greek Empire. Marx used *diadochi* for actors of the French Revolution. The real revolution was in the realm of pure thought that had effects carried out in the form of the French Revolution. He was evidently referring to the Enlightenment to complement its philosophical fermentation. However, like any such fermentation, this too met with a status quo, which ceased growth. In Marx's words:

> the industrialists of philosophy, who till then had lived on the exploitation of the absolute spirit, now seized upon the new combinations. Each with all possible zeal set about retailing his apportioned share. This was bound to give rise to competition, which, to start with, was carried on in a moderately civil and staid fashion. (33)

This scenario deteriorated, explained in the language of economics as spurious production, adulteration of raw materials, fictitious purchase, bill-jobbing and a bad credit system. The competition of philosophers turned bitter in the German context that characterised, according to Marx, the 'parochial narrowness of this whole Young-Hegelian movement'. The aftereffect of the grand philosophical revolution showed in the indulgence in 'mystification', due to an allegedly undue dependence on Hegel. Hence, any claim to advance from Hegel was nothing more than a relapse to metaphysics and morality. This is also to be understood in the context of Marx's intellectual biography which gives sufficient evidence that apart from reading Hegel and other philosophers to come up with his criticism of conservatism, he also aspired to postulate universal ideas. His praise for universalism, an Enlightenment heritage, was expressed quite early in a letter that he wrote to his father, saying, 'History calls those greatest men who ennobled themselves by working for the universal'.[15] He is known to have delved deeper into Hegelian philosophy after finding Immanuel Kant and Johann Fichte, the founding figure of German idealism, unsatisfactory for his thesis. And there is a strong suggestion that Marx also engaged with Saint-Simon's notion of socialism.[16] His criticism of the German young Hegelians in general, and Feuerbach in particular, begins to take shape in his doctoral dissertation which was a comparative reading of the philosophies of ancient Greek philosophers Democritus and Epicurus. About the same time, when everybody seemed to have become Feuerbachians, Marx chided Ludwig Feuerbach, Bruno Bauer and Max Stirner who dwelt on the basic categories of man, criticism and ego: 'The Young-Hegelian ideologists, in spite of their allegedly "world-shattering" phrases, are the staunchest *conservatives*' (2010, 36).

Though this is not suggestive of a total break between Marx and conservatism, the word conservative is italicised to suggest a dual departure that Marx sets for his epistemological reasoning. One, as already indicated, is departure from the aftereffects/residues of the otherwise promising revolution of thoughts under the Enlightenment. The second is meant to distance Marxian scheme from the conservative as well as romantic inclinations that had sought to shift the focus from intellect to the nature and the social. For Marx, the social was to be reoccupied without falling prey to pure thoughts of the Enlightenment, or to the mystified notions of the social that stem from the romantics and conservatives. Friedrich Engels provided an apt justification towards this, with the spirit of dialectic, in the Preface to *Capital: A Critical Analysis of Capitalist Production* (vol. 1):

> every new aspect of a science involves a revolution in the technical terms of that science. This is best shown by chemistry, where the whole terminology is radically changed about once in twenty years, and where you will hardly find a single organic compound that has not gone through a whole series of different names. (1974, 14)

Hence, in proposing a newly developed historical framework, it is imperative to depart from the old terminologies and their connotations.

Marx wanted to show the relationship, or lack thereof, between German thought and German reality. He thus proposed to rethink Man. Marxian imagination of man is indeed a curious case, which reveals his negotiation and departure from romantics and conservatives, in terms of way of seeing. In this regard, it is worth pondering upon the *Economic and Philosophic Manuscripts of 1844* (EPM),[17] a compilation of significant fragments, which played crucial role in the larger panorama of Marxian theses. Usually, EPM is known to have offered an initiation, with cryptic prose, into the debate on the idea of alienation among other thematic issues. But this idea is underpinned by a double-register of seeing man. On one hand, Marx could see the ideal situation in which man is *species-being*, a whole entity organically linked with nature, though distinguishable due to the sensibility he acquires from society. As he put it: 'Man *lives* on nature—means that nature is his body, with which he must remain in continuous interchange if he is not to die'.[18] And such a man is equipped with not only five sense organs but perhaps more than that—sensuality and spirituality, for instance. It is an immensely capable man that is endangered by the process of 'objectification', 'estrangement' and 'alienation'.[19] This adds another layer to the Marxian way of seeing, enabling the understanding of the anomalies of industrial society. In this wake, 'man is regressing to the *cave dwelling*, but in an alienated form',[20] and it is causing men, both proletariat and bourgeoisie, to suffer. About hard-working, sober, economical, prosaic men with ownership of private property, he noted:

> His enjoyment is only a secondary matter; it is recreation subordinated to production and thus a calculated, economic enjoyment, for he charges his pleasures as an expense of capital and what he squanders must not be more than can be replaced with profit by the reduction of capital....[21]

While presenting his imagination of man and his world, Marx not only divulged his way of seeing, but also presented a consistent critique of the approaches in political economy. Only a certain kind of empiricism could commit to seeing man as a mere abstract category in the machinery of production, circulation and consumption. This was not the scheme of seeing man in between the mathematical calculation of profit and loss, which Marx ascribed. It assumed more clarity, as far as the Marxian way of seeing is concerned, when one turns to the German ideology. This is where he emphatically positioned himself in the realm of reality:

> The premises from which we begin are not arbitrary ones, not dogmas, but real premises from which abstraction can only be made in the imagination. They are the real individuals, their activity and the material conditions of their life both those which they find already existing and those produced by their activity. These premises can thus be verified in a purely empirical way. (2010, 36–37)

What was being dismissed was arbitrary premises and dogmas. What was being restored was reality and the intellectual exercise of abstracting from the real premises. This all led to a Marxian scheme of empiricism which was in negotiation with the predecessors and yet distinguishable due to the preoccupation with real, historical man and his activities. In doing so, he subverted Hegel. Marx reiterated it eloquently in the Preface to the *Capital*:

> my dialectic method is not only different from the Hegelian, but its direct opposite. To Hegel, the life-process of the human brain, i.e., the process of thinking, which, under the name of the "the idea", he even transforms into an independent subject, is the demiurgos of the real world, and the real world is only the external, phenomenal form of the "the idea". With me, on the contrary, the ideal is nothing else

> than the material world reflected by the human mind, and translated into forms of thought. (1978, 29)

There is an uncanny Marxian hermeneutic at the core of this empiricism, that is succinctly expressed when Marx says, 'As individuals express their life, so they are. What they are, therefore, coincides with their production, both with what they produce and with how they produce. Hence what individuals are depends on the material condition of their production' (2010, 37).

This is a material, contextual and social base on which Marx is proposing a qualitatively different sense of empiricism vis-à-vis historical materialism. In the centre of such an empirical scheme is the man with his real struggles and transformation. Following such empiricism, Marx unravelled the various epochs in history that engendered corresponding sets of relationships, technology and forms of property, all coming under the scheme of division of labour. There is indeed a sense of positivism about it, as the Marxian analysis is geared to a positive reconstruction of the otherwise negative postulates of the Enlightenment encyclopaedists, as well as transformative politics in the industrial society. In Marxian way of seeing, thus, a clear sight of social structure emerges, which is 'continually evolving out of the life-process of definite individuals'. Marx persuaded us to see the real individuals, conditions and processes, steering clear of 'phantoms formed in the brains of men'. Reminiscent of the Baconian idols of mind, these phantoms were 'sublimates of their material life process' which could be empirically verifiable and bound to material grounds. But then, such ideologically coloured empirical ideas, inclusive of morality, religion, metaphysics, ideology and any form of consciousness, are only humbugs. As put succinctly:

> Consciousness (*das Bewusstsein*) can never be anything else than conscious being (*das bewusste Sein*), and the being of men is their actual life-process. If in all ideology men and their relations appear upside-down as in a *camera obscura*, this phenomenon arises just as much from their historical life-process as the inversion of objects on the retina does from their physical life-process.... It is not consciousness that determines life, but life that determines consciousness. (2010, 42)

As soon as these corrections are made in the scheme of empiricism, and reality rather than *camera obscura* is given importance, history ceases to be a collection of dead facts. Likewise, it also corrects the ideological humbug that idealists create by putting forth imagined activities of imagined subjects. Neither the empty phrases of idealists nor the verifiable abstractions of empiricists can engender the history of material qua real lives. It allows a seer to see that there is an interplay of man and circumstances, individual and collective, biography and history. Typically expressed, 'circumstances make men just as much as men make circumstances' (62). Only a speculative, idealistic and fantastic way of seeing allows perceiving man and his social world in binary opposition, akin to the opposition between nature and society that the rationalists created. Some of such ideas have been 'dominant', 'ruling ideas of the epoch' belonging to the 'ruling intellectual force' that controls means and relations of production. Such ideas have masqueraded as 'eternal law', only to be tossed away in the wake of an understanding arising from the scheme of historical materialism that enables us to see the things as they are and seek to transform them. This is not merely a political agenda, it's an epistemological proposition too, for, to reiterate, 'where speculation ends-in real life- there real, positive science begins' (38). And thus, the Marxian way of seeing, and if one can say, being sociological, summons not only a different scheme of empiricist history, positivistic–scientific formulations, but also struggle to change, typically expressed in what is famously known as *Thesis Eleven*, one of the theses on Feuerbach that Marx developed in the German Ideology, 'Philosophers have hitherto only *interpreted* the world in various ways; the point is to *change* it'.[22]

However, it is with Max Weber that the sociological way of seeing returned to the philosophical troubles about meanings that Kant tried resolving. Known to be a neo-Kantian inclination, this emphasised that an empirical discipline scientifically explaining the world in terms of what 'ought to be'[23] is impossible. One cannot validate value judgement through scientific analysis. However, this doesn't indicate a shift of understanding human behaviour from the domain of science altogether. It was, once again, a different kind of science that Weber aimed to develop, and in doing so, he developed a way of seeing distinguishable from Durkheim and Marx. Even though Weber had fed on similar kinds of predecessors, such as Simmel, Schmoller and Tönnies like Durkheim, he was to find another pathway, reading from jurisprudence, economics, history and philosophy. Like some of his other German contemporaries, Weber did not to accept the Comtean hierarchy of knowledge. Comte had proposed a hierarchy in which he deemed sociology to be like a queen at the top. However, this queen of all disciplines was deemed dependent on those placed below sociology, such as biology, chemistry, physics and astronomy. According to Comte, sociology would forge relationship of the sciences placed below in the hierarchy of knowledge. Weber expressed his discomfort with such positivistic orthodoxy in which social science had to depend on methods of natural science.

Weber considered the human world, the area of study for social science, as fraught with irrationality and epitomised by *volksgeist*. Hence, his intention was to establish a way of seeing which does not fall prey to overly simplistic dichotomies of ideographic and nomothetic domains of knowledge. Writing about economic behaviour and practices, he would be looking at religion, ideology and normative conditions in historical context. This makes him distinguishable, particularly established in the masterpiece, *The Protestant Ethic and the Spirit of Capitalism* (*The Spirit*) that originally appeared as two long articles in 1904 and 1905. These essays emphasised the role played by various denominations of Christianity in shaping up the spirit behind the development of capitalism. The climax of this development was brought about by Calvinism, which, unlike the other variants such as Lutheranism and Catholicism, paved the way for practices in the midst of disenchantment of the world. Most important among others was the idea of 'calling' that acquired a finitude in Weber's analysis, in *The Spirit* as well as in his methodological rumination that spelt out his way of seeing. It is, to put in a memorable one line, a cold and clinical way of seeing through, as popular Weberian phrase read, the iron cage of rationality. The most apt expression of it was in Weber's passionate defence for value neutrality in empirical science that solicited from teachers as well as students, seekers and seers of knowledge an extraordinary performance. The idea of value neutrality was, however, more complex than just a rhetorical question. Value neutrality, argued Weber

> is the intrinsically simple demand that the investigator and teacher should keep unconditionally separate the establishment of empirical facts (including the "value-oriented" conduct of the empirical individual whom he is investigating) and *his* own practical evaluations, i.e. his evaluation of these facts as satisfactory or unsatisfactory (including among these facts evaluations made by the empirical persons who are the objects of investigation). (2011, 11)

The calling of science, or as elsewhere Weber put it, science as a vocation,[24] characterised by value neutrality, engulfs both teachers transacting knowledge in the lecture hall as well as researchers who seek to know through investigations. Weber used evaluative phrases such as 'intellectual honesty' and 'intellectual integrity' to describe the pitfalls of the demagogues, teachers adding a personal touch to scientific deliberation. Taking a dig at such passionate teachers, Weber called them 'officially accredited prophets' who deliver 'personally tinted professorial type of prophecy' in the name of science. In his words, 'the calm of rigor, matter-of-factness and sobriety of lecture declines with definite pedagogical losses, when the substance and manner of public discussion are introduced, in the style of the press' (5). The vocation of science, as well as teaching, did not permit the personality cult that follows from the professorial prophecies of officially privileged prophets. The vocation required the separation of personal and factual, ethical and scientific, public speaking and pedagogy. This applies to students as well as teachers who needed to fulfil their tasks in workmanlike fashion, recognise facts even though they may be personally discomforting, and repress impulse, personal taste and sentiments in the vocation.[25] While subscribing to the imperative of value neutrality, one ought to be cautioned as Weber suggested that it is not about denying value judgement in the public, political and cultural spheres. The same teacher or scientist who maintains value neutrality in lectures and science can express judgements in the non-academic pursuits. And likewise, it is misnomer that one can be value neutral by 'weighing the various evaluations' like a statesman to make a compromise among them. One cannot be scientific just by showing the self-evident value judgement, and thereby taking it for granted. The specific function of science, Weber stressed, was to 'ask questions about these things which convention makes self-evident'. For example, in his discussion on the astronomical conceptions of the Chinese, Weber was keen to show that it did not lead to the same development as in the modern western astronomy; the Chinese conceptualisation was equatorial and focused on observation of circumpolar stars. However, the Chinese astronomy did not necessarily demonstrate the correctness of the Chinese astronomy through a rational procedure; there was a lack of methodological procedure and process of verifying the exactness in the Chinese astronomy. One can recall a similar position Weber took in *The Spirit*, which persuaded us to see lack of rationality in the scientific[26] as much as in economic pursuits in Asian thought systems.[27] The idea of a vocation has to be seen in this context. It is not calling with the traditionalist, specifically the Lutherean, dependence on the divinity that is invoked when the vocation of science becomes a source of the Weberian way of seeing. Instead, it was a variety that had shorn off all traditionalist outlooks, and acquired sheer 'this-worldliness', of the here and now, of performing as if there were no tomorrow. As a central dogma of all Protestant denominations, originally developed by Luther, it meant, 'the only way of living acceptably to God was not to surpass worldly morality in monastic asceticism, but solely through the fulfilment of the obligations imposed upon the individual by his position in the world' (1968, 80). Calvinism diminished the irrational impulses of the idea of calling,[28] by enforcing a religious worldview distinguishable from the orthodox Catholicism.

In this regard, it is important to recall what some of the readers of Weber have suggested. Gerth and Mills (2009) uphold the view that Weber wanted to deliver double responses to two significant names, Marx and German existentialist philosopher Friedrich Nietzsche. Both are equally significant in providing content to the Weberian way of seeing in sociology.

> With Marx, Weber shares the sociological approach to ideas: they are powerless in history unless they are fused with material interests. And with Nietzsche, he is deeply concerned with the importance of ideas for psychic reactions. Yet, in contrast to both Nietzsche and Marx, Weber refused to conceive of ideas as being mere reflections of psychic or social interests. (2009, 62)[29]

Besides, Weber dwelt on the tensions between ideas and interests. He was keen to unearth the relationship between internal states and external demands. This explains the reasons why Weber was keen to adopt a Robinson Crusoe approach to social man and his adoption of Friedrich Schiller's phrase—the disenchantment of the world. In Daniel Defoe's *The Adventures of Robinson Crusoe*, published in 1719, the protagonist was stranded on a Caribbean island for over two decades. Likewise, Weber gave a sense that social actors in the twentieth century were ultimately solitary in the modern disenchantment of the world. If the human world is such, why shouldn't the science, as well as its proponents including teachers, students, seekers of knowledge, be equally 'heartless' in their approach? The heartlessness in this way of seeing is due to the ideas, as elucidated above. The disenchantment renders the world cold. Reminiscent of the linear sense of progress of the Enlightenment, it necessitates a value-neutral science.

As discussed above, Weber's idea of value neutrality in the calling of science, helps us to further understand ethical value judgements. Revisiting Kant's *Critique*, he admitted that discussion of evaluation had a utility insofar as it aided in '*understanding explanation*'. However, 'understanding all', does not mean 'pardoning all' (2011, 14). A rather complex track, in fact more complex than Kant, led Weber to conclude that value discussions, when correctly conducted, 'can be extremely valuable for empirical research in the sense that it provides it with problems for investigation' (21). The problem of understanding was an important problem in Weber's sociology, since man understands intentions through introspection, and hence, sociologists will understand men's intentions qua motivated actions. To do so, the types of actions, such as rational, affective and traditionalist, was a conducive anchorage. And likewise, the basic types of structures, such as society, association and community, could be heuristically significant.

This was all towards the making of Weber's interpretative sociology, which 'considers the individual (*Einzel Individuum*) and his action as the basic unit, as its "atom"—if the disputable comparison for once may be permitted. In this approach, the individual is also the upper limit and the sole carrier of meaningful conduct'.[30]

This is what brought Weber (1978) to discuss another aspect of his way of seeing—the complex domain of meanings fraught with value discussions, a key target in Weber's interpretative sociology. Meanings arise in a concrete situation referring to a particular actor, or 'average or approximate meaning attributable to a given plurality of actors', or 'the theoretically conceived *pure type* of subjective meaning attributed to the hypothetical actor or actors in a given type of action'. None of these needs be an objectively correct meaning that will be taken for granted by empirical sciences such as sociology and history. The important rider in this is that all subjective meanings may not be worth pondering. Resonant with Kant, it means that the subjective meaning arising from mystical experiences cannot be adequately communicated. Only those located in experience, and can be recalled and reproduced, will be given further attention. Like in scientific observation, there are the usual social practices of interpreting meanings, seeking to verify, clarify and comprehend. To understand a meaning with certainty, there are certain bases: rational (direct observational rational understanding of a logico-mathematical kind) or emotionally empathic (explanatory understanding of artistic appreciation). The highest degree of rational understanding, with verifiable certainty, is possible when meanings have a logical or mathematical proposition, such as $2 \times 2 = 4$, the Pythagoras Theorem, or when a person acts with clear means and ends in any given situation (rationally purposeful action). Understanding such meanings, motivations, and cause and effect, entails direct observation. A lower degree of understanding, based on an empathy of the meanings pertaining to actions with many ends/values, lacks certainty. It is when one cannot be sure of one clear motive behind an action that irrational meanings can emerge. They may have an emotional appeal but there is no intellectual clarity about the certainty of the results of an action. One can develop an explanatory understanding of irrational meanings, as Weber expressed through the following examples: through observation we can understand an actor's motive behind the chopping of wood or aiming of a gun; but in addition to direct observation, it would be more helpful if we know that the woodchopper is working for a wage or is chopping a supply of firewood for his own use; or, the actor may be chopping the wood for recreation, or possibly working off a fit of rage, an irrational case. Similarly, we can understand the motive of a person aiming a gun if we know he has been commanded to shoot as a member of a firing squad. It would be more helpful if we have information about the motive behind the action: whether he is fighting against an enemy or he is doing it for revenge. Motive for revenge may be emotionally determined and thus in a certain sense irrational. Finally we have a motivational understanding of the outburst of anger if we know that it has been provoked by jealousy, injured pride or insult. All such actions with emotional determinations lead an observer to note the irrational motives of the actors. Given the complexity of the motives and actions, Weber propounded,

> *Thus for a science which is concerned with the subjective meaning of action, explanation requires a grasp of the complex meaning in which an actual course of understandable action thus interpreted belong.* (1978, 8–9; emphasis author's)

The understanding through interpretation of social actions requires performing another task—to formulate 'the average of, or an approximation to, the actually intended meaning', also to be known as pure/ideal type. These types are fraught with subjective meanings, capable of offering hypotheses, but they need to be compared with the concrete course of events. Weber proposed to construct ideal types, which, however, were neither 'idea' in semantic terms nor an absolute representation of reality in an empirical sense. Though admitting the role of the intuitions, a priori notions, and such unverified ideas as important, in the last analysis, the Weberian way of seeing in sociology solicits the following,

> A correct causal interpretation of a concrete course of action is arrived at when the overt action and the motives have both been correctly apprehended and at the same time their relation has become meaningfully comprehensible. (1978, 12)

In the end, a teleological justification for the rational meaning conquered the complexity in Weber's sociology. Unless fully grasped through the causal analysis along means-ends, meaning is not suitable for the science of society in general and Weber's interpretative sociology in particular.

Lust for Trinity: Not a Conclusion

The key thinkers revisited in this chapter are divergent in their ways of seeing. Each is distinct despite some of the shared concerns.

Durkheim took it in one direction by stressing on how one needs to look at social facts as things and how social things presuppose a way of seeing in order to be scientific. He was not only concerned with the idea of order in society but also with an ordered discipline—sociology. Marx refashioned a historically materialist sense of empiricism, which could pull off an epistemological break from the after-effects of the Enlightenment as well as a political plan for transformative struggle. There was an inherent hermeneutics in Marx' way of seeing that presented man and his consciousness in the wake of natural and anti-natural regimes of production, giving an uncanny credence to Marxian historical materialism. Weber provided excruciating details of motives, meanings, understanding—the brick and mortar in the body called 'sociological', while underlining the need of value neutrality. The latter is a paradoxical notion, since Weber did not dismiss the ubiquitous presence of values and yet proposed ways of dealing with it rather than dismissing it. In each way of seeing, there was a negotiation with and a critical revisiting of the predecessors. There were notes of departure in each strand of thought marshalled for a way of seeing. Yet, they all had something unusually common; all of them expected certain extraordinariness from the seekers of knowledge and doers of sciences of society. Each ultimately invites us to 'fight against the phantoms', idols of minds, *camera-obscura*, and the subjective meanings inaccessible to positivist, rational, scientific reworking. Everything that could be perceived as common with the ordinary folk was suspicious in these ways of seeing. Paradoxically, this was despite a clear bent of each way of seeing to the ordinary human's worldview. Non-experts were as clearly separated from experts as they are in the laboratory bound natural sciences. Each wanted to create a science of society, which aspired to arrive at indubitable, certain and generalisable principles. This is a common feat of each way of seeing that has emerged from the revisiting the trinity in this chapter. In other words, all three key thinkers of the classical sociology persuade us to adopt an Arjun-motif[31] from the 'Adi Parva' of the Mahabharata, mentioned at the outset of this essay. This Arjun-motif underlines a *cogito*, no less important than the Cartesian 'I', an extraordinary accomplishment. Each had a metaphorical bird's eye to which each was transfixed. And they expect us to be not swayed by anything that can distract us from the target. They invite us to get rid of emotions, biographical conditions, residual determinations, cultural orientations and local–contextual expectations.

On a brighter side, they were all participating with their own way of seeing in the larger-than-life paradigm named positivism. However, positivism for Marx and Durkheim was a scientific method for reconstructing the social world, whereas Weber worked on/with it towards emancipation from any emancipatory agenda. The distinction of each way of seeing provides us with an occasion to believe—there is not one way of seeing in classical sociology. And there is not one singular way of seeing, and being sociological, since the very beginning of sociology. Hence, there cannot be one-size-fits-all formula to be sociological. The pluralism inherent in the classical trinity enables us to enjoy a respite from the constraining methodological singularity of being sociological. However, it is time to get back to Bauman (2000) who made sinister observations about the classical sociology pertaining to the trinity. Bauman noted that ever since sociology came into existence it has been preoccupied with the imperative of "social order", with pattern, structure, and regularity in human affairs. The objective behind this preoccupation was to bring them about and protect them. This essentially made various human beings behave alike and in a predictable manner in the sociological way of seeing. In Bauman's sarcastic words:

> Since its inception sociology struggled with the solution to the "Hobessian problem", that is preoccupied itself with the mystery of people living with each other in a by-and-large orderly and peaceful fashion despite the fact that each one of them pursued wilfully his own gains and pleasures.... And cracking that mystery was for all founding fathers of sociology—for Marx, Durkheim or Weber alike—the major, perhaps the sole concern. (2000, 71)

As polemical as it gets, there is an evident reason that all sciences are about how things must be rather than just how they are. A modern metaphysics, so to say, this connects the ways of seeing emergent in the Enlightenment, scientific epistemology, and the classical social sciences. We can see a relation among a Cartesian supremacy of *cogito*, a Kantian call for *Sapere Aude*, and the trinity's fight against phantoms of the mind. And in a sweep, Bauman held the trinity as culprits of continuing with the agenda set by the Enlightenment. The trinity, as the Enlightenment, delivered the formula on, how things must be! Such moralistic imposition by the trinity was, ironically enough, based on the observation and explanation of how things are! Bauman's criticism of the Enlightenment-bound sociology of the trinity necessitates further explorations of the methodological ways of seeing in sociology. It means that the difference between the two aspects of explanation of the motives—namely, 'in order to' and 'because of'—demands more critical discussion. This was allegedly explained away in the works of the trinity of classical sociology. It also means the difference between subjective motives and objectively determined behaviour does not make any difference to the scientific way of seeing in sociology. The positivism of the sociological trinity did not allow for the difference of subjective meaning and objective behaviour. Arguably, this is because positivist sociology in general aimed at 'legislating existence' of humans in society in accordance with the imperative of social order. In other words, the sociology of the trinity emphasised how the human should be and what they should do in order to maintain social order. The sociological way of seeing, at least in the age of orthodoxy, is thus about ignoring the vast pool of subjectively lived experiences, the life-world of mortals in order to ennoble immortality, the immutable value orientation of the group. This is a poor substitute for the radical break that science had brought about for lay people. Failure characterises science as well as sociology, and the overarching umbrella called modernity. Modernity promised to replace uncertainty with an orderly human universe and sociologists followed suit. Bauman, however, apprehended:

> But the promise to conquer and annihilate uncertainty, if repeated nowadays, sounds hollow, while people resourceful enough to do the conquering are few and far between and altogether difficult to trust. There seem to be few takers for the orthodox gifts of sociology—and a fast shrinking demand for the kind of product which the orthodox sociologists had become past masters in assembling. (2000, 77)

This critique of modernity, and thereof gifts and promises, could be justified in the contexts where disenchantment prevailed. One can further the polemic and add a curious case to it with the following observation, hinting at a sociological metaphysics. The sociologists' way of seeing is metaphorically akin to the Midas touch,[32] and it is difficult to resolve whether it was a blessing or a curse. As one can recall in the tale, Midas, the king of Phrygia in Asia Minor, was known for his fondness for two things—gold and his daughter. Stung by a rabid desire to possess more of 'pure' and hence precious gold, he once happened to be blessed by the god of desire, Dionysus, that anything Midas touched would turn into gold. He then touched a table and it turned into pure gold. When he discovered that it did indeed work, he did the same with every object he came across—chairs, doors, walls, and so on. Midas was like the 'extraordinary' entity called sociologist, seeking to turn everything social into a scientific episteme. Maddened by the spectacular fulfilment of his desire, when he sat to eat, the bread he touched turned to gold, as did the grapes he put in his mouth, and the flower that he held to admire. He soon began to fear that the blessing was actually a curse. Melancholic, he saw his beloved daughter and hugged her tight only to find that she had turned into gold too. Eventually, he prayed Dionysus to release him from the blessing that was actually a curse. Dionysus then advised him to take a dip in the river Pactolus to find a release.

Do sociologists vying to create a science of their own, as in the case of the trinity, have known of a river like Pactolus that can cleanse off the effect of their touch? Do sociologists admit the problem with their predisposition to turn everything into indubitable knowledge? We don't know, though we do know one thing. There is contextual variation, and a corresponding difference of experience, when it comes to South Asia, where disenchantment did not replace the sources of enchantment altogether. Instead, it has been an experience of dialectic of the two, enchantment and disenchantment, as Obeyesekere (2012, 5) ruminated on the significance of modernity in the context of the Buddhist experience in Sri Lanka. Just as one does not take for granted the idea of enlightenment of the eighteenth century, one also doesn't take for granted the significance (blessing or curse) of the sociological way of seeing that comes from the sociological trinity. Hence, it makes sense to revert to Nisbet's proposed 'paradox' of sociology, conjoined with that of modernity (1967, 17). It reminds us of, to repeat the metaphor, being a blessing and a curse at once, of modernity and its sciences. And hence, Nisbet added another way of reading the trinity. He showed that the classical sociological thinkers 'never ceased to be artist!.... Each was, with deep intuition, with profound imaginative grasp, reacting to the world around him, even as does the artist, and, also like the artist, objectifying internal and only partly conscious, states of mind' (18–19).

This recalls afresh the contents and discontents of modernity, the Enlightenment propositions, and endeavours of predecessors and forerunners followed by the founding figures, the sum total of last two chapters. And what does it all accomplish for us? We begin to see the paradox of modernity, and thereof intellectual gifts everywhere, including in various parts of South Asia. For example, we get to learn that in India, sociology, and its ways of seeing, had to negotiate with not only the European masters but also its own organic intellectuals, thinkers, poets and artists to name a few. Mahatma Gandhi happened to be at the backdrop of much development in colonial and postcolonial India. Likewise, Rabindranath Tagore was an ever-available source of reference. In India, Avijit Pathak (2015) elucidates this by doing a consistent reading of both sociological as well as social thoughts to understand the negotiations that make up the intellectual traditions in modern India. One gets a sense of the making of, possibly, a different way of seeing for sociology in the Indian context, at the cusp of modernity and tradition. This indeed summons yet another exploration of sociology in South Asia, at the interface of Indology, history and varied traditions of ideas.

References

Alexander, Jeffery C. 'Beyond the Epistemological Dilemma: General Theory in a Postpositivist Mode', *Sociological Forum* 5, no. 4 (December 1990): 531–544.

Barberis, Daniela S. 'The *Année Sociologique* as Training Ground for Sociology: Durkheim, Mauss, and the Art of Book Reviewing in *Fin de Siècle* France'. In *History of Universities: Volume XXXIV/1: A Global History of Research Education: Disciplines, Institutions, and Nations, 1840-1950*, edited by Ku-ming (Kevin) Chang and Alan Rocke. London: Oxford University Press, 2021.

Bauman, Zygmunt. 'Sociological Enlightenment—For Whom, About What?', *Theory, Culture, and Society* 17, no. 2 (2000): 71–82.

Bottomore, Tom. *Marxist Sociology*. London: Macmillan, 1975.

———. 'Marxism and Sociology', In *A History of Sociological Analysis*, edited by Tom Bottomore and Robert Nisbet, 118–149. London: Heinemann, 1979.

Burawoy, M. *Public Sociology*. Cambridge: Polity Press, 2021.

Connell, R.W. 'Why is Classical Sociology Classical?', *American Journal of Sociology* 102, no. 6 (1997): 1511–1157.

Durkheim, Emile. *Socialism and Saint Simon*. London: Routledge and Kegan Paul Ltd., 1958.

———. *Montesquieu and Rousseau*. Ann Arbor: The University of Michigan Press, 1960.

———. *The Rules of Sociological Method and Selected Texts of Sociology and Its Methods*, edited and translated by Steven Lukes and W.D. Halls. London: The Free Press, 1982.

———. *Lettres à Marcel Mauss*, présentées par Philippe Besnard et Marcel Foumier. Paris: PUF, 1998.

Gerth, H.H., and C. Wright Mills (eds). *From Max Weber: Essays in Sociology*. London: Routledge, 2009.

Giddens, Anthony. 'Positivism and Its Critics'. In *A History of Sociological Analysis*, edited by Tom Bottomore and Robert Nisbet, 237–287. London: Heinemann, 1979.

———. *Capitalism and Modern Social Theory: An Analysis of the Writings of Marx, Durkheim and Max Weber*. Delhi: Cambridge University Press, 2009.

Jones, Robert Alun. 'Ambivalent Cartesians: Durkheim, Montesquieu and Method', *American Journal of Sociology* 100, no. 1 (1994): 1–39.

Marx, Karl. *Capital: A Critical Analysis of Capitalist Production* (vol. 1). Moscow: Progress Publishers, 1974.

———. *The German Ideology*. Delhi: People's Publishing House, 2010.

Mukherji, Partha Nath (ed.). *Methodology in Social Research: Dilemmas and Perspectives*. Delhi: Sage, 2000.

Nisbet, Robert. *The Sociological Tradition*. London: Heinemann, 1967.

Obeyesekere, Gananath. *The Awakened Ones: Phenomenology of Visionary Experience*. New York: Columbia University Press, 2012.

Pathak, Avijit. *Indian Modernity*. Delhi: Aakar, 2015.

Pathak, Dev. 'In Pursuit of Spectacle of Success: Implications of Dominant Rationality in the Domain of Education', *History and Sociology in South Asia* 9, no. 2 (2015): 126–145.

Rajagopalachari, C. *Mahabharata*. Delhi: Bhartiya Vidya Bhawan, 2010.

Tiryakiyan, Edward A. 'Emile Durkheim': In *A History of Sociological Analysis*, edited by Tom Bottomore and Robert Nisbet, 187–236. London: Heinemann, 1979.

Uberoi, Meera. *The Mahabharata*. Delhi: Penguin, 2005.

Vyas, Mahrashi Ved. *Mahabharta*, trans. by Pundit Ram Narayan. Gorakhpur: Gita Press, 2010.

Weber, Max. *The Protestant Ethic and The Spirit of Capitalism*, trans. Talcott Parsons. London: Unwin University Books, 1968.

———. *Economy and Society: An Outline of Interpretive Sociology*, edited by Guenther Roth and Claus Wittich. London: University of California Press, 1978.

———. 'Science as a Vocation'. In *From Max Weber: Essays in Sociology*, edited and translated by H.H. Gerth and C. Wright Mills, 129–156. New York: Oxford University Press, 2009.

———. *Methodology of Social Sciences*, edited and translated by Edward Shills and Henry A. Finch. New Jersey: Transaction, 2011.

York, Richard, and Brett Clark. 'Marxism, Positivism, and Scientific Sociology: Social Gravity and Historicity', *The Sociological Quarterly* 47, no. 3 (2006): 425–450.

Zeitlin, Irving M. *Ideology and the Development of Sociological Theory*. New Jersey: Prentice-Hall Inc., 1968.

5

THE DISPUTE(S): SCIENCE REVISITED, SOCIOLOGY RETHOUGHT

After acknowledging what 'sociological' meant in the classics of sociology, and how it critically engaged with the tenets of scientific epistemology, this chapter takes note of the critical realisation during, and after, the Second World War. The emergence of critical Marxism and clarion calls for a New Left in the Frankfurt School were historically pivotal. In the decades of the 1950s and 1960s, in the USA and Europe, a newfound radicalism among scholars and youth emerged. The radicalism found expression in the critical thinking of the Frankfurt School committed to developing a critical sociology. It was sceptical of the old variant of Marxist politics, which had resulted in the Soviet variety of authoritarianism. The school thus sought to rediscover the tenets of Marxism in scholarship as well as in activism. Some of the key influences behind the New Left were Sartre (philosophical existentialism), neo-Marxism or revisionist theories, Trotskyism, Frantz Fanon (the postcolonial socialism of the Third World), Althusser (structuralist Marxism), among others. The New Left received a major fillip due to Herbert Marcuse's sympathetic understanding and optimism about the students' movement, and C. Wright Mills' letter to the New Left that hailed the power of the peripheral social forces across the globe.[1] Not only had the historical–political milieu changed, but correspondingly, the ways of seeing were also transforming. The grand narratives of the previous decades succumbed to critical rethinking. Such a background shall aid in making sense of the challenges to the idea of sociological that follows in this chapter.

The discursive appeals unsettled the seemingly settled trajectory of 'sociological' and called for new debates, with reference to the Dispute,[2] prominently known as the Positivist Dispute in German sociology. The new debates also brought back the question of science, its nature and scope, and whether one ought to be redoing scientific epistemology. If one wonders whether the attack on the paradigm of positivism was merely an epistemological disturbance to which sociology could be immune, that was certainly not the case. And hence, it again required looking into the idea of sociological. For, this was also a time when there was a shift from sociological theories to what Horkheimer convincingly called social philosophy, or as it were, social thoughts. The Dispute centralised a key villain in scientific epistemology—scientism. It hovered in the aftermath of the Dispute too. The accused, the malaise of scientism, received and brought together in a debate fundamentally divergent views of philosophers and historians of science, namely Karl Popper, Theodor Adorno, Thomas Kuhn, Imre Lakatos and Paul Feyeraband, among others. A notion of sociological in this wake essentially connects with the subversive idea of 'beyond'. It is a beyond of positivism, which may be deemed some kind of post-positivist way of seeing. The vastness of the beyond had a distinct appeal for those intent on liberating sociology from the fundamentalist notions of sociological that emerged in classical positivist sociology. One can labour a little to think of a possible parallel from the world of art and mythology to make sense of the Dispute. Just like in the following instance from art history, the Dispute had a complex relation with the predecessors in sociology.

Spanish artist Pablo Picasso's art is his autobiography.[3] Picasso's father, an amateur artist, decided to hand over his paintbrushes to his young son and thereafter ceased to paint. Ever since, Picasso went about creating his masterpieces. This simple tale becomes a modern-day manifestation of Oedipus replacing his father, intellectually and physically. The break away from the predecessor, precursor and founding figures is, however, never clean. Picasso bore as much guilt as Oedipus did, the guilt of replacing the father.

One wonders whether this is not the case with anyone seeking to break away from the precursors, or the founding figures. Not only limited to the mythological character of Oedipus or a legend from the world of art like Picasso, the new departures of a new protagonist are invariably fraught. There is also another story in this regard, of one of the gods in the Hindu pantheon, Ganesha. He, along with his brother Kartikeya, was given a test by their parents, Shiva and Parvati. Whoever was the first to return after taking a tour of the world would be anointed as the wise one! Known for his cleverness, Ganesha did not go around the world to prove himself an independent mind and conqueror. He just walked around his celestial parents and declared his voyage over. He did not need to replace his father to become an independent mind, a free seeker and a legitimate member of the intellectual comity.

Some of these tales from mythology and history enable us to see the complexity of the debates that divulge discontent in the predecessors' ways of seeing. Do we commit an Oedipus-like act and deliver an irrevocable blow to everything given to us, and persist in intellectual freedom plagued with guilt? Or do we also tend to be Ganesha, unwilling to waste our time in shadowboxing with father(s) and instead prove the whole business of agreement–disagreement frivolous by operating with our own alternatives? We don't have an immediate answer. But the story of the Dispute about the scientific ways of seeing is a curious case that sheds light on the dilemma stated above.

In another context, the founding figures were located in the onslaught of colonial modernity. We learn that the scientific nature of anthropology and sociology both succumbed to intellectual disputes in the wake of the Second World War. Talal Asad (1973) and others were particularly interested in reminding us of the historical encounters through which anthropology and sociology were shaped in the former colonies of the empire. The recognition of the emergent template for doing sociology and anthropology owed to colonial encounters paves the way for taking note of the inherent power game in what could be otherwise deemed to be a purely academic exercise of teaching, researching, learning, writing and participating in various academic forums. In various parts of the world, there was a critical realisation about the anthropological constructions of the field, an oriental category. Colonial modernity and anthropology shaped the ideas and understanding of the other, a binary opposite of the self of the anthropologists. Moreover, Bernard Cohn's (1996, 16) exploration helps us understand the dominance of modern forms of knowledge. European modernity added more weightage to the forms of knowledge that were befitting in the framework of modern social sciences. Such forms of knowledge were employed in the colonial process of categorising and classifying the native's society in the Empire's colonies. He explained the colonial conquest of India as a conquest of knowledge through modalities, such as historiographical, observational/travel, enumerative, museological and surveillance. It meant propagating one form of knowledge over others in the colonies, and thereby discrediting the bodies of knowledge that belonged to the people in the colonies. The perpetuity of the method and questions, the field of knowledge and the inherent intellectual politics puts an intriguing exclamation mark on the progress of social science knowledge in the postcolonial world.

Given such nuggets of realisation in the backdrop, it is imperative to unearth some nuances from the fragments of Disputes. On one hand, it leads us beyond the predominant positivist ways of seeing, and on the other, we shall see science getting revisited. In this chapter, the mirror of science is cracked. There are many splinters, each reflecting one image. And sociology did not fail to recognise this; in the final analysis, there is no one way of seeing in sociology. There is perhaps not one way to be sociological. There is not one set of resources that ought to be deemed conducive for being sociological. The celebration of pluralism is not without an epistemological repercussion, as it undermines the simple formula of gatekeeping. The disciplinary guardians thus become an alter ego of Oedipus. Amidst the shadowboxing, if not total annihilation, what way of seeing comes to the fore and how does it find a place of significance in the sociological domain of enquiry? This is a probing question in this chapter that revisits the manifold Dispute as concisely as possible, and the implications it has for sciences in general and sociology in particular. Suffice it to say, this chapter shall underscore the harbinger of what can be, for the sake of convenience, called post-positivist ways of seeing in sociology. If the idea of post-positivism is a little too much to digest, we can comfortably think of a turnstile on which positivism and its beyond swing along, because the beyond of positivism does not seem to cancel some of the inherent traits.

Before taking a glimpse at the actors in the dramatic performance of the Dispute it is curious to note that positivism has its defenders even in contemporary sociology; hence, a turnstile is an appropriate metaphor perhaps. One ought not to be misled into thinking that the Dispute leads to the demise of positivism. One such defender of positivism has been Jonathan Turner (1985) whose commentaries on social theories have been read by students and professionals across the world. Without mincing words, he charged the tendency of criticising positivism as 'smug cynicism', stating,

> My belief is that "theorists" in sociology rarely theorize, and as a result, we know embarrassingly little about the social universe. This lack of knowledge is not because of positivism; on the contrary, it is because we have failed to be positivists in Comte's sense of this term. (1985, 24)

And seemingly, this is the singular reason why, for Turner, the timeless laws of the social universe, owed to the positivist way of seeing, shall invite little derision. For positivism creates immense possibilities for theorising, by keeping a larger frame of analysis in front of the theorists. Such a tendency to theorise, to develop generalisable principles and pursue logic of reasoning while reading data, has become outdated for sociologists. This shows the fact that sociologists have retreated into the meta-theoretical stratosphere. If they care for empiricism, that too only results in mounds of raw data. As a result, sociology has become a collection of facts, interpretations, grand schemes and typologies. As Turner has observed,

> I think that we ought to go back to Comte, get comfortable in our arm-chairs once again, and start theorizing. For only when theorists begin to develop abstract principles and analytical models about invariant and timeless properties of the social universe can sociology hope to cumulate knowledge about human action, interpretation, and organization. (1985, 29–30)

A similar concern is echoed in neo-functional articulations, for example in Alexander's invitation to rethink theorising (1990). This is premised upon the recognition of the epistemological dilemma—to be a positivist or to be a relativist. Such a dilemma results in a way of seeing in sociology that does not accommodate local, contextual and experiential differences. In such a version of being sociological, an inclination to relativism is deemed invalid. For, relativism is a theoretical challenge to sociological theorising, it is brushed aside as undesirable. How to factor in the relative experiences of communities along with the generalizable objective conditions, is a creative question that sociology must undertake. Against such a tendency rife in positivistic sociology, Alexander provides an imperative to find a way forward in 'hermeneutic universalism'. The latter seeks to offer universally useful formulations and understanding emanating from the social and cultural contexts pertaining to the experiences in human society. In this formulation, objectivity is eventually an ultimate goal in spite of factoring in the relative experiences in which agency of the social actors is prominent. In a sociological way of seeing, thus, as Alexander suggests:

> even while rationality is acknowledged to be an agentic accomplishment, objectivity can also be seen as an eminently worthy goal. To achieve grounded rationality, social actors promote a decentred understanding of the social and natural world, establish norms and frameworks that negatively sanction personalization and that reward not only the ability to see the world as "out there" but the willingness to "subordinate" one's personal opinions to that world's exploration. (538)

Having noted the two positions, one explicitly pro-positivist and the other moving beyond positivism, can anyone deny the significance of theorising? For we are aware that theorising happens with many other schemes at work than simply positivism. That 'theories are couched at various levels of generality' (Alexander 1990, 540), allows one to seek for a critical departure from the postulates of positivism. Likewise, can anyone deny the practice of data digging as the means and end of research in the trivial ways of being sociological? However, it would be with an awareness of the apprehensions that C. Wright Mills expressed about empirical abstractions.[4] Even though we may not be defenders of positivism, we as teachers and researchers are dismayed by the way the mounds of data are created in research without having a way of seeing, reading and presenting stories out of the data. There could be a hermeneutic critique of the divide between theorising and data digging. And there is indeed a critical take on such divides in postcolonial societies, such as Gopal Guru's famous essay in India that nails the divide between theoretical 'brahmins' (pundits/scholars) and empirical 'shudras' (workers/data gatherers).[5] But the critical recognition of such divides, and thereof knowledge politics, does not amount to reverting to positivism, necessarily. Instead, it leads us to a more critical and nuanced departure from epistemological–methodological orthodoxy. Some of these concerns may reappear for detailed engagement later.[6] In short, there is no denial of the importance of the concerns that Turner flags on the pretext of defending positivism. However, all such concerns can be taken care of, even though one does not maintain an unflinching loyalty to Comte. This is why there is an imperative of traversing the Dispute. In the Dispute, we will get to see that a critical stance towards positivism does not preclude the possibility of theorising. Such an understanding develops further in the history of sociology globally, as theoretical developments occur in departure from the positivist way of seeing, a fulcrum of discussion in the subsequent chapters. In the following section, we shall zero in on the Dispute.

The Positivist Dispute: Background, Ground and Foreground

There were other variants of the dispute, prior to the Positivist Dispute in German sociology, in the trajectory of intellectual history. These other disputes flagged issues and concerns that resurfaced in the Positivist Dispute that would follow soon after a quick glance through the history of disputes. Perhaps, the most decisive for social sciences was a discussion in 1909 that underlined the possibility and limits of a normative social and economic science.[7] This discussion was under the aegis of Verein, a social and political organisation founded in 1872 in Germany as part of a social reform movement, which shared the socialist criticism of the Manchester School.[8] It opposed the practice of studying economic life independent of the rest of society, a fulcrum of debate till 1914. In the Verein meeting of 1909, Knapp and Weber, among others, argued whether it is important for economics in particular and social science in general to participate in political life. Weber, despite agreement on the involvement of Verein in political issues, was of the view that scientific activity shall stay above political activities. One of the consequences of this meeting was the foundation of a sociological association with an agenda to professionalise sociology to make it distinguishable from politics and economics. In the first meeting of the association in 1910, Töinnes joined Weber in reaffirming the non-partisan goal of sociology, emphasising that sociologists would concern themselves only with what is, not with what should be.[9] Like Verein, there was another group of scholars in Germany known as the South-West School of neo-Kantianism that witnessed a raging debate on the character of historical and cultural sciences in the 1880s and 1890s. Windelband and Rickert were leading figures in the school, and they propounded a sharp divide between nomothetic and ideographic sciences. It was thus natural that another discussion at Verein, mainly presenting a debate between economists Menger and Schmoller, was about whether economics should follow the exactness of the historical method—deductive or inductive, abstract or empirical. A comprehension of values through a historical framework was deemed to be inevitable for economics in particular and social science in general. Needless to say, they were by and large conversing with another predominant discussions arising from the Vienna Circle[10] that had a more consequential impact on social sciences in general. The Vienna Circle comprised mathematicians, and physical and natural scientists, and advocated a radically anti-metaphysical stance, supported by an empiricist criterion of meaningfulness and a logicist conception of mathematics. Unlike the neo-Kantians, the scholars of the circle denied that any principle or claim was synthetic a priori. They envisaged scientific theories to be regimented within a logical framework. This is famously known as the positivism of the Vienna Circle, briefly discussed in the previous chapter.

The list could get longer if one goes on including many more instances of debates that seemed to have enlivened the intellectual domains in Germany. But this is imperative to take a more sustained glance through the climax in the drama, the Positivist Dispute, also known as the positivism debate in German sociology that charged the intellectual horizons in the 1960s and gave birth to new possibilities. It was an odd debate, as many commentators have suggested, in which no one claimed to be positivist and each sought to critically thrash logical positivism of the Vienna Circle as well as of social sciences.[11]

Seemingly the making of the Positivist Dispute comes into the picture with the formation of the Frankfurt School,[12] which was a contemporary of the Vienna Circle and exhibited critical engagement with the logical positivism of the circle. In the 1930s, Max Horkheimer set the stage by showing that the circle had brought about a culmination in the compromise on reason. Even though one cannot discredit the significant scepticism—for example, Hume's—and philosophical interest in the idea of intellectual rationalism that characterised the Enlightenment, there was sufficient discussion on the anomalies of science, the scientific way of seeing and the poor clones such as several social science disciplines. The critical theory of the school presented a sustained critique of and departures from many of its predecessors. In an address to the school, Horkheimer (1931) focused on those who thought the role of philosophy was over. Instead, he emphasised the role of the scholars of the Frankfurt School in building up social philosophy as a profound activity in social science.[13] And this entailed taking a critical posture on positivism in general and sociological enquiries in particular. As he observed:

> For positivism, everything is exhausted in mere facts [*Tatsächlichkeiten*]. These facts, demonstrable with the means of analytic science, are not questioned by philosophy.... In contrast, the various viewpoints which maintain the existence of such entities appear simply as "another" world view, "another" metaphysics, or "another" consciousness, without any possibility of a valid resolution of the matter ... it is in this dilemma that we find the difficulty that must be overcome.[14]

Horkheimer's criticism of positivist sociology is indeed a critique of the dilemma of social philosophy that is reflected in its inability to deal with the cultural life of humanity in wholesome manner. If at all, positivism leads sociology to perceive human life only in terms of ideological [*weltanschaulich*], sectarian, and confessional terms. Such a way of seeing is bound to the social theories of August Comte, Karl Marx, Max Weber and Max Scheler. Horkheimer's intervention anticipated critical comprehension of the classical masters, philosophies and an action plan for the group of scholars who did not take positivism for granted. Moreover, it summoned scholars to engage with a variety of sources that may be otherwise beyond the pale of preference in positivism. This was also noted in other works of Horkheimer (2013), and the essay on the dialectic of Enlightenment that he co-authored with Adorno (2003, 7). But one cannot mention this trajectory of the school without simultaneously taking a look at a significant philosopher of science, Karl Popper, a coveted target in the Positivist Dispute in German sociology raised by the proponents of critical theory later in the decade of 1960s. Popper's Logik der Forshung, also known as Logic of Scientific Discovery, had already been a point of discussion in the Vienna Circle and beyond since 1934.

To begin with, Popper's position was mistaken as following the premise of the circle, though it was a nuanced critique of logical positivism. It was, once again, the philosophy of science unsettling the methodological certainty of logical positivism and sciences. Popper deemed all the activities that displaced metaphysics or such sources in the name of science as pseudoscience. Most such pseudoscience protected itself from counter-factual evidence with a myth and community of believers. Be it Marxism or psychoanalysis, there was an evident lack of risk-taking. Those who work within the Marxian or Freudian psychoanalytic framework take them for granted, just like a student of physics does with the theories of physical science. The pseudoscience's prerequisite was a converted follower and a quasi-religious status.[15] Hence, what they performed mostly was an accumulation of corroborating evidences, confirmation of the theory dear to them and verification in the light of the suitable evidences. Such pseudoscience precludes possible epistemological progress.

Against the Vienna Circle, Popper showed that all observations were theory impregnated. All sciences stand on an a priori ground, shifting sand, and hence, any amount of verification does not result in a science with certainty. Toward this, Popper presented an elaborate thesis, in which modern science is seen as emerging from 'optimistic epistemology', which suggested, 'Man can know: thus he can be free' (Popper 1963, 7). This was when epistemology was hopeful of man's ability; in this regard, one thinks of an array of philosophers' epistemological constructions—Plato (theory of *anamnesis*), Bacon (theory of *veracitas naturae*), Descartes (theory of *veracitas dei*) and even Russell and Kant. But this optimism was Janus faced, with an epistemological pessimism that humans were depraved and incapable of self-regulation. A jump from Plato's *Meno* to *Republic* or *Phaedrus* revealed the pessimism—the divine man with essence (knowledge) becomes a prisoner of the cave (ignorance). This is consistent in Bacon and Descartes, who on one hand celebrate the inherent ability of man, and meanwhile propose to cleanse of doxa, idols, or sensations of the body.[16] Hence, the need to have a 'resplendent authoritarian theory' emerged to support an epistemological, and concomitantly political, authority. Such a theory with corresponding authority was envisaged to regulate the alleged vulnerability of mankind.

Due to such a dual epistemology, 'thus, we are split into a human part, we ourselves, the part which is the source of our fallible opinions (*doxa*), of our errors, and of our ignorance; and a super-human part, such as the sense or the intellect, the sources of real knowledge (*epistēmē*), whose authority over us is almost divine' (22). The divinity of the epistemological authority is typically expressed in positivism which blames humans for failing to follow positivist procedures for the collection and interpretation of data. Science thus becomes an authoritative source of knowledge. Revisiting Hume's scepticism, Popper proposed a way of seeing as he developed a 'critical rationalism' distinguishable from the rationalism or intellectualism of Descartes and Kant. Critical rationalism aids in detecting and eliminating errors 'by criticising the theories or guesses of others and that of our own. This is an ability that makes one admit—'I do not know: my assertion was merely a guess' (35). This furthermore dispels the certainty with which one source of knowledge becomes absolute, one epistemological authority supreme and one kind of pursuit most ennobling. In sum, this leads to the realisation that all sources are equally fallible. Hence, our contestation shall not be about the sources of knowledge; it shall instead be about the refutations of conjectures. This was the sum and substance of Popper's theory of refutation, through which he proposed to rescue science from pseudoscience based on inductivism and verification.[17] This critique of pseudoscience is towards reaffirming the imperative of science and the scientific way of seeing, no matter how incomplete and provisional, and no matter what source of knowledge is referred to.

It is in this context, with the premise of the Frankfurt School ready and Popper's work already in the public domain, that the Dispute occurred in a somewhat dramatic fashion.[18] The Frankfurt School took the initiative and invited Popper to a conference of the German Sociological Association at Tübingen in October 1961. He was specifically requested to make his presentation in concise points rather than in philosophical discourse. Abiding by the instruction, Popper's presentation included a critique of logical positivism as well as questionable tendencies in social sciences. Adorno's interjections followed Popper's presentation, and Ralph Dahrendorf, as the chair of the symposium, delivered remarks on both.

Traversing through the twenty-seven theses in his presentation, Popper established the imperative of admitting the dialectic of knowing and ignorance, a twist to the Socratic idea about ignorance. Socrates observed that acknowledgement of ignorance is a type of knowledge. Popper took it forward to emphasise that the more we know, the more aware we are of our ignorance. Our knowing enables us to see what we don't know. 'Knowledge starts from the tension between knowledge and ignorance' (1976, 88). We start with a problem, 'something' of which we are aware. Most social science is about the 'problem' for which we seek to offer a 'solution'. These fundamentals prepared the ground for Popper to deliver the most important thesis, number six, that the solution for problems in social sciences is provisional and conjectural, and based on the method of trial and error which undergoes a process of criticism and attempts at refutation. 'The so-called objectivity of science lies in the objectivity of the critical method. This means, above all, that no theory is beyond attack by criticism; and further, that the main instrument of logical criticism—the logical contradiction—is objective' (90).

If this is so, there is no reason why social sciences resort to naturalism or scientism of logical positivism that dwells upon a myth of inductivism and objectivity of natural sciences. It is 'absurd', as Popper stressed, that anthropologists masquerade as true heirs of natural sciences, believing that the objectivity of natural science depends on the objectivity of scientists. Instead, objectivity can only be described through competition (of scientists and schools), tradition (critical tradition of investigation), social institutions (publication, congresses, conferences etc.) and power of state (tolerance, or intolerance, of free discussion). Popper ends by recalling Xenophanes:

> The gods did not reveal from the beginning,
> All things to us; but in the course of time,
> Through seeking we may learn, and know things better.... (104)

All hell broke loose, so to say, following Popper as the Dispute came into shape. But ironically, the immediate cacophony was too mild because Popper and Adorno (1976) seemed to be in agreement about a wide array of issues, including the problem of science, critique of scientism,[19] the nature of social science and the slippery domain of relativism in the sociology of knowledge. Adorno, however, sought to differ on one ground, saying, 'for Popper a problem is something merely epistemological and for me, at the same time, it is something practical' (109). Adorno underlined it as a seminal problem that science, or social sciences, can be separated from reality by any stretch of philosophical rumination. Epistemological problems, since Bacon and Descartes, have been trimmed according to the conception of science. They do not reflect the 'actual process of cognition'. Likewise, Popper's idea of criticism, an essential characteristic of critical rationalism in an open society, was merely an epistemological pursuit. Facts and knowledge, for Adorno, were mediated through society. Hence, he suggested that 'Not all theorems are hypothesis; theory is the telos not the vehicle of sociology' (112). Moreover, by emphasising the significance of criticism in science, according to Adorno, Popper had done a service to the dialectician. The dialectical character of science is what critical theory, 'a critique of society', would overemphasise. In Adorno's return to dialectic, 'reality, the object of societal knowledge' is not 'imperative-free'; 'scientific objectivity and value-freedom are themselves values'; hence, 'separation of evaluative and value-free behaviour is false' insofar as they are reification (117). Reality is a totality that demands critical theory to defy the delimiting academic division of labour according to which sociologists shall not engage with psychological issues. In the scheme of dialectic, it is difficult to maintain such boundaries that eventually sustain the autarchy of science. Instead, bringing back the Hegelian dialectic, critical theory centres on the idea of speculation which started to resemble 'the Faustian cliché of the beast on the barren heath' (5), since the collapse of the Hegelian system in popular discourse. And with such a bare minimum methodical imperative,

Adorno suggested getting back to the 'dignity of objects' rather than 'the objectivity of the findings' (72).

As the chair, Dahrendorf found the debate utterly disappointing insofar as the emergence of new bodies of thought was concerned. The overwhelming points of agreement between Popper and Adorno enabled the chair to boldly guess that the discussion was dominated by a 'third man', which could be named variously as '"positive method", "metaphysical positivism", "empiricism", "empirical research", and so on' (125). Elsewhere, Giddens likened the debate between Popper and Adorno to 'Hamlet without the prince'.[20] While, this may be a playful observation, a veiled sarcasm or a serious allegation of 'political controversy for fame',[21] there is a line of thought that emerges from the Dispute. Be that as it may, Dahrendorf reaffirmed that Popper and Adorno both agreed that all sciences are theoretical. All sciences deal with problems and offer solutions. But sciences deal with unmediated and unqualified materials while the materials central in critical sociology are socio-politically determined and hence sociologists need to be political. Second, the debate aided in developing a dialectical sociology alongside Popper's critical rationalism. This was more sharply and prominently accomplished in Adorno's student and assistant Jürgen Habermas, whose dialectical concept of totality, against the functionalist concept of system,[22] emphasised the need to shift from analytical science to post-Hegelian dialectics. The latter saw the cooperation and the antagonism inherent in societal totality. Thereby, it reaffirmed Adorno's proposition that scientific problems are not detached from real life. The totality is beyond the pale of positivist comprehension, for, the scientific pursuit of positivist thinkers is predominantly guided by scientism, which is science's belief in itself. Thereby, knowledge in neo-positivist or the scientific, analytical and functional theory of systems serves only technical interest. This idea was more elaborate in Habermas' thesis on the relationship of knowledge and human interest (1987). Suggesting that humans have more than merely technical interests, the thesis was an imperative of more than merely positivistic–scientific knowledge. After all, the human world is also guided by aspirations of understanding and transformation, solidarity and synergy, intellect and emotions. The integral relation of knowledge (in plural) and the corresponding diversity of human interests indeed gave uncanny strength to Habermas' contribution.

The Disputed Sciences and Beyond

The clear demarcation of science, empiricism and positivism that may have been the harvest of the deep and prolonged ploughing may have slipped under the obscurity of debates. However, a critical revisiting allows for rethinking science, not merely as the accumulation of textbook information but beyond the haloes of inventions and discoveries. The revisiting that was set in by the Dispute, discussed above, resonated with another context. This is the context of the debate among Thomas Kuhn, Paul Feyerabend, Imre Lakatos and others in Anglo-American philosophy.[23] They responded to Popper too, though not with the stance that is central in the Dispute in German sociology. They were, however, sharing the fundamental idea that science ought to be revisited in order to develop a sense of a science that is non-innocent, theory-loaded and plagued by rivalling hypotheses. The relevance of the revisiting was in the realisation that falsification does not make scientists jettison theories; the baby is not thrown away with the bath water.[24] However, as a historian of science, Thomas Kuhn had more to add to it because he seemed to be dissatisfied with Popper's idea of refutation and falsification. For him, progress in science tells a story beyond the idea of refutation and falsification.

Kuhn's attempt to unravel the structure of the scientific revolution helps to understand the nature and scope of science, by centralising the process of scientific development. It provokes us by suggesting that our understanding of scientific development is incomplete since our questions have been ill-framed. To understand scientific development, the following questions are misleading: When was oxygen discovered? Or what is Galileo's connection to modern science? Instead, the question should be: What was the connection between Galileo's views and his group? The question needs to be about the relationship of discoveries and inventions with the peers in the community of scientists, and not just about the accumulation of information about what was invented when and how. The nature and scope of science is always in relation to a set of received beliefs that guide a vast majority of scientists engaged in what Kuhn calls 'normal science'. The latter is the domain of scientific practices characterised by puzzle solving, a kind of troubleshooting with the given tools and techniques, ideas and insights. At the repair shop, for example, where we take our bicycle to have its handle straightened, we witness a puzzle-solving activity, a more technological avatar of science as it were. The solution to a problem is already available, and hence puzzle-solving only solicits ingenuity from scientists and an adherence to a given set of rules, ideas and concepts. Unlike Popper's image of a critical rationalist scientist who thinks afresh and undertakes risk by creating new pathways, Kuhn's image of 'normal' scientists has limited independence. The puzzle-solving of such a normal scientist did not amount to a path-breaking discovery that could bring about a radical shift, or even a benign tremor, in the epistemology of science. The puzzle could be the same as a problem in science, but,

> if it is to classify as a puzzle, a problem must be characterised by more than assured solution, there must also be rules that limit both the nature of acceptable solution and the steps by which they are to be obtained. To solve a jigsaw puzzle is not, for example, merely to make a picture. (2012, 38)

This is how a scientist solving a puzzle is distinguishable from a child or an artist, or someone who does not belong to the community to which the puzzle belongs. The activities in 'normal' science characterise adherence to and affirmation of the given. Hence, Kuhn emphasised the significance of a paradigm that underpins the normal science of puzzle-solving activities. A paradigm determines the nature of the community, activities, puzzles and solutions. It is a misnomer that 'paradigm' is merely a set of rules, following which one belongs to a community and solves the puzzle acknowledged thereof. Kuhn dwelt upon Michael Polanyi's idea of tacit knowledge acquired through practices rather than a formal body of thought. This inarticulate knowledge in the background enables a scientist to perform something that Wittgenstein questioned as the following: How to apply terms like chair and leaf or game without provoking an argument? It is the paradigm, according to Kuhn, which 'may be prior to, more binding, and more complete than any set of rules for research that could be unequivocally abstracted from them' (46). A scientist gets the paradigm intuitively and consciously, to carry out the puzzle-solving in a normal science, with and without rules.

Kuhn also cleared another likely misunderstanding about normal science, which may appear as a monolithic–unified domain of practice. Within normal science, there is little coherence among the practitioners of widely separated fields; for example, a chemist and physicist will give different answers to the same question: Is a single atom of Helium a molecule or not? The chemist would call it a molecule because they are looking at it through the kinetic theory of gases, whereas a physicist would not consider it so because they do not find a molecular spectrum associated with a single atom Helium. Both engage with the same material through their respective training and practices. Hence it is easier to believe that a paradigm of one scientific discipline may not be useful in another. Indeed, a disciplinary paradigm may have vulnerability in another scientific discipline. This, however, need not mean the vulnerability of normal science as a whole. Furthermore, normal science is by and large cumulative, depending on the acquired body of theory, knowledge and methodology. But it would be a fallacy to imagine that science in general is cumulative. The mistaken idea of cumulative science is 'entangled with the dominant epistemology that takes knowledge to be a construction placed directly upon raw sense data by the mind' (96). The new science of the seventeenth and eighteenth centuries instead dwelt upon the destruction of prior paradigms. The Newtonianism of modern science destroyed the tautological scholasticism that had come from the Greeks. Likewise, there was a 'supermechanical aspect of Newtonianism' (106), which caused methodological limitations. It began to change as Albert Einstein developed the Theory of Relativity, and science moved beyond the century-old regime of Newtonianism. The sharp rupture between old and new, paradigms and practices, underlines the non-cumulative character of science. Thus, there are two levels of competition and conflict of paradigms. One is across time, which amounts to the replacement of the old with the new. The second is, as mentioned earlier, between the paradigms within normal science at any point in time, which appear like rivalling political choices in a truly democratic society. Lastly, it is important to remember what Kuhn reaffirmed throughout the discussion on the nature and scope of a paradigm—that it does not only entail cognitive but also normative function, which makes a paradigm larger than life. It enables scientists to do both, following-a-map as well as map-making. The categories of theories, methods, standards, quality, rigour and directions acquire normative character in a paradigm. All these aspects of a paradigm are marshalled to determine the legitimacy or illegitimacy of a problem, a question and an investigation. Hence, with the change of the paradigm, 'there are usually significant shifts in the criteria determining the legitimacy both of problem and proposed solution' (109).

Kuhn indeed liberated the idea of science, and the scientific way of seeing, from the positivistic rejection of the presence of theory, the a priori of science. In response to Popper's allegedly incomplete break from positivism, he sought to show the role of theories, methods, paradigms and a subjective realm of practices in the scientific community in a historical framework. In normal science, it is not merely the correspondence of theory with fact, as positivism has emphasised. Rather than correspondence, it was consensus among the practitioners, a cardinal feature of the paradigm that matters in normal science. Consensus, unlike correspondence, entails intersubjective dispositions in a community of scientists. In the face of the predominant role of consensus among the scientists, Kuhn argued that neither positivism nor Popper's, allegedly, quasi-positivism can stand.[25]

Feyerabend and Lakatos added two different and significant aspects to the idea of science and the scientific way of seeing. Though different, both had similarities in many regards. They both departed from Kuhn to arrive at two different destinations. For Lakatos, the destination was a scientific *research programme* whereas for Feyerabend it was anarchy in science. Notwithstanding the different destinations, the two shared common concerns. They both held that Popper's falsification was naïve and made no difference to the critical understanding of science; and second, Kuhn's proposition of normal science and scientific revolution only distracted from understanding the real face of science. Lakatos was unsparing in criticising Kuhn for perpetuating psychologistic rather than a logical structure of science with terms such as crisis and paradigm. There is seldom a logical way to judge the incommensurability of new and old paradigms nor is it possible to detect the causes of crises. The problem is even graver when one thinks of the monopoly of normal science that dominated Kuhn's analysis. There cannot be just one theory; there are many, and they tend to exist in competition. Lakatos emphasised a succession of theories, and not a replacement of one theory by another, which constitutes a scientific research programme. The scientific research programme is a manifestation of a remarkable continuity of various theories welded together. And finally, the history of science is a history of competing research programmes. Lakatos deemed it necessary to have competing research programmes for progress in science.

Feyerabend, in debate with Lakatos, expressed his disagreements as well as paid complements;[26] but he was primarily, and critically, responding to Popper and Kuhn. He grounded his discussion in the history and philosophy of science and found support in the avant-garde art movement known as Dadaism.[27] Feyerabend was aware of the limits of the political ideology of anarchism, and the allegations of indifference inherent to the Dadaist idea of *anything goes*. Yet his intention was to utilise the emancipatory value and passion of anarchism in order to understand science. Willing to be recognised as a flippant Dadaist, and not a serious anarchist, he articulated his objective, 'I want you to sense chaos where at first you noticed an orderly arrangement of well behaved things and processes' (2010, xv). This was indeed to show a rupture in science, unlike Kuhn's idea of normal science, which showed a closing of the mind.[28] Also, making it more nuanced than terms such as anarchism and Dadaism may connote, Feyerabend reiterated that his theses were not anti-science.

Against Method, an appropriate title of Feyerabend's book suggesting the key objective, thus, is not against science. Instead, Feyerabend was 'against ideologies that use the name of science for cultural murder' (xxvii). To work out an axis of science which did not foreclose epistemological growth, there was an explicit invocation of alternatives and pluralism in Feyerabend. And meanwhile, this emphasis on alternatives and pluralism was also to steer clear of the confusions created by his immediate predecessors such as Popper and Kuhn. Popper began with an anti-method stance and deceitfully brought method back, while Kuhn was lost in the confusing and inconsequential terminologies such as paradigm, revolution, normal science, puzzle-solving etc. Neither of them created the possibility to rethink science, which could accommodate pluralism in the way of seeing, being scientific and in methodological forays. With such understanding, Feyerabend cleared the superiority of rationalism that seemed original to Popper. The humanitarian face of Popper's critical rationalism was specialised, formalistic and elitist, 'a pale reflection of Mill' (27). Revisiting J.S. Mill's essay 'On Liberty' (1895), Feyerabend endeavoured to show that alternatives of the given ideas in science augment empirical details, necessary for the falsifying process. And in agreement with Lakatos, he proposed that these 'alternatives are not merely catalysts which can later be removed in the rational reconstruction' (28).

Then what are these alternatives? Feyerabend took an anthropological turn, informed by Levi-Strauss, to understand the significance of the primitive worldview as well as hermetic writings during the Renaissance. It enabled him to combat the triumph of scientific chauvinism. He sarcastically called out the chauvinism allegedly inherent in the dominant model of science. In the dominant model of science, the dictum was: 'what is compatible with science should live, what is not compatible with science, should die' (29).[29] To arrive at this idea, towards rescuing metaphysical as well as theoretical pluralism, Feyerabend elaborated a few theses. This began with the proposition of anarchism as a remedy for the epistemology and philosophy of science. As with Lenin and Einstein, so in politics and science respectively, adherence to one epistemology is an anomaly. A seeker of political transformation and scientific advancement should be an unscrupulous opportunist, which systematic epistemologists may not appreciate. But this is how the scientists, the harbingers of novelty in science, have been. Be it the invention of atomism, the Copernican Revolution, the rise of modern atomism (kinetic theory, dispersion theory, stereochemistry, quantum theory), or wave theory of light, they all happened because the thinkers behind them decided not to be guided by certain obvious methodological rules. In another long footnote, Feyerabend discussed the example of Niels Bohr,[30] the physicist who never deemed a finished work as a conclusion. Bohr defied the logic of scientism by dismissing simplicity, elegance or even consistency in the process of his works. Feyerabend, therefore, suggested, 'Logically perfect versions (if such versions exist) usually arrive only long after the imperfect versions have enriched science by their contributions' (7–8). It is the principle of *anything goes* that comes to aid a scientist in relating idea and action, construction and destruction, in a playful activity of passion.

This led Feyerabend to understand the significance of counter-rule behind the scientific way of seeing, being and doing. Rather than rules that many epistemologists of science were interested in, it is counter-rule that rules the scientific roost. The counter-rule instructs to proceed counter-inductively. To simplify, the counterintuitive exploration alludes to an attention to the ideas, which appear contrary to the expected ideas in the scientific epistemology. This means that scientists shall operate with hypotheses that are inconsistent with established theories. This was indeed distinguishable from Popper and Kuhn. The stance of counter-rule and the advocacy of counter-inductive investigation emphasised that thinking of alternatives in the aftermath of refutation, or destruction, of orthodox theory was like putting the cart before the horse. The alternatives needed to be envisaged at the onset and must lead to pluralistic methodology. The scheme of counter-rule solicited a passionate engagement with alternatives from the beginning to the end of an exploration. The horse of thoughts and epistemology, many and unruly, was a necessary precondition in Feyerabend's imagination of science. As he put it aptly:

> We need a dream-world in order to discover the features of the real world we think we inhabit (and which may actually be just another dream-world) … we must invent a new conceptual system that suspends, or clashes with, the most carefully established observational results, confounds the most plausible theoretical principles, and introduces perceptions that cannot form part of the existing perceptual world. (15)

This was evidently a sharp departure from Kuhn who showed the emergence of alternatives, the new in an old paradigm, only after a prolonged and sustained failure of normal science. The counter-rule would instead suggest that anything scientific starts with alternative ideas at play. Hence, despite the relative autonomy of fact as propounded by positivists, Feyerabend underlined the intimate relation of facts with theory, the empirical with insights, the material with vision. We choose facts, describe and understand them, in accordance with some or other theory. The presence of an alternative theoretical–conceptual apparatus is, therefore, a crucial precondition. Being realistic, however, Feyerabend agreed with J.S. Mill in admitting that revolutionary ideas eventually transform into obstacles to new thoughts. As he argued, 'Alternatives are still employed but they no longer contain realistic counter-proposals; they only serve as a background for the splendour of the new theory' (23). This is so due to the modern scientific epistemology, from Francis Bacon to Thomas Kuhn. Seemingly a conspiracy, the reduction of alternatives to ornamental pieces in scientific discourse is aimed at cleansing science of inconsistent materials. There are many stakeholders in the status quo of science, which may flirt with the ideas of novelty. But they all prepare us to arrive at a unanimity of opinion much akin to that of the rigid church, or as Kuhn suggested, intersubjective consensus. Feyerabend sensitised us to the pitfalls and demanded from us a more free-spirited engagement with science. This is all towards curating a new image of science and scientists based on a critical reading of the history and philosophy of sciences.

Conclusion: Sociology in the Wake of Post-Positivism

The instance of the Dispute that this chapter hinges on contributed to a new beginning in methodological thinking, ways of seeing, in sociology. At a time when practices of scholarly deliberations in social science are all about avoiding disputes of a consequential nature, the instance of the Dispute is like a polestar. It reminds us that we must indulge in a dispute, small or big, consequential or not. Such encouragement shall show not only in writings but also in deliberations despite the limits imposed by the logic of academic networking. For no dispute would simply amount to 'no social sciences'. The tendency to avoid disputes in social science is indeed anti-social scientific imperatives. Second, the Dispute, as obvious, was manifold. It was about the characteristics of scientific epistemology, highlighting that what was being taken for granted was a problematic self-belief of science in its superiority. The Dispute, and corresponding debates on science between philosophers and historians such as Karl Popper, Thomas Kuhn and Paul Feyerabend, solicit a departure from such scientism and rethink the modes of being scientific. A sense of pluralism in the way of being scientific dawns upon the scientific epistemology. There was a picture of liberal science for an open and progressive society in Karl Popper's philosophy, and discursive caution about the possible slippages into pseudoscience. Yet another picture of science, Kuhn's normal science, was an aid in understanding that science is a sociological entity because it is essentially what the community of scientists do with their methods, tools and overall paradigm. With Paul Feyerabend, we begin to understand the intricate radicalism at the core of science. This is an epistemological radicalism through which a scientist is capable of thinking out of the box, against the grain, and developing novel ideas. An idea of methodological pluralism is a major takeaway from the anarchist model of science discussed by Feyerabend. Altogether, the Dispute and the philosophical deliberations in this chapter have underscored positivism as an ingeniously constructed clone in tune with orthodox scientific epistemology. The problem of scientism was indeed a revelation of the limits of the epistemology that took birth in the history of science and the Enlightenment philosophy. This development paves the way for turning to what is termed a post-positivist way of seeing in the next chapter.

If scientism lost its superiority in the Dispute, as discussed in this chapter, positivism receive a devastating impact too. Against such a backdrop, there should have commenced a sharp departure from the positivist mode of doing social sciences, particularly sociology. There was perhaps a modicum of success for the Dispute, and hence this chapter has recapitulated the details. However, to play the devil's advocate, had it been the success of the Dispute in sociology, social philosophy and thoughts emanating from societies across the world could have joined in the league of serious discussions. Social thoughts as well as sociological theories would have come together in framing novel questions, insights, perspectives and overall, ways of seeing. As a result, as envisaged by both parties of the Dispute, many new epistemic categories and innovations in the epistemological frameworks could have been formulated. Did such radical departures happen? After all, there is always a sinister divide between thoughts and theories, praxis and epistemology.

With such realisation based on this chapter, the following chapter recounts some of the methodological rethinking, with some scepticism. For there is always an eye out for, what Sandra Harding's *The Science Question in Feminism* (1986) aimed to develop, a 'successor science'. We shall return to the science question in the next chapter in spite of the revisiting of science that commenced with Popper in this chapter. It is yet another quest of science that is more located, partial enough to be conducive to understanding women's situated knowledge in feminist epistemology. Likewise, it is evident that the prefix post in 'post-positivist' is a fraught usage. Suffice it to say, it renders the terrain of post-positivism promising as well as doubtful. The promises of post-positivism in sociology keep us all optimistic about a fruitful way of seeing., However, the doubts trick intellectual hopes, as the next chapter shall show. And thus, the perpetuity of a creative ambivalence, that is—to be sociological or not to be—shall remain a mainstay.

References

Alexander, Jeffrey C. 'Beyond Epistemological Dilemma: General Theory in a Postpositivist Mode', *Sociological Forum* 5, no. 4 (1990): 531–544.

Adorno, T., H. Albert, R. Dahrendorf, et al. *The Positivist Dispute in German Sociology*, trans. Glyn Adey and David Frisby. London: Heineman, 1976.

Asad, T. *Anthropology and the Colonial Encounters*. London: Ithaca Press, 1973.

Bottomore, Tom. *The Frankfurt School and Its Critics.* New York and London: Routledge, 2002.

Cohn, Bernard. *Colonialism and Its Forms of Knowledge: The British in India*. Princeton: Princeton University Press, 1996.

Feyerabend, Paul. *Against Method.* London: Verso, 2010.

Frisby, David. 'Introduction'. In *The Positivist Dispute in German Sociology*, edited by T. Adorno, H. Albert, R. Dahrendorf, et al., translated by Glyn Adey and David Frisby, ix–xliv. London: Heinemann, 1976.

Gedo, Mary M. *Picasso: Art As Autobiography*. Chicago: University of Chicago Press, 1980.

Giddens, Anthony. 'Positivism and Its Critics'. In *A History of Sociological Analysis*, edited by Tom Bottomore and Robert Nisbet, 237–287. London: Heinemann, 1979.

Guru, Gopal. 'How Egalitarian Are the Social Sciences in India?', *Economic and Political Weekly* 37, no. 50 (2002): 5003–5009.

Guru, Gopal, and Sundar Sarukkai. *The Cracked Mirror: An Indian Debate on Experience and Theory*. Delhi: Oxford University Press, 2012.

Habermas, Jürgan. 'The Analytical Theory of Science and Dialectics: A Postscript to the Controversy Between Popper and Adorno'. In *The Positivist Dispute in German Sociology*, edited by T. Adorno, H. Albert, R. Dahrendorf, et al., translated by Glyn Adey and David Frisby, 131–162. London: Heineman, 1976.

———. *Knowledge and Human Interest*. London: Polity Press, 1987.

Harding, Sandra. *The Science Question in Feminism.* Ithaca, New York: Cornell University Press, 1986.

Horkheimer Max. 'The Present Situation of Social Philosophy and the Tasks of an Institute for Social Research', 1931. https://www.marxists.org/reference/archive/horkheimer/1931/present-situation.htm.

———. *Eclipse of Reason*. London: Bloomsbury, 2013.

Horkheimer Max, and Adorno, Theodor. *Dialectic of Enlightenment: Philosophical Fragments*. Stanford, California: Stanford University Press, 2003.

Keuth, Herbert. 'The Positivist Dispute in German Sociology: A Scientific or a Political Controversy?', *Journal of Classical Sociology* 15, no. 2 (2015): 154–169.

Kuhn, Thomas S. *The Structure of Scientific Revolutions*. Chicago: Chicago University Press, 2012.

Mills, C.W. *The Sociological Imagination*. New York: Oxford University Press, 1959.

Mills, J.S. *On Liberty: The Subjection of Women*. New York: Henry Holt & Co., 1895.

Motterlini, Matteo (ed.). *For and Against Method: Imre Lakatos and Paul Feyerabend*. Chicago: Chicago University Press, 1999.

Mukherji, Partha Nath (ed.). *Methodology in Social Research: Dilemmas and Perspective*. Delhi: Sage. 2000.

Popper, Karl. *Conjectures and Refutations*. London: Routledge, 1963.

———. 'The Logic of the Social Sciences'. In *The Positivist Dispute in German Sociology*, edited by Theodor W. Adorno, Hans Albert, Ralf Dahrendorf, et al., translated by Glyn Adey and David Frisby, 87–104. London: Heineman, 1976.

Richter, Hans. *Dada: Art and Anti-Art*. New York: Thames and Hudson, 1997.

Samuels, Warren J., Jeff E. Biddle, and John B. Davis (eds). *A Companion to the History of Economic Thought*. Oxford: Blackwell, 2003.

Turner, Jonathan H. 'In Defense of Positivism', *Sociological Theory* 3, no. 2 (1985): 24–30.

Williams, Liz. 'Karl Popper, The Enemy of Certainty, Part 4: Lakatos, Kuhn and Feyerabend', *The Guardian*, 2012. https://www.theguardian.com/commentisfree/belief/2012/oct/01/karl-popper-lakatos-kuhn-feyerabend.

———. 'Karl Popper, The Enemy of Certainty, Part 2: The Virtue of Refutation', *The Guardian*, 2012. https://www.theguardian.com/commentisfree/belief/2012/sep/17/popper-enemy-uncertainty-virtue-refutation.

6

POST-POSITIVIST WAYS OF SEEING: RESURGENCE OF EXPERIENCE

Against the backdrop of the discussions in the previous chapter comes a question of cardinal significance: What could be the way of seeing in sociology following the critique of positivism, scientism and the consequent novel ideas of science? The question solicits a revisiting of the precise instances of seeing things, a little differently, in sociology. There is a qualitatively different notion of the sociological in the so-called post-positivist way of seeing because there is a creative engagement with subjectivism, an interpretative lens, reason, emotions and meanings. It is a trajectory of discussion on understanding, interpretation and explanation geared towards meanings. Truly a messy domain of meaning becomes an anchor to outdo the clinical clarity of scientific epistemology, or its cognate named positivism.

Phenomenology is one such instance. Frisby (1976, x), while reflecting upon the Positivist Dispute,[1] makes note of the importance of many other ways of being post-positivist, in the aftermath of the critique of modern science qua debates with Karl Popper. To name a few, they are the sociology of knowledge and hermeneutics, phenomenology and ethnomethodology among others in social sciences. This is not to suggest that these variants came into existence only after the Dispute. The intellectual history of social sciences highlighted in this chapter shows that they existed even before the Dispute, but the variety of methodological ways of seeing was rediscovered. We can recall that the sociology of knowledge was invoked as a dubious relativist variation in the debate between Popper and Adorno. Likewise, phenomenology was merely a philosophical work before its rediscovery in post-positivist sociology. Before sociology adopted a rediscovered phenomenology, the philosophy of phenomenology was significant for the philosophers of hermeneutics ever since Heidegger's endeavour to ontologise understanding. A significant change occurred with Alfred Schutz's ingenious translation of philosophical phenomenology into a body of sociological theory. Likewise, hermeneutics was largely confined to the realm of philosophy, except for Wilhelm Dilthey's hermeneutics which was a source of *verstehen*, the German term that means empathic understanding, in Weber's sociology. They all began to appear, or they were rediscovered, in social science discussions more confidently after the Dispute. For this chapter, this is the scenario, of methodological significance, that has been deemed to be post-positivist. It is, however, subject to debate whether they did indeed radically depart from positivism. Perhaps, due to such sceptical considerations, some of us prefer non-positivist to post-positivist.

To understand phenomenology and ethnomethodology, we need to first briefly touch upon the background of hermeneutics. Besides, we will also unravel the sociology of knowledge. An important implication in this chapter is about the return to the relatively subdued, or selectively used, category of experience as a premise of the post-positivist way of seeing. In the previous chapters, the experience was an epistemologically delimited premise in scientific epistemology, a conditioned entity in the Enlightenment philosophy. There are ruptures along the idea of experience in this chapter. We get a sense that the methodological debates are indeed a contestation about experience, with the following questions: Whose experience matters—that of social actors or sociologists? How much of experience makes for a sociologically convincing way of seeing? And finally, what are the politics of experience in any way of seeing? To approach some of these questions, this chapter reads methodological–theoretical debates from Europe as well as India,[2] which returns to the idea of reflexivity in the next chapter. This chapter predominantly confines itself to discussing the sociology of knowledge, phenomenology, ethnomethodology, hermeneutics and feminist epistemology while emphasising the theoretical (re)emergence of the category of experience.

The post-positivist ways of seeing in sociology hinge a great deal on hermeneutical tradition. In this regard, Mukherji (2000, 3) observed that social scientists were identical to social hermes[3] when it came to objectives and actions. Apart from factoring in a variety of psychologisms, hermeneutics 'provided a romantic critique of rationalistic Enlightenment' (24). It centred 'cult of feeling' by decentring 'cult of reason', and in the same fashion, it underlined subjectivity, cultural essentialism and the production of meanings as important features of the human world. Two broad characteristics are found within hermeneutics—objectivism that prevailed among German neo-Kantians, Weber's sociology and Freud's psychoanalysis, and subjectivism that pervaded the works of philosophers such as Martin Heidegger, Hans-Georg Gadamer and Peter Winch. However, there is a third strand too which brings in Habermas and Paul Ricoeur as the proponents of critical hermeneutics. Elsewhere, there appear three-fold divides and phases of hermeneutic tradition, namely, theoretical, methodological and philosophical (Bleicher 1980, Mueller-Vollmer 1985). However, we shall try to take a synoptic glance to develop a holistic understanding rather than following the classificatory divide. More or less, there is unanimity among the strands of modern hermeneutics, despite variation in the intellectual trajectories, in emphasising the significance of the cultural context in the production of meanings. It unlocks a domain of intellectual–interpretative politics in which knowing and not knowing, knowing and being, knowledge and self, epistemology and ontology unfold together. In implication, the total of hermeneutics leads to an idea of 'methodology of being', a way of seeing in which one sees oneself and the object of knowledge at once while one is capable of retrieving one from the other (Pathak 2019, 104). To such an issue the next chapter shall return with more discursive details.

Hermeneutics: A Way of Seeing Subjectivity

Since Friedrich Schleiermacher, the founding father of modern hermeneutics, the hermeneutic project had delivered a novel epistemological challenge to the Cartesian Cogito, which was unnervingly complacent with the purity of 'I'.[4] This project sought to highlight the limitations of Cogito in the midst of debates on meanings. Additionally, the project returns to some of the Enlightenment encyclopaedists discussed in Chapter 2 for a critical rethinking. This began to show in Schleiermacher's basic framework. He observed that a hermeneutist shall detect two broad strands in a text under discussion—grammatical and psychological. While the exploration of the grammatical aspect leads to a philological understanding, it is with the psychological exploration that an author's intention comes to the fore. It sets some of the fundamental aspects that a hermeneutist intends to discover through a text. They are: who is the author, what is the text, why and how the author developed the text when the author worked on the text, where is the author located, and which means were used by the author in the accomplishment of the text? One gets a sense of the fundamental concept of the hermeneutic circle, which brings the text and context face to face, even though Schleiermacher's preference is in the subjective intentions of the author.

In this regard, it is worth remembering that hermeneutic philosophy is a walk away from the Kantian distinction of *noumena*, the reality accessible to pure reason, different from *phenomena*, which is the domain of scientific knowledge. The Kantian distinction amounted to a divide in the realms of experiences and knowledge. Such a divide of knowledge was somewhat challenged even in Max Weber's sociology. We are aware that Weber broke away from the divide between the two domains of knowledge that Rickert and Windelband had tried to perpetuate.[5] Instead, Weber followed Dilthey who adopted a more objectivist approach to meaning, as did Freud in psychoanalysis. Dilthey attempted to show that everything subsidiary and residual in Kantian formulation becomes central in a hermeneutic engagement with meanings. Instead of getting trapped in the distinction of a priori and posteriori, there is a serious deliberation on the idea of 'preunderstanding'. The latter is loaded with historicity and guides humans in the practice of understanding. There is a sense of an uncanny parallel between scientific observation and preunderstanding, also interchangeably called 'pre-given'. It is a domain where Dilthey located a historical objectivation of experiences. Moreover, Dilthey added a category of life expressions in his deliberation. 'Life expressions' are intricately linked with 'life experience'. One is what one does, which appears to be a hermeneutic maxim. It is safe to say that Dilthey responded to Kant by making a variety of a priori experiences central, thereby suggesting that humans follow norms and customs with feelings and desires. Rather than Kantian categorical imperatives, it is human interest that figures prominently. *Verstehen* becomes a hermeneutic tool for humans to get a sense of each other. Likewise, a hermeneutist seeking to understand meanings employs *verstehen* as a methodological tool.

In this regard, Giddens (1976) put Weber and Dilthey together and argued that they both failed to defend against an allegation. That *verstehen* generates only hypothesis and not verified knowledge is a catch in both Dilthey's hermeneutics and Weber's sociology. While positivist social science benefitted from such a tricky role of *verstehen*, qualitative social science research, particularly interpretative sociology, suffered. Only with the interventions of Heidegger and Gadamer could the subjective meaning of the actor find acceptance in the realm of objective enquiry. Following Dilthey's premise, German theologian Rudolf Bultmann ventured into the area of preunderstanding often left for anthropological explorations in modern social sciences. In a hermeneutic engagement with the New Testament, he discussed mythology as a text pertaining to humans' preunderstanding, that is, pre-given. However, this approach to mythology was unlike the approach of a theologist or an ethnologist. Bultmann sought to hermeneutically demythologise mythology. For, god is not accessible, but his activities are. It is an interpretation of mythology to understand the interface of nature and culture, concrete and abstract, social and mythological. This was all still with an aspiration to find objectivity in hermeneutics which could run parallel with that of scientific objectivity.

With a linguistic turn in hermeneutics, indeed, there occurs a turn to subjectivism too. Heidegger and Wittgenstein who made reality appear as linguistically constituted and context-bound primarily accomplished this. And in this line of subjectivist hermeneutics, as it were, Gadamer is an oft-revisited philosopher. Heidegger's hermeneutic project was aimed at, among other things, 'ontologising understanding'. In the ultimate analysis, it unravels the characteristics of experience. Following Edmund Husserl's phenomenology, he presents a dual *Dasein*, being in and being there, two aspects of human existence. This duality of existence led him to unfold preunderstanding, going back to primordial times. With various usages, such as foresight, forehaving, foreconception, the being in Heidegger's framework got to enjoy a much richer variety of preunderstanding than in Dilthey's. This all led to the key *existentiale*, that is, meaning. Heidegger put it categorically that understanding itself is not interpretation. The latter is a fulfilment of understanding. It is in the act of interpretation, guided by our understanding, that we realise the essential *existentiale*. Understanding occurs in an intriguing way to a being as Being-there always discloses itself to Being-in. To quote Heidegger, 'Understanding is the existential Being of Dasein's own potentialities-for-Being; and it so in such a way that this Being disclose in itself what its Being is capable of' (Mueller-Vollmer 1985, 217).

In a more accessible sense, this means I can understand what I am because I understand what my world is. Both my world and I are disclosed to each other in terms of potentialities and possibilities. It takes place in this way because we are situated on a timeline with the past, present and future as coordinates. But an understanding, curiously, does not guarantee meaning. As Heidegger put it, 'Meaning is that wherein the intelligibility of something maintains itself. That which can be articulated in a disclosure by which we understand, we call meaning' (224). Meaning is an *existentiale* of *Dasein* that emerges from interpretation. We can hear, converse and thereby interpret the meaning from our understanding. We can do so because we all have in common Being-there and Being-in, disclosed and disclosing *Dasein*, and the basic minimum preunderstanding. Interpretation carried out in the form of assertion is 'derivative mode' as it is based on 'forehaving/foresight/fore conception'. The latter is actually the existential foundation of interpretation, arising from *Dasein*. Thus, as an offshoot of understanding, interpretation—through explication and assertion—is only the fulfilment of understanding. Similarly, a discourse that hinges on understanding and interpretation is ontologico-existential in nature.

Furthering the Heideggerian project of an ontological-existential notion of understanding, Gadamer offered a critique of the Enlightenment and its methodological preoccupations. He pointed out the methodological 'prejudice' of modern science against the 'prejudice' of socio-cultural thoughts. Thereby, tradition, religion and everything that belongs to social thought appear as an inferior counterpart of reason. The German Romantic reaction to the prejudice of Enlightenment resulted in the resurrection of the past, Christianity and tradition. This, however, only exalted tradition as opposed to reason. But methodologically, it remained akin to scientific epistemology. For example, Schleiermacher's view that narrowness of vision and over-hastiness cause misunderstanding is only slightly different from Descartes' emphasis on the same. Gadamer acknowledged the potential pitfall of Romantic hermeneutics and cautioned against endless relativism and subjectivity. Gadamer suggested, 'the focus of subjectivity is a distorting mirror. The self-awareness of an individual is only a flickering in the closed circuit of historical life' (261). But then, Gadamer also rescued the word prejudice from the negative connotations attributed to it in scientific epistemology. As tradition and reason go together, prejudice and understanding are essential components of historicity. This way, he ensured a method of play for understanding a text. In his own words, 'Prejudices are biases of our openness to the world. They are simply conditions whereby we experience something—whereby what we encounter says something to us' (1980, 128).

Gadamer departed from an unconditional antithesis between tradition and reason. The object of study/understanding and the person seeking it is on a historical continuum. This is what Gadamer called 'effective history', and the success of the hermeneutical enterprise depends on the development of one's 'effective historical consciousness'. By virtue of this, an individual can understand his/her horizon. 'A person who has no horizon is a man who does not see far enough, and hence overvalues what is nearest to him' (Mueller-Vollmer 1985, 269). We could comprehend each other's horizons because no single horizon is fixed and final. Curiously, 'the horizon is, rather, something into which we move and that moves with us' (271). It is not mere empathy because we are in a reciprocal relationship that leads us to understanding, leading to the 'fusion of horizon'. A tradition is, in fact, a site of a perpetual fusion of horizons. As Gadamer argued:

> In fact, the horizon of the present is being continually formed, in that we have continuity to test all our prejudices. An important part of this testing is the encounter with the past and the understanding of the tradition from which we come.... There is no more an isolated horizon of the present than there are historical horizons. Understanding, rather, is always the fusion of these horizons which we imagine to exist by themselves. (Mueller-Vollmer 1985, 272)

In the epistemological scheme of Gadamer hermeneutics enables for 'natural human capacity' in the universal process of understanding.

It is here that the 'I-Thou' relationship owing to the effective historical consciousness facilitates a 'fusion of horizon'. And the reason why Gadamer spent such enormous intellectual energy in elucidating the historicity of understanding is plain and simple—method begets only method, not truth. Verification and certainty, based on the subject–object dichotomy cardinal in scientific epistemology, do not take us to understand the experience of truth that is mainly in the domains of philosophy, art and history (Gadamer 1975, 10).

Thus far, the brief synopsis of hermeneutics underlines the significance of life experiences, existence, expressions, being, understanding, preunderstanding, and historical consciousness, among other things. All of these terms could be conveniently put under the category of tradition. But then, later developments in hermeneutics also cast aspersions on the validity of tradition. In a critique of Gadamer's linguistic idealism, Habermas said:

> we have good reason to suspect that the background consensus of established traditions and language games can be a consciousness forged of compulsion, a result of pseudo communication, not only in the pathologically isolated case of disturbed familial systems, but in the entire social systems as well. (Mueller-Vollmer 1985, 317)

Gadamer's idea of language as a meta-institution through which we acquire understanding was challenged. Habermas elaborated on the power that a native speaker commanded owing to the creativity of natural language (vernacular of the native). This is the relationship of power over the practical consciousness in a society. It can be used for the purpose of obfuscation and agitation as well as for enlightenment. This inherent power equation yields 'systematically distorted communication' with symptomatic unintelligibility. Habermas called it 'pathological disturbances of speech', taking cues from Freud and Lorenzer. It requires reason and rationality, which Habermas considered free from any prejudice, liberating humans from repressive consciousness. Habermas exhibited an explicit acquiescence to the Enlightenment. The emphasis on reason and rationality to deal with the pathology in speech connects him with scientific epistemology. However, this was not an unconditional acquiescence to the Enlightenment, as Habermas, in agreement with Gadamer, denounced the 'monological self-certainty' of any scientific enterprise. Nonetheless, he argued:

> The Enlightenment knew what Hermeneutics forgets … the claim to universality of hermeneutical approach can be upheld only if one starts from the recognition that the context of tradition, as a locus of

> possible truth and real accord, is at the same time the locus of real falsehood and the persistent use of force. (314)

However, it is noticeable that the (scientific) prejudice against (traditional) prejudice, which Gadamer detected in the epistemological foundation of the Enlightenment, is maintained in the hermeneutics of Habermas and subsequently in Paul Ricoeur. The latter attempted thrashing the methodological grains dispersed in the hermeneutic philosophy. However, in order to respond to the poser of the critical hermeneutics, Ricoeur reeked of an epistemological bias. For him, the aim of hermeneutics was discourse that is, and can be, inscribed and rendered into a text. Ricoeur agreed with Plato that writing is more meaningful and trustworthy than speech. At this point, it is useful to briefly refer to the celebrated synthesising of all strands apt in interpretative sociology.

Giddens', propounding the New Rules of Sociological Method, observed, 'hermeneutic, I wish to claim, does not find its central range of problems in the understanding of written texts as such, but in the mediation of frames of meaning' (1976, 64). But then, most important is the accomplishment of methodological orientation that puts self of the interpreter and the object of interpretation, under the larger ambit of understanding. No wonder, admitting its potentials, Susan Hekman (1986, 1987) highlighted the way forward coming from the hermeneutics. We return to Hekman, in the latter part of this chapter, who concertised the idea of anti-foundational epistemology by reading some of the edifying philosophers such as Heidegger, Wittgenstein, Gadamer, Richard Rorty and others.

Sociology of Knowledge: In Between Relativism and Relationism

A sub-field of sociology began to be seriously discussed in the early 1930s, after Karl Mannheim published *Ideology and Utopia*, deliberating on the nature and scope of sociology of knowledge. Mannheim's detailed thesis on the relationship of knowledge with the social, cultural and contextual heralded growing interest in a particular premise. This was a premise for the post-positivist way of seeing in sociology that centres the contextual character of knowledge. In this premise, the study of *weltanschauungen* (the study of worldview) is central. The premise of a post-positivist way of seeing, in relation with the central idea of *weltanschauungen*, was available in the critical thinking of Frankfurt School, discussed in the previous chapter. Similarly, the post-positivist quest is a characteristic of Mannheim' sociology of knowledge, Schutz' phenomenology and

Garfinkel's ethnomethodology, and in the hermeneutic philosophy in sociology. The Dispute in the previous chapter elucidated the German responses to Popper's thesis seeking to bring back the social at the interface of science, history, philosophy and sociology. Likewise, there were Anglo-American debates on science. There were other equally important strands that play a crucial role in bringing about gradual and subsequently radical changes in the sociological way of seeing, by depicting knowledge as a social entity. In this chapter, we reflect on the sociology of knowledge, hermeneutics, phenomenology and ethnomethodology in context of the previous chapter that was aimed at revisiting science and rethinking sociology. If Adorno and Habermas created the possibility of revitalising the dialectic in sociology while responding to Popper, they had simultaneously accomplished what Mannheim was seeking to do in sociology of knowledge and Alfred Schutz in phenomenology, which was to underline the interaction of the epistemological and the social, the philosophical and the political, the scientific and the contextual, and so on. The Positivist Dispute had articulated scepticism about the relativist implications of the sociology of knowledge, yet, it is important for the post-positivist quest of being sociological in this chapter.

What does sociology of knowledge have to do with a post-positivist way of seeing? And how far is it post-positivist? The answer lies in the way Mannheim conceives the sociology of knowledge as a branch of sociology which 'seeks to analyse the relationship between knowledge and existence', 'social conditioning of knowledge', and 'drawing them into the horizon of science' (1960, 237). It furthermore shows that the knowledge of society in society, as well as in the sociology of knowledge, maintains a dual composition. Knowledge entails ideology. Ideologically loaded knowledge is more inclined to maintain the ideological status quo. In so doing, one ideology also competes with other kinds. Second, there is another aspect of knowledge and that is utopia, a transcendental component inclined to threaten the ideologically sustained status quo. Mannheim imagined an inevitable presence of utopias, the reality-transcending component in the social framework of knowledge, and in a worse case, 'the complete elimination of reality-transcending elements from our world would lead us to a "matter-of-factness" which ultimately would mean the decay of the human will' (236). This apprehension is applicable to the social domain where knowledge formation happens, as well as for the sciences that are aimed at making sense of socially produced knowledge. It furthermore enumerates the historical, along with social, genesis of the ideas. Underlining the role of perspectives and thought models in the development of ideas, Mannheim discussed the example of the idea of freedom and its various forms that emerge from the conservative–romantic–idealist, and positivist–liberal perspectives. A purely formal logic, as in the orthodox social sciences and sociology, overlooks the perspectives that engender the 'qualitative elements in the structure of thought'. But the sociology of knowledge divulges the perspective and shows that the idea entails situational–relativity. Knowledge is relative to a life-situation, social position, and location. Human thoughts are in response to where they are and what they do. The relationship between belonging and knowledge is emphatic in situational relativism. This, however, is not a total relativism, in which knowledge is unequivocally tied to a situation. Any knowledge is aimed at a larger group, beyond a limited situation. Mannheim's relativism is therefore a micro context of knowledge, which is geared towards the macro context. But knowledge does not end with relativism. It instead takes us forward to the relational character of knowledge.

In terms of the relational nature of knowledge, Mannheim underlined a coming together of perspective and thought models in which an idea unfolds. Functionalist or Marxist thought models offer, in accordance with the inherent perspectives, diverse details along their respective metaphors, concepts and analyses. Moreover, the sociology of knowledge enables a shift from the particular conception of ideology (exclusive and distrustful of other ideologies) to a total conception of ideology (inclusive and able to move towards the total structure of group mind or folk mind, an allusion to a social collective). However, Mannheim rejected both, the singular individual or the group's categorical determination of thought. With this shift, Mannheim noted, 'neither the concrete individuals nor the abstract sum of them can legitimately be considered as bearers of this ideological thought-system' (52). Instead, he proposed that a thought is more concretely shaped by a relational interdependence of individual life histories and more inclusive group situations. While each particularistic ideological position sees false consciousness in the other ideological camp, the totality of the *volksgeist* in the philosophy of consciousness shows the relational existence of diverse particular ideologies. While particular ideologies indulge in distrustful unmasking of each other, the sociology of knowledge tries to understand their positions in the total structure of thought without any partisan bias. This is a non-evaluative approach, characterised by relationism instead of relativism. Mannheim clarified:

> relationism signifies merely that all of the elements of meaning in a given situation have reference to one another and derive their significance from this reciprocal interrelationship in a given frame of thought … when the social situation changes, the system of norms to

> which it has previously given birth ceases to be in harmony with it. The same estrangement goes on with reference to knowledge and to the historical perspective. (76)

Knowledge in Mannheim's sociology did not corroborate the divide of evaluative and non-evaluative, idealistic-romantic and positivistic, isolated individual thinking and a totally relativist group mind. Instead, it demands from us an ability to arrive at an intellectual synthesis of available positions. In the ultimate analysis, knowledge is product of interdependent life histories and inclusive situations upon which humans work further in unconscious manner. Keeping their own motives and interest in perspective the social humans collectively operationalise the knowledge. Mannheim showed that the convincing arguments in the history of thought have emerged from a variety of syntheses, one example of which is in the thought system of Karl Marx. Likewise, it is possible to envisage an intelligentsia that would be capable of trying out various syntheses. This is the famous Mannheim discussion on the ideal class, of intellectuals 'who feel threatened from above and below and who, out of social necessity, seek a middle way out' (137). Such a class of the bearers of syntheses shall be free from the social order and sensitive to the dynamic nature of society, its wholeness. They occupy a relatively classless stratum insofar as they are socially unattached intelligentsias. And hence, they shall be able to attach themselves to any class and fathom the particularities of ideology in the class under question. In this wake, intellectuals may exhibit 'endless wavering' that, however, should not be misconstrued by critical observers or intellectuals as a license to lack in conviction. 'The repeated attempts to identify themselves with, as well as the continual rebuffs received from, other classes must lead eventually to a clearer conception on the part of the intellectuals of the meaning and the value of their own position in the social order' (142).

There was an inherent radicalism in Mannheim's propositions of the sociology of knowledge insofar as it departed from the foundational thoughts pertaining to the Enlightenment ideas of science, epistemology, rationality and knowledge. His sociology of knowledge, as elucidated in the above discussion, underlines the presence of value judgements inherent in knowledge. There is an evident subversion of Weber's treatment of the values, discussed in Chapter 3. For, in Mannheim's sociology, the presence of values in knowledge is not antithetical to the objectivity that arises from the relational configuration of knowledge.

But there were many articulation of discomfort with Mannheim's sociology of knowledge, of which two are crucial. One was echoed in the German positivist dispute, in which Adorno agreed with Popper in the critique of the relativist tendency of the sociology of knowledge.[6] The second was in Susan Hekman's quest of anti-foundational thoughts with a comparative reading of Mannheim and Gadamer, the sociology of knowledge and hermeneutics (1986, 1987). The complaint was that Mannheim had not sufficiently departed from the foundation, and that he maintained the possibility of an objective sociology of knowledge. In other words, the sociology of knowledge still maintains a cognitive divide between the objective and subjective, the generalisable and relative frame of thinking. This led Hekman to suggest: 'Mannheim eschews philosophical and particularly epistemological issues. It also contains contradictions as well as elements of naïve historicism and a sympathy for positivism that are antithetical to antifoundation thought' (1987, 336).

In short, the criticism was that Mannheim failed to deliver a methodology that could be conducive for a somewhat anti-foundational sociology of knowledge. But then, the criticism can be turned on its back to drive home a message that despite the stress of the sociology of knowledge on the relationship of the social and the epistemological, there is a possibility of theorising even in post-positivist sociology. In other words, a theoretical body with generalisable concepts is possible even without dependence on the positivist way of seeing in sociology. This point also benefitted phenomenology and ethnomethodology, as we read in the following section.

Phenomenology and Ethnomethodology: Seeing Subjectivity Objectively

Phenomenology is often seen in relation with the German intellectual tradition, including the philosophy of Hegel. The most prominent among these, however, is Edmund Husserl's philosophy. Many renowned philosophers, including Max Scheler, Martin Heidegger, Jean-Paul Sartre, Maurice Merleau-Ponty and Alfred Schutz, have presented their respective readings of phenomenology, each of which has been revisited in sociology. Schutz's reading of Husserl, however, is most often underlined as the best possible relation of phenomenology with sociology (Wolff 1978, 538). The reason why Schutz's synthesis of phenomenology and sociology is important because, 'he was the first to do it systematically and comprehensively … he confronted this philosophy not with sociology as a whole but with a sociological approach'.[7]

Schutz aimed at revisiting Max Weber and had benefitted from direct interaction and correspondence with Husserl. Moreover, he drew upon diverse other works; for example, those of Henri Bergson, William James, Max Scheler, John Dewey, G.H. Mead, C.H. Cooley and W.I. Thomas. The first and foremost in Husserl's, and consequently in Schutz's, phenomenology is a detailed acknowledgement of the limitations of social sciences insofar as understanding 'intersubjectivity of thought and action' is concerned. Evidently, there is a pool of meanings, often taken for granted in method-driven social sciences. This set Husserl thinking critically of the rigorous social sciences which 'use mathematical language with such efficiency', and yet fail to fathom an array of questions about the human experiences. Some of such questions are:

> How does it happen that mutual understanding and communication are possible at all? How is it possible that man accomplishes meaningful acts, purposively or habitually, that he is guided by ends to be attained and motivated by certain experiences? Do not the concepts of meaning, of motives, of ends, of acts, refer to a certain structure of consciousness, a certain arrangement of all the experiences in inner time, a certain type of sedimentation? (1970, 56)

Such questions lead phenomenology to delve into the acts of interpretation in human society. Everyone, be that a common man among other men or as a social scientist, are social actors in the realms of interpretations. We all interpret others and ourselves by taking recourse to a stock of pre-interpreted experiences. Such pre-interpreted experiences are available to everyone. Phenomenology trains us to deal with such questions and ideas regarding our everyday interpretative practices. Allegedly, many such oft-encountered questions are either taken for granted or explained away in social sciences. These questions solicit psychologically informed philosophical analysis, rather than social science methods, techniques, and measurement. And that is the promise of phenomenology to deliver. It begins on the simple premise that 'I think' and 'I feel' are intricately related. This brings about an interface of experience and cogitation, of personal conscious life and phenomenological practice. To begin with, it entails reflection towards our own experience, following Husserl's theory of *noesis* that refers to the inward journey across experiences. Second, it requires us to unravel the 'intentionality of consciousness', following Husserl's discussion on *noema* that refers to the experienced, the object and process of cogitation. For consciousness is in itself, as well as *of* (towards) something. We are conscious, independent of the world at large, but we are conscious of the world at large too. This curious duality with an inherent cohesiveness of consciousness, engenders experience into an equation whereby 'each specific noesis has its specific noematic correlate' (60).

It's an exciting proposition indeed, that each of our experiences is eventually related to the noematic (consciousness of something). In fact, Schutz deems the noematic to be the nucleus or kernel of intentionality in consciousness in the ultimate phenomenological analysis. This becomes more vivid as one takes note of the way Schutz weds Henry Bergson and Husserl in discussing experiences as streams of consciousness. With Bergson, there appear two broad domains, an inner stream of experience and living within the world of space and time (the experience of individual ego with full attention to life). An inner stream of experience is pure *durée* (French for duration). Bergson explained a *durée* as characterised by 'a continuous coming to be and passing away of heterogeneous qualities'. It is not possible to be cognizant of the net of reflection in a *durée*. There are too many 'nows', appearing too frequently, to be grasped sufficiently. When I immerse in pure *durée*, distinctions become alien, taught Bergson. The world of distinction is that of *noema*, where things are finite and available for prolonged reflection. With Husserl, it is easier to draw a phenomenological conclusion about how to make sense of the dual aspect of consciousness: the knower has to step out of the duration, many nows, and then reflect upon them. We cannot retrieve for reflection, the non-discrete experience, the 'essentially actual', the indubitable 'Being-there' (*Dasein*), the passing lived-experience. We can, however, aim at that part of it which becomes discrete experience, the passed lived-experience, accessible in memory and 'recapitulative reproduction'. In this light there are two key propositions that emerges from Schutz's phenomenology:

> The limits of recall coincide with the limits of "rationalizability".... Recoverability to memory is, in fact, the first prerequisite of all rational construction. That which is irrecoverable—and this is in principle always something ineffable—can only be lived but never "thought": it is in principle incapable of being verbalized. (65)

With the basic principles laid out, it becomes possible to see the social world with a phenomenological way of seeing in sociology. In this way of seeing behaviour is equivalent to seeing meaning-endowed conduct. It is the 'behaved', rather than 'behaving', the sedimented knowledge rather than experience passing by—that enables further enquiry. In short, it enables us to be wide awake, to pay attention to life. This takes the phenomenological way of seeing a little farther in making sense of the way the social world is organised. This is the life world, an intersubjective, pragmatic, everyday world, peopled with folks with a natural attitude. While natural attitude is about taking things for granted, it is also about operating and reasoning with a given stock of knowledge. Each individual has a unique possession of the stock of knowledge, the sedimented thoughts and wisdom determined by the definition of a situation and biographic orientation. It amounts to suggesting that I would inherit a stock of knowledge as per my location in the socio-cultural and, of course, political arrangement. That I would operate with one part of folklore while someone else will do so with another. The stock of knowledge offers me one set of stereotypes, values, prejudices and notions of progress while it could be different for others in the same folk world. We all try to forge relations and impact one another in accordance with the stock of knowledge (also interchangeably called practical knowledge) that we operate with. Curiously enough, this is not a homogenous and monolithic entity. Instead, it is, incoherent, only partially clear, and not at all free from contradictions. Stock of knowledge is in continual flux, changing from one 'Now' to another, in the wake of new streams of experiences in consciousness. This multiplies currents embedded in the notion of experience.

> The emerging experience may, for example, be conceived as a pre-experienced "same which recurs" or as a pre-experienced "same but modified" or as of a type similar to a pre-experienced one, and so on. Or the emergent experience is found to be "strange" if it can not be referred. (75)

The nature and scope of the life world, the natural attitude, the stock of knowledge and perpetual process—that is, to experience—bring about novel possibilities for the phenomenological way of seeing in sociology. We begin to see that akin to experience, meaning-making is invariably an ongoing social action. Moreover, in continuation with the discussion on the life world, Husserl spoke about the diverse realms of experiences corresponding with provinces of meaning. A life world that is dominated by natural attitude is one such province, within which we are pragmatic in our actions. We are actors taking many things for granted, while reasoning with and acting upon, with clear motives of two kinds—'because of' and 'in order to'. 'Because of' alludes to the reasons, causal factors and the larger premise that drive actor(s). Whereas the 'in order to' motive is about another set of reasons why an action is performed. An 'in order to' motif elucidates the objectives, the purposive rationality and the larger vision of why an actor is practically active. There was a separation of the two motives in the Weber's sociology. Instead of the separation of the two, phenomenology depicts them together in the practical activities of the actors in the life world. They figure even in the phantasy where we are free from the pragmatic motives of the life world and yet we have its specific 'because' and 'in order to' in place as we imagine performances which we seldom perform. It is freed from the purposive fiat of the practical everyday life-world and still located within.

Likewise, the province of scientific reasoning has its own location in the life-world, with specificity of motives, purposes, relevance and activities. Husserl, and Schutz, conceptualised a divide between the practical world of actors and the theoretical world of scientists. The two, actors and theorists, are masters of their respective worlds, though theorists are located within the world of actors too. And hence,

> The "leap" into the province of theoretical thought involves the resolution of the individual to suspend his subjective point of view. And this fact alone shows that not the undivided self but *only a partial self*, a taker of a role, a "Me", namely, the theoretician, "acts" within the province of scientific thought. This partial self lacks all "essential actual" experiences connected with his own body, its movements, and its limits. (260)

The acknowledgement of the partial self of a theorist/scientist is what connects phenomenology with the revisiting of science as well as proposition of a qualitatively distinct way of seeing in sociology. Even though a phenomenologist 'brackets', in order to suspend the essentially taken-for-granted assumption, it is likely that it is only a partial comprehension of the pragmatic world. Even though Schutz proposed to have an interpretative sociology equipped with phenomenology, departing from the behaviourist assumptions, there was a possible lapse in the subjectivism. Unlike the methodological unity of the empirical sciences, and purity of method, this way of seeing enabled the adoption of a subjective point of view. And towards this, 'the safeguarding of the subjective point of view is the only but sufficient guarantee that the world of social reality will not be replaced by a fictional non-existing world constructed by the scientific observer' (271).

The operation of minds, production and perpetuation of meanings, and such details of subjective nature could be accessed with Husserl's phenomenology, and particularly a sociologically conducive reading and representation of it by Schutz. It is important to remember that Hegel's phenomenology of the mind promised to comprehend consciousness too. But it is only with Husserl, and following that with Schutz, that the consciousness was analysed through the ordinary, common sense, mundane, everyday world (Wolff 1978, 502). Likewise, it is possible to suggest that the Cartesian question of cogito[8] is a Husserl question too. But this question acquires a new lease of life of a qualitatively different kind as the external objects, the finite part of the cogitation, the noetic, come to play a crucial role. Despite the recognition of the noetic, there has been criticism of phenomenology—that it is not sufficiently historical and materialist. That, in the ultimate analysis, phenomenology is geared towards transcendental bracketing, proving that the object world becomes secondary. The neo-Marxist criticism from the critical theorists of the Frankfurt School, particularly Herbert Marcuse and Theodor Adorno, is well known. Even though the phenomenological slogan, 'Back to things', sounds anti-idealistic; it relies on the height of idealism since the 'things' are mostly to do with consciousness. It carries forward the logical absolutism that we witness in orthodox scientism, as well as a concept of essence that we critically apprehend in the Greek philosophy, Enlightenment and positivism.

From Schutz, there emerged another important intrigue about the intersubjective world of meaning. Harold Garfinkel criticised the philosophically abstract notion of consciousness in phenomenology. The complaint was about the lack of the ordinariness in phenomenology as far as the representation of ordinary life is concerned. And hence, the imperative of yet another methodological approach, another way of seeing, that could facilitate more documentation on the subjective world. As Wolff noted, 'If the subject is predominantly cognitive in Husserl and, in the sense have seen, in Max Weber and Schutz, in ethnomethodology it becomes what might be called selectively cognitive, namely specializing in method; it becomes a methodological specialist' (536).

And so doing, it rearranged the fundamental principles of sociology, controverting but building upon Durkheim because the objective reality of social facts was rethought as 'an ongoing accomplishment of the concerted activities of daily life, with the ordinary, artful ways of that accomplishment being by members known, used, and taken for granted, is, for members doing sociology, a fundamental phenomenon' (2011, vii). Clearly, it was about being sociological by finding a link between the members of society and sociologists. Garfinkel worked towards finding a bridge between the social way and the sociological way of understanding. This also means that sociological methods and techniques cannot be unwed from the social practices. It makes a departure from sociology's preoccupation with a structured common-sense world; instead, ethnomethodology tends to ask: What is the common-sense world and how is it possible?[9] The social actors' everyday activities entail methods to make such activities 'visibly-rational-and reportable-for-all-practical-purposes'. A study that dwells upon ethnomethodology is committed to deciphering these activities, methods and the accounts produced by the members. And by doing so, ethnomethodology does not intend, or is not supposed, to deliver 'supplements to "standard" procedure'. In other words, it is not a dramatic development of a new methodology that ethnomethodology seeks to deliver. It does not offer any remedy to the practical actions nor does it search for theoretically loaded 'humanistic arguments'. Keeping the sociologist's disposition to a bare minimum, and thus of methodology to maximum, Garfinkel envisaged understanding and applying people's methods as a distinguishable way of seeing in sociology.

This is once again with a promise to develop the 'inexact sciences' that was promised in phenomenology because unlike exact sciences that deal with 'objective' expressions, inexact sciences grapple with 'indexical expressions'. The indexical expressions, available in human accounts, are recognisable through some rational properties. One of the most important properties is the relation of the biography of the *user* of the indexical expression, the purpose of the *user*, the circumstances of utterance, and the conversation in which the indexical expression is reported to the *auditor* (the sociologist). Indexical expressions are contingent upon time and space, as they can mean different things according to the context (temporal and spatial). Hence, there is a fathomable fluidity of meaning that can arise from indexical expression. The speakers employ indexical expression in relative terms. They connect these expressions with their own experience, the object about which these expressions are, and others (the listener, auditor, reporter). In Garfinkel's ethnomethodological way of seeing in sociology, these indexical expressions are located in the accounts that social actors produce in the intersubjective world. This intersubjective world is, akin to that in phenomenology, a world of 'practical activities, practical circumstances, and practical sociological reasoning' (2011, 5). The way the members of the social world produce and manage the settings of everyday life is similar to the way they make their everyday life 'account-able'. The hyphenated account-able is to suggest that it is about being able to produce account, and not necessarily about the word accountable in the literal and ethical sense. Members don't only live in the practical world; they practically engender accounts of their world, meanings and procedures. Account-able, in ethnomethodology, is thus about observing-and-reporting, looking-and-telling. In this process of making life account-able, members observe rules, law-like prescriptions, which are specific to time and space and yet adequately loose. They are loose, for the conditions are not fully spelt out, and hence they offer scope for interpretative manoeuvrings. Thereby, members/actors/narrators lead their everyday life, and in the same way produce accounts to make sense of what they do, think, believe and practice. Since everyday life is fraught with the indexicality of meanings, fluidity of reason and contextual inconclusiveness, the accounts of everyday life exhibit the same too. Thus, accounts are full of usages of terms such as 'et cetera'. 'unless', 'let it pass', which reflect the relationship of the account with the real situation. This amounts to a contextual rationalism, practised and propagated by the social actors. Unlike the sciences in which rationalism is determined by scientific authority from somewhere above or somewhere else with the word of objectivity, ethnomethodology sees rationality arising from practical life and the actors' accounting activities. Second, this is a practical variety of rationalism, since the usages in an account, as in real life, are determined by their pragmatic values and utility. To make a witty proposition: if an expression is not useful we don't employ it. If a wink, in answer to another wink, is of no utility, we don't wink. The rational feature of accounts, and thereof expressions, depends on what members 'make of' their accounts. Thus, ethnomethodology is, 'the investigation of the rational properties of indexical expressions and other practical actions as contingent ongoing accomplishments of organized artful practices of everyday life' (11).

While members in everyday life conduct their common-sense practical activities with due amount of reflexivity in making things accountable, the ethnomethodologist adopts a resembling method. Garfinkel invoked Mannheim to suggest that the documentary method is central to ethnomethodology. It is through this method that an ethnomethodologist seeks to unearth patterns and homologies in the vast pool of meanings. In this method, each actual appearance is, 'the document of', 'pointing to', or 'standing on behalf of', a 'presupposed underlying pattern'. Thus, each is in connection with other such appearances and 'what is known'. The preordained information and unfolding appearance have a direct relationship in the documentary method. In a document of actual appearance, to reiterate, 'each is used to elaborate the other' (78). In this way, ethnomethodology seeks to bring together familiar scenes accessible in everyday life along with the relatively less familiar scenes due to the taken-for-grantedness. This can be also understood using metaphors from theatre and dramaturgy. In ethnomethodology, the foreground, the on stage, the background and the off-stage are brought face to face to divulge meanings. This may be fraught with shock, when one seeks to disturb a familiar scene in order to comprehend the structures of everyday activities. Bewilderment, consternation and confusion could be conducive to generate socially structured affects of anxiety, shame, guilt and indignation. This is also called 'breaching experiment', in which the commonly taken-for-granted sense of what is normal is violated in order to get reactions. A breach in the normal situation, leading an actor to reactions, indeed reveals pragmatic rationality, an actor's belief and mechanism to maintain order in everyday life. The instance of a breach compels an actor to more forcefully, and at times aggressively, reaffirm the pragmatism and endeavour to restore the normal order. And in the final analyses, such actions of the ethnomethodologist and reactions of the members of society aid in divulging structured patterns and affects. In the details of the method, ethnomethodology propagates what is often reviled along the lines of ethics and feasibility. It is the notion of 'ethnomethodological indifference', which is at the core of the experimental tendencies in the method. This is an indifference to any moral judgement that might interfere an ethnomethodologist's approach and activities to understand the everyday social world. When a familiar scene explodes, with bewilderment and anger, to facilitate an ethnomethodologist with documentary evidence of how everyday life is organised, there is an instance of ethnomethodological indifference. An ethnomethodologist is indifferent to the judgement on the social actors' accounts and methods. With this tendency, ethnomethodology tries to distinguish itself from the sociological debates on value neutrality. The latter is woven around the distinction between 'is' and 'ought'. 'Ethnomethodological indifference' (109), is an indifference to this distinction about what is and what ought to be, or what is good and bad for society. However, the implications of this indifference are also dubbed as methodological sadism in the name of objectivity.[10]

A brief note on both, phenomenology and ethnomethodology, however, opens the possibility of understanding knowledge as a social construction. It also elucidates that the notion of objectivity emanates from the subjective actors' objectively implemented knowledge and actions. And in this wedding of the two, subjectivity seems to have an upper hand than the predominant notion of objectivity underpinning scientific epistemology. The role of subjectivity in the above discussion, however, is balanced with the idea of intersubjectivity of the social actors in everyday life. This begins to unfold more concretely in the feminist interventions in the realm of empirical sciences.

Anti-Foundational Quests and Feminist Epistemology: A Way to Another

As though the above-discussed plunge into the subjectivity of social actors, and thereby an objective way of seeing such subjectivity, were not sufficient, there is another strand that pointed towards *another*, of science and sociology. What does *another* mean? The answer unfolds as we proceed in this section. The discussion in this section further underlines the complication in the idea of experience.

According to Susan Hekman, during the early stage of sociology, it was deemed necessary to get rid of idols, phantoms and prejudices in objective social sciences. An objectively determined nature of human experience was central in the classical sociology of the trinity. Such an emphasis on the objective reality was, furthermore, in light of the foundational thoughts emerging from the Enlightenment. Hekman deemed Heidegger, Wittgenstein and later, even Richard Rorty as anti-foundational philosophers and in the context of their interventions she proposed a rejection of foundational thoughts. The Enlightenment was not merely a suspect, it was deemed to be a body of thought that ought to be replaced by an alternative. This rejection was not merely about post-positivist advances; instead, it held an anti-positivist stance that aimed to radically change the vocabulary of social sciences altogether. It sought a fundamental change in the methodological grammar of seeing and being in sociology. In short, anti-foundational impetus was to give a rebirth to the way of seeing in sociology. Such radicalism shaped up the quest of another, that is, a full-bodied replacement of the orthodox epistemology and sociology.

Hekman noted:

> what the anti-foundational philosophers suggest is not a search for 'truth' conceived apart from history and culture, but, rather, an examination of the relationship between human thought and human existence … the kind of 'sociology of knowledge' that can be found in the works of Wittgenstein, Heidegger and Gadamer offers an understanding of what the social sciences are about that definitively rejects the Enlightenment conception of knowledge. (1987, 9–10)

While there could be a sense of departure and negotiations in post-positivist sociology, this particular section brings forth the epistemological interventions in science and sociology the feminist standpoint theory. The theoretical debate starts with a realisation that various waves of women's movements and feminist activism also rendered feminism as an epistemological field. The various interventions on feminist standpoint theory are testimonial to not only the epistemological bearings of feminist activism and women's movements across globe but also shapes up ways of seeing in sociology that could be in proximity with feminist politics.[11] Meanwhile, the consequence of the variety within feminist epistemology also amounts to suggesting that there cannot be one feminist standpoint. This was most systematically put in Sandra Harding's *The Science Question in Feminism* (1986) that enumerated at least three components of feminist epistemology: feminist empiricism, feminist standpoint theory and feminist postmodernism. Instead of putting each separately, it is worth playing with the enmeshed discourse that serves feminist epistemology better.

One variety of the feminist standpoint theory operates within the dichotomy of the abstract world—of science, which is inclined to the masculine ruling class and oppressors. The other is about the concrete world—of feminist epistemology, which is inclined to women's lived experiences and everyday life. While this dichotomy is the strength of this theory, it also delimits its outreach, particularly in the face of questions arising from postmodernism, post-structuralism and epistemological relativism.

Adopting a social constructionist perspective, yet one rooted in Marxian historical materialism, Nancy Hartsock in 1975 proposed an idea about the possibility of developing a methodological approach to life and politics in a dualistic structure of reality. This dualistic structure placed oppressor and oppressed on two sides. It dwelt on the object–relation theory through which Hartsock sought to transcend positivism. The latter was allegedly infused with abstract masculinity and epistemology pertaining to the sexual division of labour. Hartsock aimed at steering clear of the perversity of the ruling class epistemology, and to arrive at the experiences of women. However, this attempt faced a postmodern challenge as Foucault would deem both—counter-discourse and hegemonic discourse, or in Hartsock's vocabulary, oppressor ruling class and oppressed women—partial and perverse. With emphasis on object-relations, Hartsock holds the ground that the perception of reality is formed in the relation of the self with the other, the oppressed with the oppressor, and hence it is worth disclosing women's experiences to know what they are, what they do and what they tend to seek. Without disagreeing with the basics, Dorothy Smith proposed to rethink the conceptual apparatuses in sociology, which tended to be abstract and opposed to the experiential–embodied lived reality of women. She sought to bring about what she called a Copernican shift in sociology by showing women's phenomenological everyday world in relation with Marxian understanding of the material condition. This makes Smith distinguishable from Schutz's phenomenology in which material and historical conditions were neglected. But both Hartsock and Smith, and others who follow the dichotomy, did not tend to recognise the 'difference', the marked subjectivities from diverse contexts, in short, diversity and locatedness (Hekman 1997, 345–350).

For, the diversity and located-ness of women's experiences need not sit comfortably together. This is most crucially identified in Patricia Hill Collins' attempt to build up a Black feminist thought, dwelling upon an approach of an 'outsider within', to underline the uniqueness of black women's experience as different from their white counterparts. This way of seeing endeavoured to suggest that oppressed women's perspectives need not be absolute, situated knowledge need not amount to total knowledge, and yet, one need not succumb to relativism of knowledge. This was an attempt to redefine the idea of objectivity, centred on the location of black women and their experiences in relation with white women, black men and white men. Collins deemed the experiential accounts of black women 'relatively' objective. And on the other hand, Sara Ruddick explored maternal thinking from a feminist standpoint, dwelling upon Wittgenstein's philosophical proposition, challenging the universality of experience. Acknowledging storytelling as method women employ to articulate maternal thinking, Ruddick explored situated reasoning in the role play associated with social and stereotypical roles, including that of a mother. In her autobiographical accounts, she furthered the critique of the universal reason that prevailed upon academic scholarship. Through the mothering practice related to childcare, a mother develops an experiential account, a valid sociology of social roles and struggles. The most systematic attempt to put together the ambivalence about a universal truth approachable from a feminist standpoint dealing with the apprehension of relativism was put forth by Sandra Harding, which underlined the importance of instability in feminist theories in an unstable world. There cannot be one coherent theory of an incoherent world. Hence, it is imperative to adopt a postmodern standpoint approach committed to revising notions owed to the conventional meta-theories of science. This was Hardings' resolve for the seemingly irresolvable dichotomy of essentialism versus relativism, and pluralism versus located-ness. Recognising the many ways of seeing within feminism addresses essentialist unity of all the oppressed voices. Yet the objective character of location vis-à-vis women's lives takes care of the apprehended slip to relativism. The determination of the two sides of the dichotomy, diversity and located-ness, could therefore be avoided if it were a postmodern feminist standpoint that can embrace each side with equal ease—the possibility to be universal, essential, specific, located and lived exist together. This, however, does not cancel the basic tenet, in continuity with the conventional standpoint, which underlines the importance of the accounts of the oppressed. The higher the level of oppression the stronger objectivity in the women's accounts arising from lived experiences. This idea of objectivity departed from the masculine science that advocated objectivity as a way of detached narration.

It amounts to suggesting a middle ground between the scientific–objective accounts based on detachment. Such detachment-based accounts were fully distorted and partial. The imperative of a less partial and distorted account of women's lives summons a middle ground. The less false stories mediate between transhistorical universals and relativism. Unlike postmodernism, Harding was keen to tell less false stories of women's lives than tell one true story, more situated stories than one grand narrative.

Hekman moved ahead in solving the dilemma of recognition (diversity) and difference (distinction), a postmodernist challenge to the feminist standpoint, by suggesting that Thomas Kuhn was more important than Karl Marx. This needs a modest recalling of a particular lesson from the previous chapters. The perpetuity of normal science ought to be replaced by the radical steps forward in order to bring about the essential transformation of knowledge. That the character of science was more conducive than a bipolar social structure was crucial in the formulation of a feminist science. Steering clear of the modernist dichotomy of the universal and the particular, Hekman stated that feminist epistemology would deliver a new paradigm in which 'politics is defined as a local and situated activity undertaken by discursively constituted subjects' (1997, 357). And likewise, political resistance would be viewed through the locally discursively constituted formation. Since there was no Archimedean point of neutral observation, it was imperative to explore the various discursive factors that inform observations and, consequently, understanding and explanations. It was a novel variety of feminist empiricism that turned away from dislocated empiricism of scientific epistemology. Instead, it turned to a located, contextual empiricism. Such empiricism was at the core of the feminist standpoint, leading to an idea of 'successor science'. Donna Haraway (1988) emphasised on this newfound feminist science that is more attuned to 'another' story rather than the abstractions of truth and reality.

Making radical departure from the Enlightenment philosopher's policing of knowledge with the weapon of objectivity, Haraway admitted the significance of a social constructivist perspective. The latter in feminist standpoint allowed for the understanding of the conspiracy of scientists, and thereof a parable of objectivity and scientific method. She showed the prevalence of a scientific mythology, and asked a fundamental question: Who have been the victims of the scientific mythology? Haraway noted:

> The only people who end up actually *believing* and, goddess forbid, acting on the ideological doctrines of disembodied scientific objectivity—enshrined in elementary textbooks and technoscience

> booster literature—are nonscientists, including a few very trusting philosophers. (1988, 576)

The scientific mythology found legitimacy from the separation and distinction of a 'proclaimed to be superior' totalising epistemology from an allegedly inferior relativism. The scientific mythology benefitted from the absolute legitimacy of grand narratives over other kinds. Haraway persuaded us to tear through what she deemed to be the 'philosophical verbiage'. This was necessary in order to 'unmask' the dominant doctrines so as to fathom 'a feminist version of objectivity'. This paved the way for Harding's idea of successor science in which ethics and politics, rather than epistemology, was prominent. In such an alternative version of science, transcendental objectivity was replaced by situatedness. In this wake, local experiential narratives and an embodied vision superseded grand narratives and disembodied ones. Haraway questioned the myth of infinite vision, the ability to see across contexts. She envisioned feminists to have a situated vision in which the separation of subject and object collapses. And thus arose Haraway's feminism as 'another science', which was 'the sciences and politics of interpretation, translation, stuttering, and the partly understood' (589).

In feminist science, one is answerable for what one sees and the way one sees. It is not merely fact and epistemology but an acknowledged role of politics that feminist science encourages.

Conclusion

In spite of the length and the density of exegeses in this chapter, the discourse is yet not exhaustive. One has safely edited out some of the variants that sit pretty well with the basic premise of post-positivist social sciences; for instance, the constructivism of Peter Berger and Thomas Luckmann (1967, 1), an important leaf in the larger ambit of the sociology of knowledge and phenomenology, among other things. This variety of a social construction of reality approach found great deal of acceptance among sociologists, as in the case of the feminist standpoint debates. One can also argue against the absence of an adequate recognition of postmodern theoretical reasoning, which presented a reasonable critique of the foundational–scientific–Enlightenment premise, by proposing a shift from grand narratives to micro narratives (Lyotard 1984, 5), and from legislators to interpreters (Baumann 1989, 3). The onerous cutting to size is, however, not at the price of this chapter's basic objective, which is a possible outline of post-positivism. This indeed called for many jump cuts while also weaving strands in order to engender a debate which could emphasise the imperative of going beyond positivism in creating newer methodological possibilities. More precisely, the discussion in this chapter, enables us to think of *another* way of being sociological. This is a radical departure from the sacred tenets of the scientific epistemology as well as a negotiated paradigm in social sciences, namely, positivism. Moreover, this chapter has centralised the contested nature of human experience, and hence the legitimacy of diverse ways of seeing. Experience is no longer an assiduously tailored idea befitting for the scientific epistemology and positivism. The experience that was befitting for the positivist framework enjoined upon the social scientists a responsibility to be an exceptionally detached human. After going through the discussion in this chapter, experience is liberated from the epistemological straitjackets. Experience is everywhere, everyday and of everyone. In this wake, we begin to see the chance to be sociological in a slightly different light.

References

Adorno, T., H. Albert, R. Dahrendorf, et al. *The Positivist Dispute in German Sociology*, translated by Glyn Adey and David Frisby. London: Heinemann, 1976.

Alexander, Jeffrey C. 'Beyond Epistemological Dilemma: General Theory in a Postpositivist Mode', *Sociological Forum* 5, no. 4 (1990): 531–544.

Baumann, Z. *Legislators and Interpreters: On Modernity, Post-Modernity and Intellectuals*. London: Polity Press, 1989.

Berger, P., and T. Luckmann. *Social Construction of Reality: A Treatise in Sociology of Knowledge*. New York: Anchor, 1967.

Bleicher, Josef. *Contemporary Hermeneutics: Hermeneutics as Method, Philosophy and Critique*. London: Routledge and Kegan Paul, 1980.

Chakravarti, Uma. *Gendering Caste: Through a Feminist Lens*. Calcutta: Stree, 2006.

Fanon, Frantz. *The Wretched of the Earth*. London: Penguin Classics, 2001.

Frisby, David. 'Introduction to the English Translation'. In *The Positivist Dispute in German Sociology*, edited by T. Adorno, H. Albert, R. Dahrendorf, et al., translated by Glyn Adey and David Frisby, ix–xliv. London: Heinemann, 1976.

Gadamer, H.G. *Truth and Method*. New York: Seabury Press, 1975.

———. 'The Universality of Hermenuetical Problem'. In *Contemporary Hermeneutics: Hermeneutics as Method, Philosophy and Critique*, edited by J. Bleicher. London: Routledge and Kegan Paul, 1980.

Garfinkel, Harold. *Studies in Ethnomethodology*. Cambridge: Polity, 2011.

Giddens, Anthony. *New Rules of Sociological Method: A Positive Critique of Interpretative Sociologies*. London: Hutchinson and Co., 1976.

Giddens, Anthony. 'Positivism and Its Critics'. In *A History of Sociological Analysis*, edited by Tom Bottomore and Robert Nisbet, 237–287. London: Heinemann, 1979.

Guru, Gopal. 'How Egalitarian Are the Social Sciences in India?', *Economic and Political Weekly* 37, no. 50 (2002): 5003–5009.

Guru, Gopal, and Sundar Sarukkai. *The Cracked Mirror: An Indian Debate on Experience and Theory*. Delhi: Oxford University Press, 2012.

Haraway, Donna. 'Situated Knowledges: The Science Question in Feminism and the Privilege of Partial Perspective', *Feminist Studies* 14, no. 3 (1988): 575–600.

Harding, Sandra. *The Science Question in Feminism*. Ithaca, New York: Cornell University Press, 1986.

Hartsock, Nancy. 'Fundamental Feminism: Prospect and Perspective'. In *Building Feminist Theory*, edited by Charlotte Bunch, 32–43. New York: Longman, 1981.

Hekman, Susan. *Hermeneutics and the Sociology of Knowledge*. Notre Dame, Indiana: University of Notre Dame Press, 1986.

———. 'Anti-Foundational Thought and the Sociology of Knowledge: The Case of Karl Mannheim', *Human Studies* 10, no. ¾ (1987): 333–356.

———. 'Truth and Method: Feminist Standpoint Theory Revisited', *Signs* 22, no. 2 (1997): 341–365.

Lyotard, J.F. *The Postmodern Condition: A Report on Knowledge*. Minnesota: University of Minnesota Press, 1984.

Mannheim, Karl. *Ideology and Utopia: An Introduction to the Sociology of Knowledge*. London: Routledge and Kegan Paul, 1960.

Menon, Nivedita. *Seeing Like a Feminist*. Delhi: Zubaan and Penguin, 2012.

Mueller-Vollmer, K. *The Hermeneutics Reader: Texts of the German Tradition from the Enlightenment to the Present*. Oxford, UK: Basil Blackwell, 1985.

Mukherji, Partha Nath (ed.). *Methodology in Social Research: Dilemmas and Perspective*. Delhi: Sage, 2000.

Pathak, Dev Nath. *Living and Dying: Meanings in Maithili Folklore*. New Delhi: Primus, 2019.

Said, Edward W. *Orientalism: Western Conceptions of the Orient*. New Delhi: Penguin, 2001.

Sartre, Jean-Paul, 'Preface'. In *The Wretched of the Earth*, edited by Frantz Fanon. London: Penguin Classics, 2001.

Schutz, Alfred. *On Phenomenology and Social Relations*, edited and translated by Helmut R. Wagner. Chicago: Chicago University Press, 1970.

Turner, Jonathan H. 'In Defense of Positivism', *Sociological Theory* 3, no. 2 (1985): 24–30.

Wagner, Helmut R. 'Introduction: The Phenomenological Approach to Sociology'. In *On Phenomenology and Social Relations*, edited and translated by Helmut R. Wagner, 1–50. Chicago: Chicago University Press, 1970.

Wolff, Kurt H. 'Phenomenology and Sociology'. In *A History of Sociological Analysis*, edited by Tom Bottomore and Robert Nisbet, 499–556. London: Heinemann, 1978.

Part 3

DUSK

7

INTRIGUES OF EXPERIENCE(S): RETURN TO REFLEXIVITY

The famous ghazal singer the late Jagjit Singh has among the songs to his credit a famous one penned by a popular cinema lyricist and poet Javed Akhtar, which has a verse,

क्यूँ डरें ज़िंदगी में क्या होगा, कुछ ना होगा तो तजुर्बा होगा

'Why fret about where your life is heading?
Even if it comes to nothing, at least it will be an experience'.[1]

In case ghazals of such kinds are associated with a particular class in India to cater to a niche audience, popular cinema could arguably vouch for the masses. Popular cinema, incidentally, also (re)presents ample imaginative renditions on the idea of experience. It is useful to recall a rather philosophically profound musical drama, written by a renowned modern litterateur in Hindi, Bhagwati Charan Verma, and adapted into the film *Chitralekha* (1963, directed by Kidar Sharma). The movie debated the vulnerability of norms; it also emphasised the experiential journey, rendering it through the famous song penned by the poet and lyricist Sahir Ludhianvi:

संसार से भागे फिरते हो भगवान को तुम क्या पाओगे

'How will you reach god, if you shy away from experiencing this world?'.[2]

Interestingly, the song underlines the importance of experiencing this world if one aspires to sense what the divine may be like. Another more recent movie, a Rajat Kapur directed *Ankhon Dekhi*[3] (*Seen Through One's Own Eyes*, 2013), narrated a tale about the protagonist's quest for experiential knowledge over what was heard, preconceived or given. The film delivered a debate on the ordinary quest of experiential rationalism, which may cause consternation in society since socially, we tend to take our knowledge of the world for granted.

The list of such popular engagements is certainly much longer. Literary, cinematic and poetic tropes all offer a medium to encounter layered notions of experience. Various categories, including, caste and class, nation and patriotism, gender and racial differentiation, violent and humoured dispositions, mediate such ideas of experience. Almost everyone's biography presents an encounter with notions of experience, which unfold in ordinary ways in everyday life. If popular culture abounds with references and discussions on the category of experience, it is imperative to juxtapose it with methodological positions and fathom the complex notion of experience. Hence, it was not surprising that, at one point in time, the National Council for Educational Research and Training (NCERT)—the central body of the Indian government responsible for preparing school textbooks and curricular visions—prepared a vision plan known as the National Curriculum Framework-2005.[4] This stressed on experience-based learning, given that students come into school with prior experiences. And hence, schools would benefit from connecting textual knowledge within the context of children's experiences. It enjoined upon the teachers and schools a responsibility to reorganise the idea of teaching with a constructivist approach, enabling learners to realise that learning is not confined to classrooms and schools. The objective was to transform school pedagogy so that it could be sensitive to the idea of experiential learning.[5]

The idea of this chapter is not to give a detailed discussion on the popular conception of experience. Instead, it is to highlight the significant recognition of experience in the domain of popular culture, everyday life as well as (school) education. Hence, while discussing the methodological significance of experience in sociology, one ought to be aware of the general importance it has in our daily life. Given the ubiquity, it could certainly be a topic for full-fledged exploration on some other occasion.

Contesting Experience: In between Universal and Local

Experience, central to the post-positivist ways of seeing, was not entirely absent in scientific epistemology. It was a particular kind of experience that was configured in the philosophical meditations of Descartes, the wisdom capsules of Bacon, the methodologically detailed discussion of Locke, and so on and so forth. The category of experience was not absent in the wake of Newtonianism, nor was it insignificant for the forerunners of sociology. Positivist sociology underlined that part of experience which could be free from prejudices and could aid in generating generalisable principles, propositions and perspectives. In the post-positivist scenario, this is no longer the kind of experience that scientific epistemology propounded as a premise of relatively indubitable knowledge.[6] It is not an experience of a detached observer. Instead, the so-called detached observer is as capable of getting attached as the subjects. And the experience intricately associated with the existence of the people can be only partially recapitulated and reproduced in social sciences. Moreover, it is a complex category of experience riddled with partisan values and heterogeneous perspectives and divides along various lines including class, caste and gender. Besides, the divide along socio-political lines, such as those of the coloniser and the colonised, also figures in the realms of experience. The colonisers and their native counterparts imbibed the values of the colonisers. This was almost following the footsteps of the 'intimate enemy'[7] that natives internalised the values of the oppressor, shaping the trope of experience of colonial modernity. Sociologists and anthropologists also tend to exhibit socio-psychologically subservient behaviour as they imitate their sources of influence—the theoretical masters in Western universities. This was the case of mimetic modernity across the colonies. However, there is a flip side to it—violent expressions of victims' experience, a reactionary epistemology guiding one to cynically dismiss everything pertaining to Western knowledge. The question is whether to reproduce the dichotomy of Western and Eastern or to find a more equitable relationship between them. Unfortunately, there is manifold reproduction of the dichotomy in social everyday life and in scholarship. At times, there is cultural and political justification for the aggressive rejections of Western ideas. Simply replacing a non-Indian name of a road with an Indian name, for example, is deemed as a self-glorifying act of decolonising. Unfortunately, it does not serve the decolonising impact since the epistemological base pertaining to colonialism remains intact. Any justification of a rejectionist act remains ignorant of the fact that Western ideas have undergone a historical process that has made them the ideas of the host society. The rejections do not necessarily provide any alternative to the experiences dominated by the knowledge of the powerful elite. A class of educated modern Indians adopted the values of modernity during colonial rule. This could be deemed a mimetic modernity of the natives modelled upon the modernity of a class of rulers who Nandy (1983) called intimate enemy. In both instances—of subservient mimesis and violent reaction and rejection—we notice the presence of historical encounters. Experiences of both types, who copy modernity and who reject it, are in the light of the historical conditions. History and experience are integral to each other. An example of such a relationship between historical encounters and experience occurs in Frantz Fanon (2001) who sought to understand the political experience of the colonised in the wake of postcolonial Africa in the early 1960s. In a provocative Preface to Fanon's *The Wretched of the Earth*, an incisive account of the interface of encounters and experiences, and politics and expressions, Jean-Paul Sartre wrote:

> In the colonies the truth stood naked, but the citizens of the mother country preferred it with clothes on: the native had to love them, something in the way mothers are loved. The European élite undertook to manufacture a native élite. They picked out promising adolescents; they branded them, as with a red-hot iron, with the principles of western culture; they stuffed their mouths full with high-sounding phrases.... It was the golden age. (2001, 7)

This is about *naked truth* obscured by the *walking lies* at the intersection of historical encounters and politico-epistemological experience. Needless to say, Sartre articulated it with due sarcasm and intended consequences from political and philosophical interpretations. It was to suggest that the natives in a decolonised (or a decolonising) world would be violent, and that does not seem to matter to the former masters, because dogs that bark don't bite! But in the ultimate analysis, the barking dogs operate with troubled, chequered experiences, leading to far-reaching consequences. Fanon detailed the phenomenon and its consequences. As he noted, 'the colonial world is a Manichean world' (28–32), which has cultivated dehumanised natives, the others, the animals. But the animals worked with diverse strategies—strength and weakness, violence and spontaneity, national consciousness and national culture. 'While the politicians situate their action in actual present-day events, men of culture take their stand in the field of history' and this is while 'colonial domination was indeed to convince the natives that colonialism came to lighten their darkness' (168–169). Fanon appealed to the colonised to steer clear of sterile litanies and nauseating mimicry of Europe, which is 'never done talking of man, yet murder men'. This was aimed at freely making inroads into the self without falling prey to 'naturalism' or to the evolutionary logic of 'catching up'. Naturalism and catching up, unfortunately, became the buzzword in the postcolonial Global South, including India. Fanon's appeal to all the natives of the postcolonial society was to dwell upon the troubled historicised experience. This was truly an invocation of a qualitatively different kind of experience, an invitation to chart out new trajectories for the erstwhile victims of colonial domination.

This was a revolutionary capitalisation of the historically troubled experience leading to a new world away from the ravages of colonialism. Elsewhere, a decade-and-a-half later in the late 1970s, Edward Said (2001) aided in understanding the creation of the other, the Orient, in the history of colonialism. Having fed on many sources, informed by Michel Foucault's idea of knowledge as a power construct, Said sought to show the overpowering experience of the epistemologically superior over that of the 'other'. As to what Orientalism means, Said reflected:

> Orientalism is a style of thought based on an ontological and epistemological distinction made between "the Orient" and (most of the time) "the Occident".... My contention is that without examining Orientalism as a discourse one cannot possibly understand the enormously systematic discipline by which European culture was able to manage—and even produce—the Orient politically, sociologically, militarily, ideologically, scientifically, and imaginatively during the post-Enlightenment period. (2001, 2–3)

The construction involved works at various planes of expression by novelists, poets, philosophers, political theorists, economists and imperial administrators. Thus, the phenomenon of Orientalism underlines the relationship of knowledge and power, texts and contexts, experience and politics, enabling one to see that nothing is as innocent as it appears. Marshalling historical evidences to strengthen this thesis, Said also underlined the perpetuity of Orientalism in academic, cultural, political and civil society programmes. He thus arrived at the conclusion that connected the politics of experience, Orientalism and ways of seeing:

> I consider Orientalism's failure to have been a human as much as an intellectual one; for in having to take up a position of irreducible opposition to a region of the world it considered alien to its own, *Orientalism failed to identify with human experience, failed also to see it as human experience*. (328)

The added emphasis in italics is on a particular kind of epistemology that played a role in encouraging and strengthening Orientalism. That epistemology enabled us to make sense of a select variety of experiences and intellectually disabled us to approach the experiences that weren't a fit for it. Reminiscent of Fanon, Said believed that the answer to Orientalism was not Occidentalism. It is not a caricature of the West, as Fanon stated, that can dent the epistemological status quo of Orientalism. The endeavour to decolonise the Third World needed a more creative and autonomous response, which perhaps was conspicuous by its relative absence in the sociologists' duel with Louis Dumont on the topic 'For Sociology of India' in the journal *Contributions to Indian Sociology*, discussed more elaborately in the next chapter. As Said advised, decolonising demands starting on a novel experiential journey, exploring alternative epistemologies that could deliver us ontologically sensitive ways of seeing. Suffice it to say, that the politics of experience in a plural world comes to the forefront in the above discussion.

This perhaps hitherto holds true despite the rise of a global South Asian scholarship, which in part sought to 'provincialize Europe', and in another part proposed to show the ambivalence of the self in postcolonial ruminations (Chakrabarty 2000, Bhabha 2008). Closer to sociology and anthropology in India, there was a realisation that the trope of experience could come to shape the way of seeing in sociology. It is pertinent to mention the experience of T.N. Madan, then a postgraduate student at Lucknow University, on a field trip for training in a village in Ranchi (then in Bihar, now in Jharkhand). He noted:

> Everybody in our group, I found, was asking the villagers questions about their family and economic life, religious beliefs, and similar matters of significance, without any regard for their feelings of convenience. My shyness crippled me, but I did manage to take photographs of an old woman's funeral procession and cremation, without first seeking anybody's permission to do so. As we came back from the village, I had the uncomfortable feeling that there was something improper about such field trips. (2011, 247)

Madan struggled with the divide between the subjective and the objective until he began to reflect on the issue critically. He feared, like many others, 'subjective bias'; and he coveted, like many others, 'scientific objectivity'; and then he took recourse to Dumont's anthropology, along with other American anthropologists, to get methodological enlightenment (pun intended); the solace was in the realisation that anthropology is 'one's cultural experience—one's personal anthropology—as well as knowledge of ethnography to make sense of the cultures one writes about' (255). This is truly a benign but broad recognition of a sociologist's cultural experience in the way one is doing research, writing and, in the same vein, the way one is framing a course and teaching. We don't get to learn from Madan the fine details of such an experience. There is a strong methodological promise in Madan's debate on insider–outsider,[8] a page taken from the works of M.N. Srinivas (1976, 4). The debate establishes that an anthropologist who is an 'insider' in society is equally an outsider. This is because an anthropologist approaches society in a manner owed to the training in formal anthropology. As an insider as well as an outsider, an anthropologist has to find a sort of equanimity, available to only exceptionally trained minds. It, however, seldom leads us to develop an epistemological perspective on the ontological characteristics of experience. The ontology of experience will take into account the challenges of context and social determinants. In the insider–outsider debate, there is no hint of the power relations, autonomy question and the kind of sensibility that Fanon noted for the intellectual practices in postcolonial societies. But we ought to be generous to the sociologists who operated with utter fogginess about the issue that has become detrimental to the advancement of sociological knowledge, which is, what makes a thing sociological?

The turf of experience is indeed thoroughly contested. Upon this terrain, it is possible to mount further contestation. We do so by briefly reflecting upon the feminist intervention followed by what could be termed as exploration of Dalit epistemology, in social sciences.

Feminist and Dalit Ways of Seeing

There need not be a fixed way of seeing like a feminist but there is a possible feminist way of seeing. Since it is from the position of marginality, the feminist way of seeing acquires a peculiarity; it is 'a gesture of subversion towards power' (Menon 2012, ix), to disorganise and disorder the settled field, resist homogenisation and open up multiple possibilities. The location of marginality enables the feminist way of seeing to see even the seemingly invisible in society. Metaphorically speaking, the seemingly invisible is the 'nude-make-up', which hides the make-up and makes the make-up-clad face seem to be without make-up. The nude make-up, in a manner of speaking, an invisible veneer on truth, is rendered visible through the feminist way of seeing. All of us habitual of working on Microsoft Word documents know that the function of formatting makes the typed-out text visibly sorted, organised and convenient for a reader. But then, there are hidden details of the typing, characters such as the markers of spaces, paragraph and tab marks that we don't want to be visible on a document. By pressing the display button, we can get to see what is invisible in a Word document. Likewise, in society, various practices and details of actions are concealed. That's the function of the feminist way of seeing, making the invisible, visible. Steering clear of nude make-up—or Microsoft formatting—a feminist can see the underlying 'processes of gendering', almost exposing the veneer on concealed truth. Though it engenders theory from location, like the situated knowledge of the feminist standpoint theorists, it is relevant on a universal scale. It means that there is another kind of science that departs from Enlightenment science, which celebrated knowledge from nowhere, so to speak. Hence, one can arrive at the gendered nature of power at a location and simultaneously one can allude to similar phenomena across locations. Menon employed this way of seeing to reveal the gendered characteristics of judicial, legislative and socio-political processes. And in so doing, the various kinds of sources—literary, artistic and cultural texts—can be useful.

A similar way of seeing, elsewhere, enabled Uma Chakravarti (2006) to unearth the interface of caste and gender in Indian society. The wherewithal to do so involved revisiting ancient texts at the cusp of history and mythology. Many of our old texts pertaining to socio-normative orders hinged on the categories of sex, gender and caste. Revisiting Dalit texts while engaging with the historical documents in colonial and postcolonial India, and progressive social thoughts, Chakravarti presented an axis on which experience of women in a patriarchal caste-based society is central. It helped to understand the historically evolved gendered experience that could be fathomed if approached with due sensitivity to diverse sources. Likewise, a resonance of the marginalised experience, of the Dalit, the downtrodden in India, becomes crucial amid the experiences of the privileged. Taking note of this, Guru and Sarukkai (2012) deliberated on the divide of the theoretical Brahmin and empirical Shudra,[9] of the theoretical West and empirical East. The theoretical Brahmins are located closer home as well as in the Western hemisphere, who would expect the native scholars to generate only empirical details and leave the theory-building to the privileged scholars. Since experience is not a prerogative of the privileged, be it in a caste hierarchy or an international power order, theories can seldom be absent anywhere. Likewise, there can be experience-based ways of seeing of the groups in the margins too.

In a famous debate that was an outcome of a sustained dialogue on the complicated nuances of experience and theory, published as a book titled *The Cracked Mirror: An Indian Debate on Experience and Theory*, Gopal Guru and Sundar Sarukkai enriched the contested terrain of experience. Unlike the usual expectations of a formal debate, held on a certain date at a certain place, this was a long dialogue through correspondence and exchange of ideas. In such an intimate way, this was a debate in which debaters didn't seem to be out to unmask, aggressively trashing each other in an intellectual duel. There was little room for mutual hostility and egoistic dispute. Instead, both with deep interest in the intellectual history of India and profundity of meanings, complemented each other to underline the issues with the idea of experience, lived experience, self and reflexivity while engaging with some of the most important issues of Indian society, including untouchability. As the outcome of the debate shows, there was a collegiality and complementarity between the two scholars. Guru undertook a praxiological perspective owed to the theory of praxis in the writings of the Marxist thinker Antonio Gramsci. Connecting theory and experience, he emphasised the need for Dalit scholars to return to the issue of Dalit experience. Allegedly, Dalit scholars tend to value the experiences at the institutes of higher education such as Oxford and Cambridge. Guru appealed to them to make a moral choice and return to the Dalit experience. The Dalit experience is far more pertinent realm of interpretation and understanding than the theoretical idea of Dalit experience accessed from afar. And Guru's appeal for return is not to be mistaken for a walk back into pure empiricism of a positivist nature, because the latter is tokenism in academics as well as in politics. Guru expected the Dalit scholarship to theorise on the basis of lived experience and serve both politics and academic objectives. Sarukkai enhanced the scope of discussion by making a return to the core, pertinent, question: What is lived experience? In a system of thought where objective thinking was separated from the broader notion of experience, the idea of lived experience appeared to be exclusive. But in the traditions of thought in India, self, experience and knowledge are intricately tied together with the vernacular categories such as *anubhava*. Usually, the translation of *anubhava* into English will be experience. But, *anubhava* is not just the English translation. Instead, it carries the relationship of experience, cognition and the self, among other things. Unlike the connotation of *anubhava,* arguably, the English word experience is shorn of the individual undergoing it. Moreover, the word experience is often confused with the cause and materiality of experience. It does not acknowledge that the cause and materiality would mean little without the actor, the experiencer, who is the key person behind an experience. And hence, almost to compensate the loss, in English there is a separate entity called lived experience. Sarukkai noted:

> Lived experience suggests an immediacy that is not present in the other idea of experience ... the words of experience in different languages exhibit hidden presuppositions about experience. "Experience" in English does not have a sense of the "lived" in it. As is well known, this word is derived from the Latin *experintia*, which, among other things, supports the meaning of proof and experiment. (55)

Sarukkai and Guru were approaching the distinction of experience in the context of India in order to highlight its relationship with the specific local context. The attempt was to deliver a more context-sensitive understanding of experience. This reminds us of Sri Lankan anthropologist Gananath Obeyesekere's (2012, 1) discussion on the 'lived' idea of Enlightenment, which he interchangeably termed awakening, in his discussion on the phenomenology of visionary experience. Cartesian meditations lead us in one direction but the lived nature of our experiences in the socio-religious scheme amounts to a departure from Enlightenment rationalism. Both, a generic experience that aided scientific epistemology and a lived experience of a phenomenological nature walk together for many of us. The South Asian cultural lexicography, thus, offers us more than the empiricists' idea of experience. Such non-empirical notion of experience pertains to the associated terms, such as vision. Unfortunately, under the dominance of scientific rationality, visionary experience is subject to rational suspicion; such non-empirical vision gets recast in a scientific language as psychologically determined dreams, hysteria and pathology. The problem arises when a secular approach to science renders the visionary experience inspired by religious tradition into scientific categories befitting scientific epistemology. But then they are experiences in their own right, which demand from the social scientists an approach to unravel the meanings in them. Having understood experience this way, one arrives at the inseparable knowledge, experience and self. We endeavour and succeed to acquire scientific knowledge of a range, for example, the existence of a molecule of an element, the composition of a gas such as ammonia, the physical properties of a colour, and name it. Yet we seek to develop an experience of them along with the a priori knowledge. Epistemically, having a subjective experience is special; it affirms the free will as well as agency of the actor who experiences. And therefore Guru's advocacy of the lived experience of Dalits for theorising a Dalit worldview is crucial. For lived experience is not like mere experience, which can be reduced to cause-and-effect in the ultimate objective analysis—a typical feature of scientific epistemology. It means that lived experience is experience without choice, while experience could refer to a controlled situation in which one enters/exits with a choice. The experience of Dalit oppression is a lived experience, different from the experience of a participant observer who can enter and exit the situation at will. Thus goes the dictum: *Lived experience is not about freedom of experience but about the lack of freedom in experience.* Even more complex, when one factors in the emotional content of lived experience. But then, the validity of lived experience cannot perhaps cancel out that of experience which may be with freedom and choice. As Sarukkai noted:

> we can theorize about another person's experience because there is a space within that experience that is not related to the experiencer.

> For example, consider the element of oppression which a Dalit experiences. The Dalit who experiences oppression legitimately owns that experience of oppression. However, the experience of oppression also involves an oppressor, either as an individual or a system, and the Dalit has no control or ownership over this oppressor. (39)

This provided an opening in the realm of experience for those who may be outsiders to the group that has undergone the experience without choice. In spite of this very incisive argument, one cannot ignore the evidence of emotional bearing in the experience of those who have, for example, experienced as victims. The story of experience, however, had been thoroughly complicated in the debate. In spite of the philosophical resolves and attempt to sort out the intrigue of experience, there will remain always a question or two about the nature and scope of experience. Hence one could think of it, analogically: there is no pond of experience without muddied water!

The challenge to the category of experience also emerged in the domain of feminist social science in India that asked a cardinal question: Whose experience constitutes feminism in India?[10] This is pertinent since many of the feminist thinkers in India were somewhat at a loss in the face of the above question. After all, in the history of India, we find examples of iconic female visionaries and social reformers working towards uplifting women in Indian society. One such example is Pandita Ramabai from the early twentieth century, who was a foremost social reformer, proponent of women's education and crusader against child marriage. Her criticism of hierarchical caste structures and location of women are one of the earliest examples of reflection on the intersection of caste and gender in India. Given her commendable knowledge of Sanskrit literature, she was endowed with the epithet Pandita. Such an awareness of female historical icons lead us to diverse other questions: How to address an example such as Pandita Ramabai's feminism given its local characteristics? How do we adjudge the experiences of Hindu upper-caste women, appended to the imagining of a nation? Many feminist social scientists including Uma Chakravarti presented a critical reading of the cultural nationalism of the Hindu upper-caste women, which may yet not exhaust the politics of experience. Likewise, how to adjust the experience of a prominent female political leadership in colonial India such as Sarojini Naidu in the scheme of feminist understanding of women's experience? Or shall we be content with the Sri Lankan feminist scholar Kumari Jayawardena, who had propounded a unique parameter for feminist activism in the Third World. Her validates experience of all such women who have contributed to the movement for equality and transformation in structures in the Third World.[11] Feminism in the Third World is not an imported Western ideology; instead, it is a product of the societal and political needs emanating from the context. It is shaped by the manifold struggles against colonial dominance, against inequality and poverty. More as a homegrown praxis, feminism is an offspring of the struggle for social reforms and the fundamental rights to vote and education.

This is the trope on which there appeared an intervention by Madhu Kishwar (1991), inviting responses from social scientists who cared for women's experiences. Kishwar alleged feminist perspective to be too Western to adequately deal with local women's issues in India. Such a critical approach led Kishwar to underline ideological constitution of the feminist perspective, and the alleged epistemological superiority and the value orientation of progress associated with the Western models of thought. Kishwar's criticism was inspired by an apprehension that an attempt to codify Hindu law eroded the diversity in Hindu culture. And she sought to rescue diverse living traditions from the homogenising tendency of a nation state modelled upon Western concepts of statecraft. As such, this critical perspective on feminism is an attempt to highlight the significant diversity of women's experiences. But then, as many feminist scholars responded, it runs into many levels of problems. Mary John (2014) put various positions concisely to help understand the problems as well as find a ground where the universal can meet the local on the trope of feminism in India. It was understood that Kishwar's understanding of diversity was essentialist in the sense that it was essentially middle-class, upper-caste women who were hailed as the bearers of Indian culture. The nineteenth-century reform movement and subsequent national culture engendered new gender norms resulting in the 'subjectification of women, the re-fashioning of family ideals, the intensification of conjugality and the forging of new patriarchies' (55).[12] This entailed a resurrection of Hindu iconography and idioms from Sanskrit classics depicting the Indianness of an empowered woman. With the resurgence of a political Hindu Right, the essentialist notions of diversity, community and image of women have yet again found prominence. It is, however, at the price of seeing multiple overlapping patriarchies across spheres, public or private, state or civil society.[13] Perhaps, one ought to be mindful of ever-evolving contestations and diverse voices, as far as feminism in India is concerned. Feminist way of seeing in sociology, if any, ought to be read in close association with discourses in institutionalised academics, civil society activism, negotiations and contestation with state and thereof machinery and the ever-expanding framework of analysis in the wake of globalisation.[14]

However, the feminist way of seeing cannot be accomplished without some initiatives at the level of civil society along with political mobilisation. The latter can engender many levels of activism-based collaborations, interventions and solidarity.[15] Historically, leaders and intellectuals in modern India envisaged the active participation of the marginalised, in social and political life. This is evidenced even in the many articles Mahatma Gandhi wrote to highlight the caste and gender anomalies of Hindu society. His criticism of the social hierarchy in which women were placed at lower pedestal was primarily from a moral vantage point. He went to the extent of considering women far more superior in moral strength than men in Indian society. In a way, Gandhi was a proponent of the diversity of experiences of women, the Harijans and others.[16] In the same breath, it is pertinent to recall Savitribai Phule, a significant social reformer, poet and teacher in nineteenth-century India. Her active role in teaching female children from underprivileged sections of society in Maharashtra and crusade for widow remarriage are crucial components in her biography. One of the first resounding thoughts on experience-based learning and teaching in the field of education came from Phule's modern reformist initiatives. Another 'mahatma' in modern India was Jyotirao Phule, also known as Jyotiba Phule, who developed a vision of an informed and educated womankind and the lower caste. Education was envisaged as an integral tool for social transformation by Mahatma Phule, which can usher in a new order conducive for social equality. The trope of modern Indian thoughts gets thicker as one goes on adding more radical stances from, for example, B.R. Ambedkar. The contestation about experience, along the lines of caste and creed, assumed dramatic escalation in Ambedkar's various writings. His biography subsumed an experiential journey with many revolutionary moments, be that subversion of the ancient book of law, the *Manusmriti*, or conversion to Buddhism. The centrality of experiences and encounters in Dalit thoughts is thus a foregone conclusion. What is more crucial to mention here is the fact that the contestation about the experience of Dalits had more radical voices in post-independent India. A Dalit-feminist activist Ruth Manorama[17] has, however, also sought to emphasise the distinction of the Dalit women's position in the largely male-dominated Dalit discourses on the experience of discrimination and humiliation. The uniqueness of the Dalit women's experiences reveals the double inequality they suffer. The Dalit women are not equal to their male counterparts in status as well as they have absolutely inferior social status in comparison with the non-Dalit women.

The various instances of the complexity of experience from the history of modern India, discussed above, persuade us to return to the key issue on the anvil. All such instances of 'complication in experience', as it were, date back in time. The ancient systems of logic in Indian tradition underlined that human experience brought together the empirical and perceptual; while the empirical is out there, perceptual understanding is based on a rationality that alludes to non-empirical factors such as emotions, intuitions and feelings. There was a contested relationship between rational verification through empiricism and the perceptions of reality; neither is any less important in experience, and thus the complexity in the idea of experience.[18] Reason and emotion, epistemology and ontology, and mind and body come together in this scheme. And with various agencies, stakeholders and experiencers coming into picture, the matter gets more exciting for further explorations. Ways of seeing, thus, do not remain a philosopher's helpless muse. The muse, too, has a say, and perhaps has always had a say, which we begin to hear in the background of the above discussion.

Reflexivity: Meanings, Limits and Possibility

Foregrounding the complexity of experience leads to an intellectual anxiety. While many sociologists in India may bury their heads in the sand, like an ostrich, in the face of such anxiety and hide themselves in a conveniently constructed comfort zone, the point is to deal with the discomfiting and yet promising challenge. The anxiety is aptly summed up in the question: Are we headed toward a nihilistic epistemological, or, if it sounds better, ontological relativism? The insider is insider, and outsider an outsider, and the twain shall never meet! In this wake of contested experience simple rumination on the insider–outsider, or living intimately with strangers may not hold ground for long.[19] There is a lurking sense of relativism underpinning the advocacy of lived experience. That the Dalit way of seeing is one thing, and the non-Dalit way of seeing is another, is an epistemologically divisive politics of experience. That the feminist way of seeing shall be an exclusive endeavour of those who swear by feminism is a little too simple formulation on ontologically distinguishable experiences. Even though we have heard of the possible ways of overcoming such anxiety, we return to the resolve most sociologists are most enamoured with. This is the resolve in reflexivity.

And this idea of reflexivity shall not be confused with M.N. Srinivas', and many of his students' or protégés', anxious methodological self-defence. They shared an anxiety about studying one's own social world. Srinivas had to explain the validity of his work to sociologists and anthropologists in the First World, to the likes of Edmund Leach, Radcliffe Brown and Louis Dumont. And in that mode of defence, Srinivas said:

> The sociologist who is engaged in the study of his own society is likely to be influenced by his social position, not only in his observations but also in the problem he selects for study. But this need not always be a source of error- it might even be a source of insight. (2009, 161)

But we ought to pay extra attention to his very next sentence that makes it clear that the idea of reflexivity was more a camouflage than a stance for many of the sociologists and anthropologists in India: 'Insights, however, have to be subjected to rigorous testing before they can become valid generalizations' (161).

The divide of subjectivity and objectivity seemingly forecloses the rise of reflexivity. Srinivas, like others, got down to the typically extraordinary methodological act that characterised most of the classical sociologists. It is all about obtaining an observer's 'detachment', the illusive act that no one is sure about. Fieldwork, arguably, was a means and ways of attaining such detachment through both, intellect and emotions.[20] This sociologist in Srinivas' imagination was like a novelist who could 'get under the skin of the different characters he is writing about' (164). Far from the possible is this extraordinary expectation—a detached sociologist getting under the skin of characters in the field. Attachment would, perhaps, serve them better to help get under the skin of a character other than oneself. And besides, what is the relationship of the other and the self in this scheme of being sociological? The question makes the whole formulation somewhat pathological, almost suggesting a split personality of the sociologists.

Instead, the discussion is more likely to dwell upon the serendipitous methodological wonder that Srinivas attained by recalling the details from his field notes that were burnt down in the arson. In 1970, the anti-Vietnam war protesters set fire at the Center for Advanced Study in Behavioural Sciences at Stanford University, where Srinivas was a fellow. His collection of data, research notes and the drafts of the manuscript of his monograph were burnt. He was left with nothing except his memory related to his fieldwork-based data. Seemingly, a helpless anthropologist is better than an anthropologist with certitude. Thus Srinivas had to recall the field data, notes and insights from memory, almost as stories. The value addition of recalled information is explicit in his landmark monograph, *The Remembered Village* (1976), which presents a far more nuanced methodological insights beyond the moribund divide of subjective and objective. The ability to think and write, as though one was thinking of and writing a work of fiction, is indeed a much-needed reflexive stance in sociology. Srinivas noted, 'My mind, and my entire personality, had been involved in that experience, and what did I remember of it? I should try to do a book on Rampura based solely on memory. Indeed, I should forget that I had made any field notes' (1976, xii).

Experience, along with remembering and forgetting, became an exquisite category in this simple, ordinary and hence, significant act, far removed from the extraordinary expectations of a trained sociologist-anthropologist. The methodological anxiety about the binaries, that is, truth and lies, objective and subjective, intellect and emotion, could not stop such a creatively ordinary way of seeing in sociology. Given this, it is likely to indulge in a grotesque wishful thinking that all anthropological and sociological data shall get destroyed so that a methodologically refreshing proposition could emerge. Having said that, one shall note that Srinivas distinguished, and so did his admirer and chronicler T.N. Madan, his anthropological-sociological works from a few stories that he wrote. Informed by his fieldwork, Srinivas is known to have written a story titled *The Image Maker*.

Ashis Nandy had an insightful observation when he asked Madan whether reading Srinivas' anthropological works along with his fiction was '(a)n admission that Srinivas, by crossing the barriers between literature and the social sciences, has only enriched the latter? Or (was it) a homage to the creativity that, when forcibly distanced from hard empiricism, reaches a paradoxically a higher order of empiricism?'.[21] Nandy's question, along with the instance detailed above, holds a promise for a far more liberated idea of sociology, and a more nuanced answer to the question of what is sociological. Perhaps this is one of the finest instances of reflexivity, which entered inadvertently in Madan's homage as well as in Srinivas' oeuvre. And it all only sustains our interest in getting further into the problematic of experience.

The impact of the post-positivist turn on sociological methodology is most definitively expressed in the discussions on reflexivity. The idea of reflexivity has a trajectory spanning various domains of practices such as arts, humanities and science. It presents to us an inventory with diverse meanings and usages of the term. Paradoxically, while there is an abundance of reflection on the idea of reflexivity, there could be utter fogginess about what it exactly means. In this regard, it is worth recalling a daunting confession that 'there could be infinite sayings about reflexivity, and still reflexivity would not be captured. Reflexivity will exhaust us long before we exhaust it' (Ashmore 1989, 26). The discussion that follows, hence, does not aim to present an exegesis on the term and its various usages. It is wiser to have a selective discussion with a passing awareness of the length and breadth of the references and discussion on the term. The idea of reflexivity seemed to have acquired greater centrality in the post-positivist varieties of sociology in which agency/actor is predominant. The allusion to reflexivity began to appear in some of the post-positivist methodological positions, such as in the sociology of knowledge, phenomenology and ethnomethodology, and in post-Popper history and philosophy of science.[22] Reflexivity also became a catchword in debates on ethnography, famously known as writing culture debates.[23] In a response to postcolonial world fraught with fragments, an array of anthropologists posed questions to ethnographic practices: Who attributes meanings, an ethnographer or social actor? Who writes culture, the people or the anthropologist? The debate brought about a reflexive turn in ethnographic practices, casting aspersions on the ennobled notion of objectivity. One began to see the making of the ethnographic 'other' in conventional anthropological research. But then, furthering the premise of reflexivity, there have been anxious explorations of epistemology, representational practices and ethnography moving beyond the narrow focus on textual analysis. It aimed to make the issue of representation, rather than the ethnographic other, the central concern.[24] In other words, the key question of the writing culture debate, who attributes meaning qua who writes culture is reframed as: Who all are represented and how much in an ethnographic work today?

More important than exhausting a vast trajectory on reflexivity, and by implication exhausting ourselves as the pithy warning read earlier, is a debate with eclectically chosen sources. What follows is an attempt is to read Alvin Gouldner and Pierre Bourdieu together. Perhaps any discussion on reflexive sociology has to start with Gouldner's response to what he perceived as 'the coming crisis in Western Sociology' (1970). It was based on a critical realisation that positivist sociology operated with disabling paradoxes, one of which was about the split personality of sociologists. One has to be one thing in professional sociology and quite another in everyday life; a progressive Dalit sociologist thus could be a hard-core Brahmanical figure in a day-to-day set-up; a deeply Brahmanical and patriarchal person could be thoroughly Marxist sociologist. In other words, it is methodological dualism that splits a sociologist into two distinct parts, one possesses Olympian power (to order) and the other is ordinary mortal (living in disarray); on one hand, a scholar is the metaphorical owl of Minerva, and on the other, a mere owl, as it were. But there is another paradox that '*those who supply the greatest resources for the institutional development of sociology are precisely those who most distort its quest for knowledge*' (Gouldner 1970, 498; italics original).

The Machiavellianism of the above-mentioned sociologists shows in the judgements they make even though they claim to be value neutral. Sociology has the potential to be a thoroughly value-loaded pursuit of knowledge and yet it masquerades as value-neutral science of humans. This is why Gouldner, to reiterate a point made above, deemed sociologists to have a split personality. The split is due to the methodological binaries of personal and professional, subjective and objective. On the whole, the methodological split amounts to what Gouldner called a crisis in the Western sociology. In the background of the realisation of this crisis, Gouldner invited us to do sociology of sociology. This meant subjecting the methodological ways of seeing in sociology to a critical analysis. Such an exercise is essentially reflexive in nature. A sociology that promotes such self-critical examination of the ways of seeing is a sociology of sociology, qua reflexive and radical sociology. Such an endeavour would be radical in nature since everything taken for granted and intimate to a sociologist would be on the anvil of critical discussion. This, Gouldner envisaged, could allow sociologists to see themselves as a 'total man'. The totality of personhood expected from male as well as female sociologists enhances the sociological way of seeing. It is like looking into a mirror and developing an understanding of oneself before, or while, understanding the world. Evidently, Gouldner expected reflexive sociologists to see themselves in relation with the rest of the world, including the people they studied. It demanded a recognition of a deep kinship with their human subjects. And thus, they needed to be seen as 'brother sociologists' rather than alien 'others' or mere objects for the sociologists' superior theories, concepts, methods, techniques and insights. In sum, reflexive sociology expects a transformation of the sociologists' way of seeing the other; it demands a self-critical understanding of how and what one sees, and on the whole, a transformation of the sociologist's self and his praxis. Gouldner concluded:

> The core of a Reflexive Sociology, then, is the attitude it fosters toward those parts of the social world *closest* to the sociologist—his own university, his own profession, and its associations, his professional role, and importantly, his students, and himself—rather than toward only the remote parts of his social surround.... A Reflexive Sociology is not a bundle of technical skills; it is a conception of how to live and a total praxis. (504)

In a convincing and provocative style, Gouldner went on to suggest that a reflexive sociology shall not perpetuate a series of mistaken distinction between, for example, the personal and the public, the everyday life and the occasion of political act. Radicalism of reflexivity results in a rejection of old-style closed-door office politics and solicits innovations in public politics. For, an adequate critical introspection in any field will amount to necessary reinvention of the way of seeing.

However, before one is fully convinced of the radically formulated idea of reflexive sociology, it is wise to turn to Pierre Bourdieu for a critical appreciation of the idea of reflexivity. Needless to say, Loïc J.D. Wacquant, a student, made Bourdieu, the teacher, far more accessible. Wacquant used to walk with his teacher and have long conversations. Those interludes were extensions of the systematic lectures that Bourdieu delivered. A discourse on the idea of reflexivity, too, emerged during one such conversation in which Wacquant (1992) noted that Bourdieu anticipated reflexive gestures in a qualitatively different manner than Gouldner. He quoted Bourdieu, saying:

> In Gouldner, reflexivity remains more a programmatic slogan than a veritable program of work. What must be objectivised is not (only) the individual who does the research in her biographical idiosyncrasy but the position she occupies in academic space and the biases implicated in the view she takes by virtue of being "off sides" or "out of the game". (1992, 71–72)

In the same breath, Bourdieu was wary of the anthropological turn to reflexivity that was allegedly vulnerable to nihilistic relativism. A genuine reflexivity in social science stands guard against 'epistemocentrism' or 'ethnocentrism', and is characteristically 'anti-narcissistic'. It means reflexivity is not a licence to perform an unsubstantiated iconoclasm. Reflexive sociology or the sociology of sociology is not a prerogative of methodological specialists, narcissistic epistemologists or sociologists of knowledge or science. It is instead a fundamental dimension of sociological epistemology, 'a necessary prerequisite of any rigorous sociological practice' (68) in which it is possible to perform what Bourdieu called 'participant objectivation'. It means that every sociologist, with whatever theoretical orientation and perspectives, cannot objectivise others unless one objectivises one's own interest, motive, and objective behind objectivising others. This was more firmly put in Bourdieu's reflection on *Homo Academicus*: 'Sociology can be an extremely powerful instrument of self-understanding of one's own conditions of production and of the position one occupies in the social world …' (62).

This proposition has emerged from what Bourdieu practised as a sociologist. Wacquant observed, looking at the intellectual and personal trajectory of Bourdieu:

> From his early investigations of marriage practices in the isolated village of the Pyrenees mountains where he was raised to the hunt for Homo Academicus gallicus, the tribe he joined as result of his upward social climb, Bourdieu has continually turned the instruments of his science upon himself—if in a manner not always immediately perceptible to some of his readers. (36)

It is a brand of reflexivity that has three distinct features. First, it seeks to unravel social and intellectual unconscious embedded in analytical tools and operations. Second, rather than a lone intellectual adventure, reflexivity is discussed as a collective enterprise. And third, it provides the epistemological security to sociology rather than an assault on the already insecure and vulnerable disciplinary practice. The third one is important in that it confirmed Bourdieu's reflexive sociology was not anti-objectivity; instead, it sought to increase the scope of objectivity in knowledge in social sciences. It works towards strengthening the epistemological design of sociology in such a manner that it facilitated institutional practices rather than sporadic individual idiosyncrasies. As part of the reflexive practices, for a more nuanced notion of science and objectivity, Bourdieu critically unmasked methodological fetishism; this was resonant with C. Wright Mills' critique of the methodological inhibition of sociologists. The criticism underlined the transformation of methodology into a fetish, a quasi-sacred entity that sociologists held as unquestionable. Such unreasonable aura about the methodological way of seeing caused inhibitions among them. As a result, a methodological advancement towards reflexivity remained elusive for the sociologists. This critique also revealed the anti-theoretical or sophistication of methods and techniques devoid of theoretical insights. And the flipside was equally problematic. The hypersensitivity for methodological freedom amounted to a misinterpretation of methodological pluralism, which Bourdieu called polytheism, anything goes, epistemological anarchism, Feyerabend's Dadaism. Reflexivity rescued sociology from sentimentalist wildness, as it were, since the sentimentalism gives birth to a methodologism in sociology that is not conducive for the reflexivity. It is an iconoclastic confinement in which a sociologist is akin to a narcissist. Another tendency of an equally objectionable kind was theoreticism, a practice of meta theorising that is entirely disconnected from the empirical world. It is a 'theoreticist theory', perpetuated in the self-enclosed, self-referential realm of discourse, a separate institution of theory. Reflexive sociology can grapple against both the dominant tendencies. There is a return to intellectual balance that this version of reflexivity envisaged.

For Bourdieu, reflexive sociology envisioned a 'total science of society' inclined to fathom 'total social facts'.[25] This was an anti-Cartesian conception in which various aspects of society, including the knower and object of study, were in an intricate relationship. Reading selectively from phenomenologists and hermeneutists, from Husserl and Heidegger to Marleau-Ponty and Wittgenstein, Bourdieu dwelt upon the idea of 'ontological complicity' (1992, 20).[26] It meant that there was a 'preobjective' contact between subject and world, actor and structure, a springboard of intersubjective meanings. Since it is a pre-objective level of experience, reflexive sociology has to be making efforts to the mutual possession qua ontological complicity, of social agent and the world. Such an orientation enabled Bourdieu to develop a stance of reflexivity, which discredits the two antinomies that plagues sociology in particular and social science in general. These are antinomies of Social Physics and Social Phenomenology, and more precisely, objectivity and subjectivity. In the same series of antinomies, it is possible to perceive the confrontation of methodological holism (of positivist) and methodological individualism (of post-positivist). This is to seek for a resolve of the methodologically antithetical ways of seeing. Bourdieu proposed to develop a way of seeing that departed from methodological monism according to which either positivist or post-positivist, structuralist or phenomenological, can be of utility. Instead, a total social science steers clear of mechanical structuralism as well as teleological individualism, because the former puts agents 'on vacation' and the latter renders agents as 'oversocialized cultural dopes' (10). Agents on vacation means the theoretical negligence of the role of an actor's agency in society. A total science of society seeks to see the social world through praxiology, weaving structuralist and constructivist approaches. Moreover Bourdieu deemed it to be 'structuralist constructivism' in dialectical relation with 'constructivist structuralism' (11). The conceptual–theoretical spinning in the two usages in inverted commas are to suggest the imperative of unravelling the complexity of human experience. This is so because the social universe leads a double life, also called 'double objectivity' of society, since there is objectivity in subjectivity. The first is in the 'objectivity of the first order', constituted by material resources (including capital). And the second is in the 'objectivity of the second order', constituted by a system of classification, schemata, symbolic templates and practical activities such as conduct, thoughts, feelings and judgements. The neat duality of the universe indeed summons a double reading, qua way of seeing, qua 'double focus analytic lenses', by the sociologists of a total science of society. One reading takes recourse to social physics, the positivist way of seeing that prevails in structuralism. However, it presupposes standing firm with the following conviction—social science cannot treat social facts as things, as the Durkheimian percept did. This is because social facts are contingent upon society, an ever-dynamic entity. Despite socio-centrism, Durkheim did not sufficiently unravel the relationship between the categories of understanding in collective representation, underlying mental schemata and social structure. Durkheim and Mauss both lacked in unearthing the causative mechanism behind social classification. Bourdieu used socio-centrism to show the homology of system of classification, categories of understanding, mental schemata and social structure. They are genetically linked and constitute the durable and transposable dispositions internalised by the individuals. And hence, we ought to operate with the dialectic, as mentioned earlier, between objectivity of the first order and the second order, constructivist structuralism and structuralist constructivism. Eying double objectivity, Bourdieu emphasised that symbols were not only collective representations but also instruments of domination. It amounted to suggesting that the sociology of knowledge, or of cultural forms, was a political sociology qua sociology of symbolic power. An individual can be within structural limits and yet can transform the world by transforming its representation.

This particular way of seeing enables us to see the continuum of power and culture, politics and performance, transformation and everyday life. Thereby, there emerged a primacy of relationship in Bourdieu's reflexive way of seeing against any methodological monism qua the bipolar views, in which actors and structures were separated. Instead, Bourdieu's reflexivity allowed seeing the actors and structure as related through connecting concepts of habitus and field. Habitus, a disposition, tendency, propensity or inclination, is a way of being, a habitual state or it is akin to the intention in action, an idea taken from John Searle's philosophy. As an organised and organising principle, structured and structuring disposition, habitus is the strategy generating principle enabling the agents to cope with unforeseen and ever-changing situations. It is thus a system of lasting and transposable dispositions that bring together past experiences, ongoing moments of perceptions, appreciations and actions as an integrated whole. Habitus, therefore, shall bear an iota of indefiniteness.[27] On the other hand, a field is a replacement for society and consists of a set of objective, historical relations between positions anchored in certain forms of power (or capital).

The field is,

> a patterned system of objective forces (much in the manner of a magnetic field), a relational configuration endowed with a specific gravity which it imposes on all the objects and agents which enter in it. In the manner of a prism, it refracts external forces according to its internal structure. (17)

Besides, a field is a space of conflict, competition and various stakes of authorities. While there are clear rule governing agents in the field, there is also adequate malleability, making a field a 'structure of probabilities'. A field thus offers rewards, gains, profits or sanction, with due amount of indeterminacy. The relational conceptualisation of field and habitus, thus, befits Bourdieu's reflexive sociology in which not only self and other is a debated binary but also many related binaries slip under criticism. The key point emerging from the above discussion is the relationship of the self (of the knower) with the empirical–historical milieu. Besides, there is an inherent epistemological urge. This is about not missing sight of the relationship of sociology or what makes a sociological way of seeing, with philosophical-epistemological interrogation of what Wittgenstein called 'forms of life'. This was the mainstay in Peter Winch's reading of the philosophy of Ludwig Wittgenstein. In the wake of the full awareness of the politics inherent in selecting a vantage point as one's own, there is a newfound relation of sociology and philosophy. Winch's proposition in engagement with Ludwig Wittgenstein is,

> It is true that the epistemologist's starting point is rather different from that of the sociologist but, if Wittgenstein's arguments are sound, that is what he must sooner or later concern himself with. That means that the relations between sociology and epistemology must be different from, and very much closer than, what is imagined to be the case. (Winch 2012, 40)

This means that sociology is supposed to give an account of 'the nature of social phenomena', and that is equally a valid concern in philosophy. Unfortunately, the epistemological imperative necessary for sociology in order to present an account of the social phenomena is 'misbegotten' the moment a phenomenon is 'misconstrued' as a 'scientific problem'. The words in inverted commas are as they are used in Winch's discussion so as to highlight the waywardness of a philosophically malnourished sociological approach. This was the case with many of the classical sociological approaches too; for example, Durkheim enjoined sociologists to follow rules and create the idea of social fact without giving voice to the people to whom the social facts belong. Pareto is another example; he too advocated that sociologists develop empirical models to explain the behaviour of people without any epistemological explanation; and in the same breath, Weber's interpretative approach did not give a clear account of 'the *logical* character of interpretative understanding' (105; italics original). *Verstehen* or, for that matter, intuition, or what Karl Popper had called mental process, can engender hypotheses, to be systematically tested through the 'method of selection by elimination'. Winch is critical of a tinge of psychologism in the predecessors' works that does not explain what interpretative means other than plain and simple causal explanation. Through critical understanding the limits of the dominant (conventional, officially more legit) way of seeing in sociology, Winch arrived at Wittgenstein's basic formulation in which, rule, behaviour, language and understanding unfold together. This requires a thorough investigation into the abundance of a priori that aid humans behave, emote, enact and be. It also solicits our awareness that the notion of following rules is inseparable from the notion of making mistakes. It is all summed up, as Winch suggested, 'it is clear that men do decide how they shall behave on the basis of their view of what is the case in the world around them.... A man's social relations with his fellows are permeated with his ideas about reality' (21–22). And hence, to be sociological, we ought to be seeking for an 'epistemological discussion of man's understanding of reality'. Winch quoted Wittgenstein, 'if you are seeing a thing you are seeing identity too' (26). And thus, Winch's proposition joined in the array of strands on reflexivity preparing the sociologists to see something more than merely scientific–empirical issue, and to seek something more than causal explanation of the human behaviour.

Possibility of Holistic Hermeneutics

Yet another consequence of revisiting reflexivity could be recognition of the sources beyond the pale of formal social sciences. A synopsis of the long trajectory of hermeneutics in the previous chapter enables us to turn to discussions on experience from the various (pre-modern) texts. Cobbling together the various strands may amount to a novel interjection on the turf that this book has laid out.

In this section, there is an attempt to share one such strand. Certainly, this is not the only one. It derives from a tale from the fifth chapter of the *Brihadaranyak Upanishad*.[28]

As the story goes, three disciples of Lord Brahma (the god of creation who appears as teacher in this tale), namely, a god, a demon and a human spent years under his tutelage. They fulfilled the prerequisite to prove their competence and eligibility to learn the final and most important lesson that Brahma would impart. First it was the god's turn. The teacher uttered only one letter, 'D' (in the Devanagari script, द). God interpreted the letter as 'D' for *daman* (दमन), which means supressing sensory desires. The interpretation was motivated by the imperative for gods to avoid falling into the abyss of desires. The teacher responded affirmatively, telling his pupil that he had got the answer right. When it was the human's turn, the teacher yet again uttered the same letter, to which the human disciple uttered *dān* (दान), charity/philanthropy/parting with one's possession to prevent humans from falling prey to avarice. Brahma was satisfied with this answer as well. The demon, when it was his turn, construed it as *daya* (दया), meaning kindness/compassion, else demons would be rampant in destruction, which also met with the teacher's requirements of a right answer.

Ādï Śaṅkara,[29] the ancient philosopher renowned for his treatise on Adwaita Vedānta (doctrine of non-duality), points out two features underpinning the act of understanding and interpretation by the disciples in the aforementioned tale. First, each of the three disciples analogically indicates a distinct property/feature/socio-cultural constitution. Each thus propels a distinct interpretation of the utterance 'D' (द), and each is hence correct. Second, each has fulfilled a common prerequisite; in this tale, each disciple observes celibacy and affective devotional proximity with the teacher. Hence, despite difference of dispositions, each of them was able to offer an answer that, though different, met with the teacher's expectations. A one-point observation with regard to the aforementioned tale is: How does the teacher know and understand all three disciples' validity of understanding? The answer lies in the dialectics of ontological epistemology and epistemological ontology. A further endorsement emerges from the Upanishadic lessons.

Śaṅkara argues, intellect resides in *hridaya*.[30] The equivalent in English for this word is heart. But in Śaṅkara scheme it is not merely a biological organ. It can be construed as an amicable union between reason and emotion, intellect and affectivity, the objective and subjective. Thus, the Upanishad confidently argues that 'only heart knows the truth'.[31] In yet another insightful adage, *eko aham bahusyam,*[32] which means one yearns for and endeavours to become many. The Upanishad points out my existential joy and fear arising from my ontological being, despite my transcendental tendency. It is a significant paradox that constitutes my realm of being, understanding and meaning.

To understand and interpret, one has to realise oneself existentially and ontologically. While the knowledge generated thereby has epistemological relativism, it is ontologically transcendental. In implication, it transcends the divide of subject and object because talking about the self is also talking about the so-called other and vice versa. The alleged epistemological relativism is thus nullified, as all understanding is in terms of probabilities. The transcendental tendency of the above-mentioned hermeneutic conclusions are by no means merely a theological illusion. At this point, it is imperative to take note of the critical realism that perceives humans in terms of meta-reality, and describes transcendence as an everyday feature. It is, categorically, in contrast with the conventional notion of transcendence as an esoteric philosophical conceptualisation. A significant philosophical approach to this issue emerged from Roy Bhaskar who noted, 'Transcendence, transcendental identification in consciousness and transcendental agency are indispensable feature of all human beings, social life and indeed a necessary condition for any human act at all' (2002, 10). The non-dual, Bhaskar's 'transcendental self', resides beneath the duality and heteronomy of the visible world and its people. This self is connected to everybody else by the virtue of residing in the 'cosmic envelope'. There is, however, an important rider: 'Although we are all connected at the ground state, at the cosmic envelope, we can only act in the physical world from we are and we are unique, bounded and clearly demarcated, concretely singularized beings' (14).

Furthermore, 'you cannot live in a non-dual state, but you can minimize the splits in your being and you can eliminate inconsistency with your ground-state as that you are effectively a whole autonomous being' (110).

Thus, placing Bhaskar, alongside the discussion on hermeneutics, with Schleiermacher, Dilthey, Heidegger, Bultmann, Gadamer, and the instance from the Upanishad, there develops a sense of holistic hermeneutics. They all suggested one thing in common: Be one with your 'field' in order to talk about it not only epistemologically but also in terms of being. This is qualitatively different from the technical idea mentioned in most of the research proposals, which is rapport building or immersion into the field. Paradoxically, such textbook notions of research are accompanied by a 'detached understanding'. Most of the textbooks and formulas of doing research prescribes such paradoxes. This is also a little more than some of the self-reflexive accounts emerging from sociologists whereby we tend to be professional seekers who perform an extraordinary vocational cunningness. We show that we can empathise and hence we can know. But the truth is that we operate with the self of the seeker of meaning divided into various parts. The proposition in this wake is to not only seek but also carry out a constant appraisal of what you as a researcher mean. In simpler words, do not divide the pursuit of knowledge into the domain of heart or mind. It indeed only occurs when the dichotomies dissolve.

> By *holistic hermeneutics* in this wake I mean a philosophical discourse that puts the subject and object of a research, the researcher and the researched, the subjective and the objective, in one paradigm. To understand this paradigm, a researcher has to become both the disciples and the Upanishadic teacher. For the latter knows the validity of diverse interpretations of a single utterance. (Pathak 2018, 60)

There is a trope of possibilities that emerges from the above discussion for furthering the project of methodological explorations. For example, one can engage with three instances: Nagarjuna's Buddhist epistemology, Lokayata's materialism, tantric orientation, and examples from the annals of modern thinkers such as Rahul Sankrityayan's epistemological ontology in the idea of *ghumakkadi* (wandering) based on which he wrote a *ghumakkad shashtra* (a treatise on wandering). Likewise, one can make methodological return to some of the modern thinkers of India, such as Mahatma Gandhi, B.R. Ambedkar, Rabindranath Tagore and so on. The selections can be justified on the ground of the methodological focus in the selected works. I recall a postgraduate student building up a methodological premise for doing sociology by critically reading the English translation of an ancient text, Vatsyayana's *Kamasutra*, and kick-starting a debate on the ambivalent relation of attachment and detachment that plays a crucial role in the way Vatsyayana saw and recorded the details of sexual practices. Likewise, another student revisited *shunyata* in the Buddhist philosophy of Nagarjuna to offer an alternative vantage point for the idea of objectivity, inseparable from subjectivity, in the sociological way of seeing. If the teachers encouraged, the young scholars show the way forward by exploring methodological ways of seeing in the works of ancient sages, seers, prophets, mystics as well as the modern thinkers. These are meagre indicators of the enormity of the methodological possibilities entailed in the body of ideas. Suffice to say, there could emerge a homegrown idea of reflexivity in sociology and anthropology in South Asia, adding novel length and breadth to the practices. Such is the promise of the post-positivist milieu in sociology that could lead to manifold methodological enquiries, some of which are presented in this chapter.

References

Asad, T. *Anthropology and the Colonial Encounters*. London: Ithaca Press, 1973.

Ashmore, Malcolm. *The Reflexive Thesis: Writing Sociology of Scientific Knowledge*. Chicago: The University of Chicago Press, 1989.

Bhabha, Homi K. (ed.) *Nation and Narration*. London: Routledge, 2008.

Bhaskar, Roy. *Reflections on Meta-reality, A Philosophy for the Present: Transcendence, Emancipation and Everyday Life*. Delhi: Sage, 2002.

Bourdieu, Pierre, and Loic J.D. Wacquant. *An Invitation to Reflexive Sociology*. Chicago: University of Chicago Press, 1992.

Chakrabarty, Dipesh. *Provincialising Europe: Postcolonial Thought and Historical Difference*. Princeton: Princeton University Press, 2000.

Chakravarti, Uma. *Gendering Caste: Through a Feminist Lens*. Calcutta: Stree, 2006.

Chaudhuri, Maitrayee (ed.). *Feminism in India*. Delhi: Women Unlimited and Kali for Women, 2004.

Clifford, James, and George E. Marcus. *Writing Culture: The Politics and Poetics of Ethnography*. California: University of California Press, 1986.

Cohn, Bernard. *Colonialism and Its Forms of Knowledge: The British in India*. Princeton: Princeton University Press, 1996.

Fanon, Frantz. *The Wretched of the Earth*. London: Penguin Classics, 2001.

Freire, P. *Pedagogy of the Oppressed*. New York: Herder & Herder, 1972.

Ganeri, Jonardon. *Philosophy in Classical India*. London: Routledge, 2001.

Gouldner, A. *The Coming Crisis in Western Sociology*. New York: Basic Books, 1970.

Guru, Gopal. 'How Egalitarian Are the Social Sciences in India?', *Economic and Political Weekly* 37, no. 50 (2002): 5003–5009.

Guru, Gopal, and Sundar Sarukkai. *The Cracked Mirror: An Indian Debate on Experience and Theory*. Delhi: Oxford University Press, 2012.

Hooks, Bell. *Teaching to Transgress: Education as Practice of Freedom*. New York: Routledge, 1994.

Jayawardena, Kumari. *Feminism and Nationalism in the Third World*. London: Zed Books, 1986

John, Mary E. 'Feminism in India and the West: Recasting a Relationship'. In *Feminism in India*, edited by Maitrayee Chaudhuri, 52–68. Delhi: Women Unlimited and Kali for Women, 2014.

Kishwar, Madhu. 'Why I Do Not Call Myself a Feminist', *Manushi*, no. 61 (1991): 2–8.

Kumar, Radha. *A History of Doing: An Illustrated Account of Movements for Women's Rights and feminism in India, 1800–1990*. New Delhi: Kali for Women, 1993.

Madan, T.N. *Pathways: Approaches to the Society in India*. New Delhi: Oxford University Press, 2000.

———. *Sociological Traditions: Methods and Perspectives in the Sociology of India*. Delhi: Sage, 2011.

Matilal, B.K. *Perception: An Essay on Classical Indian Theories of Knowledge*. New York: Oxford University Press, 1992.

Mauss, M. *The Gift: The Form and Reason for Exchange in Archaic Societies*. New York: Routledge, 2002.

Menon, Nivedita. *Seeing Like a Feminist*. New Delhi: Zubaan and Penguin, 2012.

Murthy, Laxmi. 'Silences and Solidarities: Sexual Violence and Impunity in South Asia'. In *Another South Asia!*, edited by Dev Nath Pathak, 125–142. Delhi: Primus, 2017.

Nandy, Ashis. *The Intimate Enemy: Loss and Recovery of Self Under Colonialism*. New Delhi: Oxford University Press, 1983.

Obeyesekere, Gananath. *The Awakened Ones: Phenomenology of Visionary Experience*. New York: Columbia University Press, 2012.

Pathak, Dev Nath. 'A Quest of Alternative(s): A Conversation with Ruth Manorama', *Indian Journal of Women and Social Change* 1, no. 2 (2016): 1–9.

———. *Living and Dying: Meanings in Maithili Folklore*. New Delhi: Primus, 2018.

Sangri, Kumkum. 'Politics of Diversity: Religious Communities and Multiple Patriarchies', *Economic and Political Weekly* 30, no. 51–52 (1995): 3287–3310 and 3381–3389.

Said, Edward W. *Orientalism: Western Conceptions of the Orient*. New Delhi: Penguin, 2001.

Sartre, Jean-Paul, 'Preface'. In *The Wretched of the Earth*, edited by Frantz Fanon. London: Penguin Classics, 2001.

Srinivas, M.N. *The Remembered Village*. New Delhi: Oxford University Press, 1976.

———. *Social Change in Modern India*. Delhi: Orient Blackswan, 2009.

Winch, Peter. *The Idea of a Social Science and Its Relations to Philosophy*. London: Routledge, 2012.

Zenker, O., and K. Kumoll (eds). *Beyond Writing Culture: Current Intersections of Epistemologies and Representational Practices*. New York: Berghehn Books, 2010.

8

DIEHARD DEVILS: MYOPIAS AND UTOPIAS IN SOCIOLOGY IN INDIA

Some often-heard barbed remarks from ordinary folks looking at sociologists in India are worth mentioning: Sociologists in India see everything bad in the social world. They elucidate something we all more or less already know; they reaffirm, almost like a truism, that social, political and economic institutions are unequal and bad; the market is exploitative; the family is oppressive and undesirable; the state is, obviously, the worst of all; everything is bad except that sociologists can get to see this badness, theoretically and conceptually; the only good thing for sociologists is that they can see the badness of the world, ironically, with value-neutral objectivity!

Even if there is an exaggeration entailed in recounting these barbed remarks, one cannot overlook the fact that they offer a potent opportunity for critical self-reflection. How free are the folks called sociologists in India from the delimiting mathematics of good, bad and evil? A probing question could be: how much methodological playfulness, or interest in epistemological–philosophical reasoning inherent in the way of seeing in sociology, is evident in South Asia? This chapter narrows down the discussion to the case of sociology and anthropology in India, a story that has appeared in various ways in several accounts in contemporary sociology that centralised the intricacies of doing sociology. However, seldom has a story led to the diagnosis of what sociologists and anthropologists meant by the ways of seeing. In the context of this book, the diagnosis is not merely to perform crisis mongering because here, the story connects the crisis with the lack of methodological adventurism necessary for answering the question about being sociological. The idea is to take a bird's-eye view of the absence of discussion on the complexity of experience that underpins the sociological ways of seeing. This is despite the fact that an exceptional sociologist and enticing teacher such as Rabindra Ray had ruminated on the idea of *darshan*,[1] which invited the inauguration of a debate on the sociological way of seeing. Ray noted:

> Darshan is a point of departure, not a form of encyclopedic ultimate knowledge. Darshanic practice is a process that continually amends

> its viewpoint in order to illuminate the path of action. Darshan inaugurates the possibility of both spirituality (aadhyatm) and knowledge (gyan), which together concretize the meaningfulness of human life. The objective of darshan is to fashion the methods of human thought with which humans (manushya) can give concrete form to the meaningfulness of their lives. (2019, 2)

It will be a loss of sociology and anthropology in India if categories such as *darshan*, or its cognates from various civilisational discourses, do not aid in debating the idea of being sociological.

To put it simply, the previous chapters in this book underlined the intellectual freedom available in the larger body of social sciences to rework thematic issues, methodological playfulness and intellectual eccentricities. This was so in spite of the epistemological constraints visible across intellectual history due to the dominant scientism and its methodological incarnation in social sciences. We observe such freedom and playfulness in D.P. Mukerji's wishful thinking about the enormous possibilities in doing sociology, discussed in the Introduction and this chapter. Along with Mukerji, other sociologists manifested a sociology in which methodology appeared to be an area of enquiry. This chapter builds upon such possibilities and constraints that were present in the trajectory of discussion on the sociological way of seeing, in the previous chapters. This is a discursive trajectory marked by some of the following key thematic characteristics: scientific epistemology, responses to it in sociology before sociology and afterwards in classical sociology, sociology of sociology, foundational and anti-foundation approaches, and the so-called post-positivist deliberations that centralised the ontological complexity of experience. Is this what we encounter in the realm of sociological practices too? While rhetorically we may have brought about what is famously known as an interdisciplinary turn in an equally powerful rhetoric of reflexivity, our practices do not seem to vindicate our stated objectives. In the realm of practices, the strength of gatekeepers is far more superior to the courage and conviction of the intellectual daresayers, free-floating scholars and creative anarchists, that is the sociologists and anthropologists willing to take risks and transcend boundaries. The dim possibility to chance upon methodological innovation, if any, in the realm of sociology in India is a case in point. Being sociological, to put it provocatively means to be methodologically monolithic in India. This is where a creative ambivalence degenerates into a disabling dilemma that adds a negative connotation to the articulation, 'to be sociological or not to be'.

The dilemma has an uncanny clarity along linear anxiety and thus an ominous conclusion—nothing is possible beyond the sociological orthodoxy. This chapter unravels the strength of such linear anxiety while wishfully aspiring to transcend the linearity, thereof dilemma, and looking forward to the possibility of being sociological and yet not be chained to intellectual paranoia. How to sustain such wishful thinking in the wake of myopias,[2] the narrow vision of objects that become utopias,[3] an imaginary and indefinitely remote place? The usage of myopia alludes to a sinister development in sociology in India; it is a theoretical–methodological short-sightedness that enables one to see objects closer to eyes but disables a farsighted vision. Analogically, this means that sociologists have been comfortable with the disciplinary comfort zone within which, paradoxically, the grand vision of sociologists, if any, unfolds. Most sociologists, barring the exceptional ones who usually get marginalised, do not tend to question the way of seeing that they employ without adequate critical thinking. The greatest myopia is related to the central question this book articulated at the onset: What does it mean to be sociological? Obscurity reigns high when we seek an answer to this question in the annals of history and the practice of the discipline in India. The radicalism of self-reflective sociology, leading to the sociology of sociology, does not venture too far in India. This is revealed in the various compilations of essays mapping disciplinary history and practices. Second, we encounter the dominance of paradigms, theories and methods related to the concoction of myopia(s) and utopia(s). Imagine the fate of a discipline that languishes in a swishy comfort zone with great arrogance in their ability to solve the problems, and imagine a future, of a society. Sociology in India delivers to us a thick corpus of prognostic analyses of problems, seldom leading to remedy. It is mostly the case of rhetoric breeding more rhetoric that sociology is condemned with. The evidences of a lack of intellectual risk-taking in sociology in India also shows in its failure to recognise the nature and scope of crises despite strong crisis-mongering by scholars in sociology in India.

Such a rumination as in this chapter is imperative, given that even among sociologists there have been perpetual concerns about the kind of questions and approaches that have dominated sociology at a time in a place. Highlighting the significance of centring civilisation in the purview of sociological knowledge, T.K. Oommen made an exceptional remark worth recalling:

> In fact sociological investigations in the last hundred years or so were primarily addressed to the task of understanding states/nations which are believed to be "societies". Because of this fallacy of misplaced concreteness the very possibility of asking meaningful questions has been aborted.... The manner in which questions are

> formulated in contemporary social science has relegated sociologists to the background.... Authentic sociology ought to be synthetic, not insular or alienative; a synthesis of traditions, life-styles and cultures. (Oommen 1990, 12–13)

Stepping Stone

The discipline spans a wide gamut of thematic areas to map with such certitude that a fluid framework degenerates into rigid righteousness. The prophetic counting of the wide array of themes itself may vouch for a disciplinary broadness that allows a researcher greater leeway to utilise insights from other disciplines in his/her sociological research. But then, this self-congratulatory temper takes a nosedive as we peruse the details. Perhaps, the beauty of the social sciences lies in the fact that disciplines speak to each other with substantial openness, and research in any discipline is bolstered by drawing upon other allied disciplines. Or, at least, that ought to be the case. This is the self-congratulatory mainstay in the survey of sociology conducted by the Indian Council of Social Science Research (ICSSR), published as trend reports on 'Indian Sociology', in which the editor Yogendra Singh, an institution-builder sociologist, noted:

> evidently, the direction of the theoretical choices, selection of substantive themes for research, organization of its funding and support, the orientation determining the content and direction of research, its design and purpose, etc., constitute the context that a trend report should encompass. However, to overcome the issues of complexity and multidimentionality in the scatter of thematic coverage, and for operation reasons, it has become imperative to set some "boundary conditions" while selecting themes. (2014, 7)

The drawing of the 'boundary conditions' was indeed an inevitable necessity in reporting on the trends since there was not much deliberation on the inherent intellectual politics of inclusion and exclusion concealed in the details. It all appeared as a euphemism for the rigidity of the disciplinary boundary of sociology in India. And it is within such boundary conditions that a twofold casualty happened in the trend report. One, it seldom tackled the fundamental question headlong: What makes a sociological way of seeing? And two, there seemed to be an ominous division of intellectual labour following which some sociologists would refer to the methodological orientation while others would do sociological research. In this division of labour, methods and techniques became superior to the larger methodology, somewhat akin to the superiority of Newtonianism over philosophy. However, we will turn to the problematic of reporting on the trend in the latter section. For now, we continue with the preliminary task of setting the stepping stone.

There was an archaic articulation pertaining to the fortification of sociology in the 1950s, exemplified in Pitirim Sorokin's much-talked-about book, *Fads and Foibles in Modern Sociology and Related Sciences* (1953). The book had set an angry and anxious tone against the rise of American sociology that was, allegedly, not leading to scientific–empirical research. But, seemingly for the rest of the world, Sorokin's intolerance for the so-called unscientific themes and analyses in the so-called scientific social sciences was a manifesto for how to remain sociological. Any new areas of enquiry, newly framed questions or methodological adventurism, became an instant suspect in this scheme of reasoning. It is, curiously, hitherto a prevalent trend in India where novelty is simply rebuffed as mere buzzwords, *fads* and *foibles*. Furthermore, areas such as the arts (literature, cinema, folklore, performance, theatre etc.) can also be of particular use to the social scientist and works located within the social sciences can only be enriched by borrowing insights from literary/cinematic works. Every so often, social scientists utilise literature to add depth to their work. To cite one example, Shiv Visvanathan (2003), in a critical engagement with the official discourse on nationalism, highlighted the importance of literary works in interrogating the mainstream idea of the nation. Similarly, works produced in disciplines such as cultural studies, comparative literature, art history, performance studies, etc., are often of considerable sociological significance, and many courses taught as a part of master's programmes in sociology in several universities include papers from other associated disciplines. Consequently, as a student of sociology, one inevitably traverses multiple disciplines, unhindered by rigid disciplinary confines. One of Karl Popper's arguments emphasised that we are students of problems, ones that may cut across disciplinary boundaries. Our sources include works from multiple disciplinary domains, which are relevant to the questions we raise.

However, a researcher's individual attempts to initiate dialogue across disciplines through his/her work are often met with resistance and ridicule during interviews and presentations in universities. Research on topics which do not squarely fall within any of the staple sub-fields of sociology (for instance, sociology of religion, education, caste, etc.) often finds a particularly unreceptive academic environment. One is often asked to justify their presence in a sociology department. It has been perennial, and hence, one can recall the ridicule that came in the way when the likes of Partha Nath Mukherji and T.K. Oommen undertook the study of social movements (in Chapter 1 of this book).

Reflecting upon the straitjacketing of knowledge as disciplines get professionalised, Feyerabend (1988, 7) provocatively elucidated the scholars' training within a specific discipline conditioned in the 'logic' of the discipline, separating one area of study from the other disciplines. A part of this training consists of inhibiting personal interests, emotions and context, which could result in a blurring of disciplinary boundaries; for instance, a person's religion, beliefs, cultural background, and even sense of humour etc., are not supposed to have even the slightest connection with their activities in the domain of knowledge production. Everyone may have it and yet everyone has to hide it for professional legitimacy! Consequently, imagination is restrained to the extent that a researcher's very language, style and question are not their own. Feyerabend's proposition, *anything goes*, necessitated a radical departure from such (social) scientific activities and rigid traditions; and he insisted on embarking on a quest for an education that would foster a humanitarian attitude, encourage individual liberty and not curtail one's imagination. With a normative sacrifice of imagination and eccentricities, eventually, innumerable works within the ambit of sociology must raise questions of 'sociological relevance', in addition to drawing upon theoretical perspectives that are established as key to the discipline. The problematic, the notion of being 'sociological', remains unquestioned. It leads to asking: Does a research work located within the institutional confines of a sociology department have to fall into the established sub-fields and staple areas of research? Often, works of interdisciplinary nature and approach seem to exist precariously, with secondary status, in sociology departments.

In sociology in India over the last few decades, there emerged a few chronicles and analyses dealing with the development of the discipline, the constitution of major areas of study within sociology, intellectual traditions of research, the professionalisation of the discipline, theoretical and methodological perspectives, and intellectual biographies of institutions and scholars.[4] Chroniclers state that

> Indian sociology attained a professional character when the University of Bombay started a post-graduate course in economics and sociology in 1914, the University of Calcutta began to teach sociology to the post-graduate students from 1917, and an undergraduate course in sociology was introduced in Mysore University in 1917.[5]

Amidst the erudite recounting, the basic question is missed: The relationship between the history of sociology in India and contemporary practices where ambiguity about the ways of seeing, essentially being sociological, surfaces. In such accounts, there is also a sign of the pioneers of sociology inclined to multiple sources and thematic areas of research. The ideas from diverse sources amicably entered the otherwise guarded disciplinary borders. And yet these chronicles also show a contemporary picture in which critical engagement with the methodology is nearly drowned in the din about the lack of theorisation in India.[6] Paradoxically, the pioneers paved the way for methodological enquiries in sociology in India that do not find even lip service in contemporary practices. The story is not new; the only difference being that the retelling in this chapter coincides with the central question of the book.

Dawn and Dusk of Sociology in India

It is important to briefly re-narrate the ways in which sociological knowledge came to be established as a discipline during and after colonial rule in India. As a feel-good departure, one can recount its seemingly glorious beginning in a socio-political milieu constituted by colonialism and the indigenous intellectual responses to it.[7] In this recapitulation of an oft-heard narrative, the attempt is to embolden the marks of intellectual openness, if any, in the contributions of predecessors to the field. This is of considerable importance because an obsessive distinction of non-sociological and sociological plagues us even today. The beginning is associated with the political, social and cultural encounters between the colonial rule and indigenous people. The ideology of nationalism provided a significant fillip to sociology and social anthropology in India. Indological studies thrived as British scholars and officials sought to acquire knowledge regarding Indian socio-cultural life. Interpretations of ancient Indian literature by the likes of Max Müller attracted the Western-educated Indian elites to interpret Indian culture, resulting in reformist tendencies, and encouraging studies of the past and present social institutions among native elites. It is yet another consequence of larger significance that some of the homegrown anthropologists began to challenge the stereotypical formulations. For example, Gananath Obeyesekere's incisively alternative readings of several issues, including the popular thesis on cannibalism,[8] and an unrelenting critical engagement with American anthropologist Marshal Sahlin,[9] is a classic case. Sahlin had presented an essentialist idea of Hawaiian natives, generalising an ethnocentric view of the indigenous folks. Criticising it as a narrow Western view of native culture, Obeyesekere tried to show the rational cognitive system and practices of the natives. It resulted in a qualitatively distinguishable development in Obeyeskere's anthropology. Methodologically, Obeyesekere was at liberty to weave various strands in accordance with questions and themes of enquiries. He had read psychoanalysis and Romantic poetry in English, Buddhist texts alongside anthropology and sociology with equal ease. He wove personal experiences and public issues in his explanatory narratives without qualms. Therefore, the pursuit of being sociological, in Obeyesekere's anthropology, offers ways of seeing beyond colonial binaries.

One wonders whether this was manifest in the critical engagement with Louis Dumont that various sociologists and anthropologists undertook in India. In one of the earliest critical debates on the nature of sociology in India, Dumont made propositions that attracted the attention of Indian sociologists who responded to them. The debate and responses appeared in nine volumes, from 1957 to 1966, of the journal *Contributions to Indian Sociology* (co-edited by Dumont and Pocock). Sociologists from India critically engaged with Dumont's proposition, which was allegedly aimed at an essentialist understanding of an unchanging Indian society. Given that the debate was the first-ever formal attempt in the journal to situate sociology in the country squarely within the realm of Indian experiences. Anyone reading the intellectual history of sociology in India seldom fails to note it. The sublime ghost of Dumont haunted sociology in India too deeply to let novel methodological engagement come to the fore. Every reaction, or sophisticated response, to Dumont's formulation, seemed to be reinforcing the 'purity-pollution' based cognitive scheme of the institution of caste in the sociological writings of celebrated sociologists. There might be a few exceptions to cite,[10] notwithstanding, leading to another cognitive logjam, a shift to the axis of left–right in ritual performances. The debate on 'For a sociology of India', however, was about the relationship between Indology and sociology, as though it was a remedial mantra of some self-fulfilling prophets of modern society. The exceptions also did not disrupt the methodological wherewithal; it was a safe debate, as it were, in which departure(s) from Dumont did not trigger a new epistemological–philosophical reasoning with the prevalent ways of seeing in sociology. Hence, the perpetuity of the then-popular theoretical stances—functionalism, structural functionalism and even structuralism—was a common tendency.

After Dumont stopped publishing the *Contributions to Indian Sociology* in 1966, T.N. Madan, with support from an international group of scholars, started a new series of the journal with the same title in 1967. Madan (2011) mentioned in a self-congratulatory note that this new series aimed at the diversity of thematic issues and new approaches to sociology. He went on to edit the new series for twenty-five years. In a rare critique of the new series of *Contributions to Indian Sociology*, Thapan and Lardinois (2006) observed a general lack of broadening of the scope. In implication, it was about the feeble way forward in the way of seeing in sociology in India. Criticism of the earlier version of the journal edited by Dumont was equally interesting. M.N. Srinivas found the Dumont and Pocock-edited volumes filled with insufferable evangelical zeal, while Bailey and A.K. Saran[11] also criticised the propositions provided in the journal. Yet, the sociologists from India persisted with their loyal responses, envisaging an advancement in the way sociologists saw the world. The new series of the journal advanced a way of seeing Indian society, with smartly deployed syntagmatic–paradigmatic analysis following the structuralist anthropology of Levi-Strauss. Yet, the series maintained a prominent place for the analysts' judgement. A structuralist analyst writing about Indian social reality employed the analytical lens borrowed from Levi-Strauss but seldom questioned the judgement inherent in the analysis. No matter how profoundly such judgements are justified, employing anthropological models and charts, one is left hungry for a debate on the existential details of the methodological process the analysts undergo.[12] This gives a reason to wonder whether ways of seeing in sociology can be adequately understood so long as there is an unflinching loyalty to these various theoretical perspectives and conceptual models. Does putting together a few of 'isms', or highlighting the preference for one over another alone fulfils the need to undertake a critical examination of the idea of sociological? There has been an ominous lack of systematic discussion on the ontological terrain in which experience assumes more significance than it does in scientific epistemology. Experience remains a curtailed episteme conducive to a perpetual fogginess about its relationship with the way of seeing. It is only in the last decade that a creative and critical debate between Sundar Sarukkai and Gopal Guru illuminated the epistemological issues in the way we approach the experience of caste.[13] Along with such debates, we see that making sense of the sensory experience of caste in everyday society need not depend on conventional sociological–anthropological sophistication. Instead, an ingenious discursive enquiry could suffice to unravel the ontological complexities.

Coming back to colonial India, the ideology of nationalism was accompanied by increasing awareness regarding religion, sect, caste, region, language, and aspects that influenced the socio-historical climate in which sociological knowledge found a foothold. Administrative exigencies had prompted British officials to collect information about the cultural, religious, economic and social life of the people; and the wealth of data collected through the Census also became valuable for social analysis. In addition, missionaries wrote important works on social institutions in India. Srinivas and Panini (1973) traced the origins of sociological knowledge in India to works such as *Hindu Manners, Customs and Ceremonies* by Abbe Dubois (1906), which was one of the earliest systematic studies on caste relationships. Towards the late nineteenth century, attempts were thus made to place data collected through literature, censuses, surveys, etc., in a comparative and theoretical framework, a development which gave a boost to the growth of sociology and social anthropology. These attempts were largely outside academic institutions, as sociological knowledge was yet to be professionalised into a concrete discipline in India. By the early twentieth century, empirical investigation by the European sociologists' and anthropologists' forays into India, for instance, Rivers' intensive fieldwork in India, contributed to the initial stage of professionalisation of sociology (Singh 2004, 4). It is important to emphasise that during this phase, scholars who contributed to laying the foundations of the discipline in India brought to the table ideas and influences from diverse fields of knowledge, pursuing sociological research in an interdisciplinary vein rather than following a lip service that is by and large a fad today.

Among one of the earliest scholars who sought to initiate studies of social institutions in academic spaces was Brajendranath Seal. He undertook lectures on 'comparative sociology' in Calcutta in 1917, and his interests included statistics, which he saw as an instrument for social analysis (Madan 2011, 28). A.R. Wadia in Mysore introduced lectures in social philosophy and sociology at the University of Mysore. An activist by temperament, he considered sociology to be 'applied philosophy'. In contemporary times, there is a possibility that philosophical interest in sociological research could invite flak for an alleged deviation from the discipline. However, Wadia set an important precedent, which also resonated with other scholars elsewhere. At Lucknow University, for example, scholars such as Radhakamal Mukerjee, D.P. Mukerji and A.K. Saran among others were not averse to deeper engagement with philosophy. Madan (2011) and Thakur (2014), respectively, inform us about the engagement with philosophical notions while endeavouring to rescue the doyens of sociology and social anthropology from disciplinary amnesia. It seems a philosophical impetus that underpinned early sociological thinking in modern India began to fade away or was subsequently marginalised, a concern to which we shall return later in this chapter.

Moreover, a milestone in the professionalisation of sociology in India occurred when the department of sociology and civics was established at the University of Bombay in 1919, to promote the study of social institutions in India, particularly with reference to their impact on the economic and industrial life of the people (Savur 2016, 35).

Patrick Geddes, a sociologist, town planner and ecologist by profession, played a major role in this development. Geddes advocated a scholarly approach, markedly interdisciplinary in orientation. Taking a stand against specialism, Geddes placed emphasis on synthesis (Munshi 2000, 485), clearly suggesting an imperative for sociologists to read from diverse sources and apply myriad insights. In his approach to the study of the interaction between human beings and their natural environment, Geddes borrowed from disciplines as diverse as sociology, botany, biology, geography and town planning.

In fact, Geddes made a case against increasing specialisation in academics, a common trend that plagues social sciences in general today. He held specialised knowledge to be inadequate for arriving at a deep understanding of the ever-increasing complexity of social life. A staunch critic of ways in which universities of the time imparted education, Geddes called for greater unity between disciplines and argued that universities have a limited role in making knowledge from diverse fields popular. Therefore, he supported a 'public sociology' geared to communicate sociological ideas to the people beyond academic spaces, a lesson even the best of Geddes' admirers in India don't seem to follow. His scholarship and holistic approach to sociological knowledge influenced several scholars, including the likes of G.S. Ghurye and Radhakamal Mukerjee, who contributed to the professionalisation of the discipline in India in their own ways.

It was Ghurye's work which lent tone and temper to research in the department of sociology in Bombay.[14] His approach to the study of caste in India, his assertion of a Hindu point of view and 'Hinduisation' of sociology, and his privileging of a Brahmanical perspective have been criticised duly and widely. However, Ghurye's wide-ranging interests point to his predisposition to cross-disciplinary orientation. His entry to sociology was through a reading of the *Manusmriti*, and he wrote extensively on themes such as religion, Rajput architecture, and literature (for instance, Shakespeare and Kalidasa). Furthermore, he encouraged students to take up studies on the fast-changing urban social contexts, on processes of industrial development in India, which created the ground for the introduction of new sub-fields in Indian sociology. Perhaps, this was not in Ghurye's imagination that there would be a subjectively constructed hierarchy of these sub-fields in sociology; that the sociology of caste would not interact with the sociology of performance; and that a course on modern Indian social thought would be deemed secondary in comparison with sociological theories. Irrespective of whether one agrees with the ideas presented in Ghurye's work, alleged to be an armchair scholarship, his engagement with diverse areas within the discipline deserves respect. Besides, he rejected the distinction between sociology and social anthropology, a stance shared as well as rejected by an equal number of professional sociologists.

A brief detour into the debate regarding divisions between sociology and anthropology seems crucial. Many highlighted the futility of this divide, suggesting that the fluid border between sociology and anthropology in India, exemplified by certain universities, signals Indian sociological scholarship's early encounter with interdisciplinarity. There is an irritating flipside—no one has bothered to provide the details of the nature and scope of the much-talked-about, and little-practised, interdisciplinarity. Seemingly, when anthropology was not sociology, sociologists perceived it fairly radical to engage with it. Patel (2016) aggressively warned of the colonial–historical and political conditions under which this disciplinary divide was created and perpetuated. The division between sociology and anthropology was part of the political project of colonialism, which engendered a distinction between studies of two kinds of societies. A study of 'us', or modern Western society, came to be associated with sociology, whereas the study of the 'other', the latter being a politically charged category, was posited as 'anthropology'. This political project historically implied the 'othering' of non-Western cultures, and this approach continues to organise research and teaching well into contemporary India too. One can indulge in conjecture to suggest that, lately, sociology joined hands with anthropology to perpetuate the project of othering that summons another detailed investigation. It works better for both, sociology and anthropology, to maintain the 'other' as an object of study.

Particularly from the late 1960s, anthropologists, in a markedly reflexive tenor, described anthropology as a 'handmaiden of colonialism'.[15] Comparatively, sociology did not have direct links with administrative exigencies or practices of the colonial state, leaving adequate room for diverse conversations between different ideas from multiple sources and different traditions. The initial period of professionalisation of the discipline in India was therefore marked by diversity, unlike scholarly practices in anthropology. As works based on empirical investigation and fieldwork by anthropologists came to dominate the landscape of sociology/anthropology in India, particularly after the increasing influence of the structural–functional method, the distinction between the two, sociology and anthropology, shrank (Srinivas and Panini 1973). However, academic borders stemming from compartmentalisation in Western universities continued to exist, and attempts were made to label disciplines based on the 'methods' of study. The commonly held assumption was that intensive studies of communities, villages, etc., were the domain of anthropologists, whereas quantitative and survey methods to study subjects spread over larger regions belonged to sociologists. One begins to notice the fortification of the disciplinary boundaries along the lines of methods and perspectives.

Unlike such latter professionalisation, Radhakamal Mukerjee staunchly advocated the unity of disciplines and started a combined department of economics and sociology at the University of Lucknow in 1921. He advocated a comparative and multidisciplinary approach to arrive at a fuller understanding of social reality. He saw society and civilisation as a whole that demands a holistic way of seeing, and accordingly advocated an integrated study of economics, political science, social philosophy and sociology. Mukerjee's sociology stemmed from his project to formulate an 'Indian economics' and a 'universal economics' made up of the building blocks of 'regional' economics. He posited the 'region' as a complex of geographical, biological, economic, social and cultural aspects, and hence laid stress on studying ground realities from multidisciplinary, historical and comparative perspectives. Through his work on the role of social institutions such as caste and religious beliefs in the rural economy, He added a socio-cultural dimension to economic analysis and also sought to formulate a sociology of values, which he posited as a fundamental unit in the explanation of social relationships and behaviour. A combination of sociological and psychological perspectives is consequently discernible in some of his work. Crucially, Mukerjee also wrote a number of important essays on the issue of art and its relationship with society, civilisation, religion and polity (see Chapter 1). One of the essays, titled 'The Meaning and Evolution of Art in Society' (1945), was published in the *American Sociological Review* with an unusual editorial note, which read, 'The Editors think that American sociologists will be interested in the contemporary thinking of an eminent Indian sociologist in the eventful year of 1945' (496). It was evident that the world at large was curious about an Indian sociologist's venture into the domain of art though they themselves preferred to keep their positivist hands clean. Mukerjee endeavoured to create a larger premise that could guide sociologists to develop ways of seeing in sociology that were sensitive to plural sources, issues and questions. The above-mentioned instances flag an openness to the diversity of issues through which the pioneers of sociology at Lucknow envisaged doing sociology. Such predisposition to diversity was, however, relatively dimly represented in Dumont and Pocock's editorial venture, 'For a Sociology of India', as well as in the aftermath that brought about the new series of the journal under the editorship of T.N. Madan, incidentally, a former student of Radhakamal Mukerjee. Indian society was primarily viewed through the issues that were the mainstay of the journal. Many themes of enquiry which were central to the sociology at Lucknow became marginal and methodologically unfeasible. For example, the absence of visual art gradually degenerated into an illicit fear of visuals in sociology and anthropology in India.[16] A significant claim of the visual turn many decades later in *Contributions to Indian Sociology*,[17] thus, became mere lip service akin to the methodological debates that seldom paved the way for a reflexive reading of the complexity of experience. Visual sociology as a sub-discipline seems to be much lower in the hierarchical, metaphorical purity–pollution, scheme in sociology in India.

Likewise, D.P. Mukerji (1958), another scholar in the Lucknow triumvirate, envisaged sociology as a discipline with a broad purview that cuts across disciplinary borders. Marked by a Marxeological perspective—an ability to read and apply Marxist insights without ideological indoctrination—his scholarship was a substantial reflection on Indian music, literature and arts. His work on Indian music locates different styles of music within a socio-historical context. Such areas of research interest have been hitherto marginalised within sociology in India. In *Diversities* (1958), explicating the general features of various new Indian literatures, Mukerji discusses ways in which social and economic factors across historical phases have impacted literary production in India. Mukerji's approach to literature is holistic enough to debate literary form, themes and values and the changes therein contingent on socio-political situations. He deliberated on the change in the scope of literature in the aftermath of technological innovations and industrialism. In the same vein, he unravelled the relationship of music with history. His approach suggests that the 'sociological' significance of a work is determined essentially by the nature of analysis and the ensuing debates. The subject matter of any kind of research, whether it engages with literature, music, caste, religion, family or kinship, need not solely determine its sociological worth, or the lack of it. Mukerji's work on music and fiction is as sociological as his other works on Indian tradition, the middle class, caste, religion, social mobility, etc. Affirming the wide range of his academic and personal interests, he, too, acknowledged the expanse of his sociological canvas. Furthermore, he hoped that subsequent generations of sociologists would witness the end of academic specialisations and appreciate the 'unity of all knowing' (Mukerji 1958, 8). Or, perhaps, he pinned too much hope on the philosophically impoverished inheritors, the torchbearers, of sociology in India. He prophesied that like other sciences, sociology has a floor and a ceiling; however, what makes sociology different is the fact that its floor is the ground floor of all kinds of social disciplines, and its ceiling is open to the sky. Mukerji thus seems to suggest that the analytical purview of sociology is necessarily wide and all-encompassing, more so than any other discipline within the social sciences. This is certainly a lesson that appears to have been conveniently forgotten in most of the professional practices of our times as myopias masqueraded as liberating utopias.

While the aforementioned suggests an intellectual openness among sociologists, it also hints at the diversity of the subject matter. Social institutions such as caste constituted the fulcrum of the discipline from the very outset. In addition to Mukerjee and Mukerji, D.N. Majumdar, the third influential scholar at Lucknow University, played an important role. Trained under Ananthakrishna Iyer and S.C. Roy at Calcutta, Majumdar undertook empirical studies of castes and tribes, employing survey research across different parts of India. He argued that sociologists should study social change. He also believed that sociologists' knowledge about social relationships and institutions should enable them to predict and control change, and thereby direct the course of social progress. However, he deemed any logical deduction from a priori assumptions a distant practice for a proper anthropologist. Emphasis on the study of tribes, caste, national integration and the Indian civilisation was also at the centre of works by N.K. Bose, another significant scholar trained in anthropology at Calcutta. Akin to the academic interests of several sociologists of the time Bose also engaged with processes of social change. His association with Mahatma Gandhi is well known. He not only joined Gandhi in the Salt Satyagraha and served in prison but also intellectually engaged with him in his famous book, *My Days with Gandhi* (1953). The book accomplishes one of the earliest instances of psychoanalysis in sociology in India, setting precedence for anthropologists to decipher the enmeshed nature of personality, intellect, culture and politics. Analysing the interviews of Gandhi, in the style of a storyteller, Bose set the parameters for studying individual personalities of socio-political significance. And this all was still cast in the framework of the rapid social change that India was undergoing. Alongside, Bose maintained a distinct position against narrow rulebook-based research, that is, fieldwork. It was instead a broader and nuanced notion of methodology which probably provided one of the earliest answers to the dilemma that imperils sociology in India to date. This was the dilemma pertaining to the distance between the self of the researcher and the object of study, or objectivity and subjectivity. Madan made a commendable observation on the emancipatory and methodologically significant nature of anthropology in the time of N.K. Bose. 'In our day with Bose, social anthropology was presented to us as a part of our own lives, not a study of other cultures. The objective and the subjective were both accommodated in his method' (2011, 246).

Significantly, analysis of social change and development in modern India was an aspect that dominated sociological research during this period. Social sciences in India during the 1950s and 1960s must be viewed in the context of the political situation of the time, when India embarked on planned development with the establishment of the national planning commission. Sociological research often collaborated with the state, furnishing data and insights, aiding the formulation of development programmes. There was an increasing demand for a research institute which would facilitate development strategies. This was the context in which the ICSSR was founded in 1969. However, even as there were demands for sociological research geared towards analysing change and development, research in economics earned priority in terms of allocation of resources and funding. Increasingly, the importance of a scholar came to be gauged by the size of the grant they could obtain. Sociologists began to appear as competitors of economists, not only in attracting grants but also in thematic interests and methodological orientations.

The 1950s saw a range of works engaged with political, economic, cultural and social changes. The sociology of education also made headway and gradually got established as an important sub-field within sociology. The foremost, however, was the studies of village communities that gained prominence during this period. Among others, S.C. Dubey (1958) made a contribution with his work on the village development programme in India, placing it in the wider context of the planning framework. Dubey's study took into account the socio-cultural factors in select villages in Uttar Pradesh, and highlighted the difficulties, successes, expectations and limitations of planned village development programmes. Village studies and community development thereby became established as a significant sub-field within sociological knowledge. While such sub-fields were important, one wonders why no one really bothered about foreseeing the foreclosures inherent in these sub-fields. To reiterate a point raised earlier, one sub-field, ironically, does not seem to interact with another. It is as though one hand in the body of sociology were not related to the other. This is hitherto a dramatic manifestation of sub-disciplinary silos within sociology and anthropology in India.

Sociological studies of village communities also entailed an analysis of politics at the micro level. In sociological studies, regardless of the specific theme, there was interplay of micro-level change and broader processes at the macro level. Curiously, the micro and macro levels were only employed to see processes and changes, and not the idea of sociology itself. No one seemed to consider, on a macro level, the relationship of village studies with the rest of the sociology. Hence, a gradual emergence of a monolithic notion of sociological set in. This was the implication of the attempts to standardise sociological knowledge in the context of a state-led expansion of the higher education system and the university, along with various centres including ICSSR.[18] Moreover, the ICSSR carried out bibliographic surveys of the social sciences, including sociology and social anthropology, with the aim to chart out specialisations in each discipline and accordingly aid research. Therefore, during this period, sociologists made conscious efforts to define and standardise the borders of the knowledge in sociology. On the whole, Indian academics of the time supported the project of higher education and joined in what was known as the project of nation building. The proliferation of works on social change and development can be viewed in this context. Also, attempts to standardise the discipline and define its contours were associated with the agenda of the state to locate the discipline within the borders of the nation state. Sociology and social anthropology in India thereby also sang to the tune of what is famously known as methodological nationalism.[19] Though there were minor whimpers, mostly as reactions to various impacts of nationalism, the larger tribe of sociologists and anthropologists seemed to toe the dominant line. Therefore, the boundaries of a discipline, which had historically been porous, came to be too fixed to allow for critical rethinking on the ways of seeing in sociology. It is important to note that the state and its agenda, factors such as funding, etc., had a significant role to play in defining and freezing the contours of knowledge produced in the discipline. Needless to reiterate, professional sociologists and anthropologists have been accomplices in the institutionalisation of the myopias in the name of standardisation.

However, even during this phase, when sociological knowledge was being moulded according to demands of the state, awareness developed regarding the pitfalls of these disciplinary practices. It is important to not ignore them even though there was a larger support to the status quo. For example, M.N. Srinivas (1973, 1994), supportive of sociology's role in the formulation and implementation of policies regarding development, warned against a situation wherein government funds would be accessible only to the kinds of research that met the demands of the state on various matters. He pointed out that dominant state-oriented disciplinary practices could push to the margins some of the significant alternative practices and perspectives or non-conformist/anti-status quo research; and, that the latter would face funding-related problems. Furthermore, Srinivas also cautioned against a 'double conformism' by sociologists in India; one was conformity to what was prevalent among sociologists in India, and the second was conformity to the practices of the Western counterparts. Obviously, this word of caution about conformity did not receive much attention, until similar concerns were articulated in the critical discussions on Euro-centrism globally. One can easily conjecture the impacts of all this on ways of doing, seeing and being in sociology in India.[20] In this regard, it is worth recalling Patel's (2013, 105) discussion on the link between Orientalism and Euro-centrism. Arguably, the two determined the social science language in modern India. In this language, the binaries of universal (the West) and the particular (the East) were key coordinates. India's particular was in its traditions, an area of study in anthropology within which the themes of religion, caste, and family and kinship were prominent. In the early twentieth century, sociology in India perpetuated the language organised by anthropology and hence the binary of tradition and modernity was pivotal. These binaries played crucial role in nationalist thought, which influenced the sociological ideas of G.S. Ghurye and D.P. Mukerji. The combined project of Euro-centrism and Orientalism, or the interplay of colonial modernity and methodological nationalism in the early sociological formulations in India was predominant and has a perpetuity in sociology and anthropology in India. This critical apprehension, however, cannot deny the emancipatory disposition that was couched in nationalist zeal among the pioneers of the disciplinary practices. The sense of interdisciplinary characteristics and the interest in a wide array of issues, set in the early days, seems to have undergone dramatic decline ever since sociology and anthropology lost their intellectual politics. Hence, one can say that the doctors who diagnosed the problem in sociology, a few of them mentioned above, seldom provoked anyone to find a way out. Curiously, none of the diagnostic analyses really shows or proposes 'another' way of seeing alias being sociological, since they seldom get down to the epistemological–philosophical reasoning. The latter seem to have better resonance in the sociological thinking in the early days of sociology in India. The politically correct diagnosis (mostly in the twenty-first century) thus turns out to be an intellectually incorrect exercise as far as the health of the disciplinary practices is concerned. Also, such arrogant diagnoses hardly turn the lens of examination on the doctors who may be themselves ailing. Be that as it may, most of the critical rethinking on the sociological thoughts of the pioneers of sociology in India seemed to be doubtful of the intellectual credentials of the pioneers. Allegedly, since they were under the pale of colonial modernity, nation state, tradition, they were deemed epistemologically, and methodologically, dubious. Such an approach to the pioneers' legacy may not be suitable for the growth of sociology. The critique of nationalism in the thoughts of the pioneers is, perhaps, myopic enough to ignore the importance of the epistemic appeals available therein. Since those epistemes from their body of work were not thrashed out for the development of concepts and theories, the early childhood of sociology in India was a little too prolonged. Rather than working out concepts and theories and taking them to the empirical grounds, the early childhood of sociology has been merely a turf of heroic contestation among commentators and analysts. Hence, the epistemological legacies available in history did not translate into the muscles and arteries of sociological practices. No wonder that Tom Bottomore deemed the development of sociology in India nothing more than infantile in the decade of 1960s, pointing out a helpless dependence on the theories and concepts, methodology and perspectives, borrowed from the British universities. His complaint was the undergrowth in the nature and character of the discipline, in spite of the milestones laid by the pioneers of sociology in India, that made it 'remote from the major intellectual controversies of the times' (Bottomore 1962, 98).

The reason why it is imperative to take note of the currents and counter-currents and ensuing development of sociology and social anthropology in India, is twofold. One is to suggest the possible openness in engaging with diversity of intellectual resources, undertaking varied exciting themes of enquiries and writing to provoke further intellectual development. There is plenty of evidence of creative intellectual promiscuity in the posterity of the discipline, duly noted in various accounts. However, another strand suggests the advent of certain tendencies of the fortification, standardisation and exclusionary ways of practising sociology. No wonder, the prevalence of methodological nationalism encouraged undue naval-gazing; it was paradoxical since it classified the thematic areas of knowledge production in sociology and also foreclosed the possibility of nuanced critical engagements with local intellectual traditions, which were only for the sake of writing interesting polemics and not for developing theories, concepts and methodological orientations. But then, as the case usually is, there is always the existence of exceptions that threaten the status quo, or so we wishfully think.

Enigma Called Exceptions

While the 1950s and 1960s were largely dominated by works which sought to aid in development policies, in the 1970s, social scientists played a significant role in critiquing development-related policies through empirically informed research (Singh 2004, Savur 2016). Significantly, this was paralleled by an increasing dominance of Marxist and neo-Marxist theoretical perspectives in sociology. A.R. Desai's scholarship had set a new trend in sociological research in Bombay.

Perhaps, Desai can be credited for encouraging a critical perspective during a time when conformism marked disciplinary practices across the country. He reformulated old courses taught at his department in the wake of the critical understanding of society and polity in India. Desai's academic concerns included the development of nationalism in India, rural sociology, development, etc. (Kar 2015, 17). His Marxist perspective provided an alternative view in the sociological landscape of the time.

Nevertheless, research largely remained within the familiar contours of the discipline. The focus was on social structures and institutions, though, gradually, micro processes of everyday life, short-lived current affairs, etc., began to make marks too. An example of new thematic areas was the sociology of social movements. As mentioned earlier in this chapter, Oommen's (1972) work on the Bhoodan-Gramdan movement was greeted with professional scepticism. Studying social movement was not so common during the time. Oommen mentions another factor that made his work unconventional; it was his effort to make a theoretical contribution through an empirical study, when theoretical research and empirical enquiries were largely distinguishable from each other. We know that this is not very different today; young researchers are hardly encouraged to dabble seriously in theories along with their empirical data. This work of Oommen critically engaged with the category of 'charisma', conventionally understood as a system-changing force, and showed it to be a system changing and a system-conserving force. He posited 'social movement' as a concept, engaging specifically with the idea of a 'charismatic movement', a novel concept then unexplored by social scientists. Though Oommen was not inclined to unravel his ways of seeing, the epistemological constituents of methodology, he did indulge in theorising.

Among the more contemporary sociologists, Dipankar Gupta's (1982) work on the Shiv Sena in Bombay presents another instance of an unconventional approach or so was the claim. Gupta's study of the political outfit was historically grounded and empirically informed, drawing upon socio-political, economic and cultural factors associated with the rise of the Shiv Sena movement in Maharashtra. Gupta, however, almost like an anxious student of sociology, made a clarification at the outset of his work that his approach was squarely within the borders of the discipline. And, thus, the claim to be unconventional became suspect. What was unconventional if there was an uncritical adherence to the disciplinary boundary and methodological stratagems? He highlighted the various approaches to studying social movements—the sociological, historical, psychological and sequential—underlining that each approach necessarily drew upon the others. It's no surprise then that the ridicule and scepticism that Oommen received for his research on the ground of being unconventional did not haunt Gupta who seemingly played methodologically safe. There was a strategic avoidance of intellectual risk-taking as far as a critical discussion on the way of seeing in sociology is concerned. In Oommen's and Gupta's larger bodies of works, one seldom comes across any appeal for methodological innovation, pushing the disciplinary boundaries. The standardisation had a sway over the imperative of discussing the fundamentals of the craft. Hence, philosophy was only a passing reference, an ornamental mention, let alone the need to discuss why their respective works could be deemed sociological. After all, philosophically impoverished typology building or politically correct analyses alone could not substitute methodological nuances. They were not oblivious of the complexity of experience, and yet they executed more or less a sociology without delving into the diversity of experience. For example, in the pages of such safe sociology, there was little engagement with gendered aspects of social politics. One wonders whether sociology of caste could be without a reflection on the intersections of caste and gender. Even the attention to caste remained largely epistemological, without dealing with the ontological experiences pertaining to the everyday life. Myopia masquerading as utopia began to show its true colours. It invites polemics, which demands reading these instances provocatively, as done in this chapter. However, one cannot dismiss the fact that there are instances, though few and far between, of possibilities of headway for methodological thinking. Despite the sociological orthodoxy of perspective at work, Srinivas did bring about an element of memory and imagination in his ethnographic account, as mentioned earlier. And likewise, Madan grappled with the complex experience called fieldwork, which led him to understand the relationship between text and ground reality. This is one common thread that binds Srinivas and Madan. Both also showed their respective love for engaging with, and writing, fiction. It showed clearly a reflexive tendency that was available, if one indulged, to sociologists so as to get a sense of what being sociological meant for them.

At this point, it is important to dwell upon ways in which certain contemporary sociologists have responded to quandaries faced by the discipline in India. Ironically, such responses do not deal with questions such as what do disciplinary innovations entail, what does sociological knowledge signify, how does one engage with the peripheries of the discipline? Beteille (2003), emphasising the significance of 'newness' in sociological enquiry, noted that disciplinary innovations do not result from a dramatic breakthrough. 'Newness' is the often unanticipated result of loosely organised collective effort that takes place over a long stretch of time. New areas of sociological research open up when alternative theoretical perspectives, concepts, methods and procedures are articulated. Beteille mentioned village studies as an example of the source for newness in perspective on Indian society and culture. Reading between the lines, it is all truly hilarious. If village studies was also a landmark in standardising sociology, what kind of newness can one expect? How could a standardised sociology yield newness in terms of themes of enquiry and methodology? If it was all about a disciplinary submission to the status quo, what theoretical, conceptual and methodological innovations could one anticipate? Everything that Beteille counted as new seemed to be the vagaries of old, imported from Western sociology. The newness was only in the fact that the conceptual lens was imported. Obviously, many celebrity sociologists of contemporary India did not have the adequate self-critical lens to see things properly before exclaiming congratulatory proclamation, essentially, a newness of perspective. This was almost an outdoing of the propositions for exploring a new sociology for postcolonial societies that the pioneers had delivered.

Moreover, Srinivas' writings resulted in establishing the importance of the field view as opposed to the book view, an intellectual development that initiated a rethinking of ways in which scholars looked at social realities. Needless to say, it was truly a methodological advance. However, one ought to be looking at it with a critical perspective too, since one kind of fetish, pertaining to armchair scholarship based on a book view was replaced by the field view;[21] this was also likely to become another fetish in time to come. Phrases such as field work and participant observation are invoked today as fetishes in order to earn instant disciplinary legitimacy. In the ICSSR trend reports, the switch from the book view to the field view is marked as a milestone. However, this is done without realising the need for a serious critical engagement, asking: What does it really mean in terms of philosophico-epistemological-methodological terms? The question is important since only by shifting the view from one source to another, one does not get to understand the cultural politics of experience entailed in the ways of seeing. The idea of a field view is almost a fad, with other associated phrases in sociological research. One gets to sense that an unfathomable taken-for-grantedness prevailed in the ICSSR report regarding the themes of research and methodology. Hence, there is a somewhat blindfolded celebration of the milestones in the trend report. Everything that was elucidated by the pioneers of sociology in India as crucial factors seems to have become a forgettable relic of past in the trend report.

More importantly, this change took place through small steps taken over a course of time. Sociological knowledge is therefore cumulative, and its growth is not the result of a radical departure from the existing knowledge or an individual scholar's exceptional creativity. Beteille, arguably, diminished the sense of a 'paradigm-shift' in Indian sociology or a radical break from the existing body of sociological knowledge and its replacement with an alternative sociology. Seemingly, sociology becomes what Kuhn had discussed as normal science (in Chapter 5). Ironically, Beteille was unable to understand that overtrained sociologists seldom undertook intellectual risks. For all the ills, he squarely blamed government agencies, community development organisations or, more recently, NGOs; this was without a clear sense that institutions and individuals are equally responsible. He pontificated in favour of intellectual autonomy for practitioners of the discipline, without paying any attention to the fact that intellectuals escape from autonomy for a variety of self- interests.

A more nuanced argument in favour of intellectual autonomy of the discipline was made by Pathak (2003). Demands of the market can pose a threat to the richness of sociology, with the discipline being packaged such that it would meet the requirements of an ever-expanding industry. In a situation in which the order of the market dictates the content of sociological knowledge, originality is lost, and the discipline begins to lose its strength. The originality of sociology lies in the fact that it is fundamentally emancipatory; it encourages perspectives which dissent from the dominant contemporary 'technologised' culture. During times when a consumerist and technology-oriented culture reigns supreme, the discipline of sociology remains one of the few spaces which permits critical thinking and allows one to look at social reality beyond its surface. This space can be kept alive only if it retains the individuality of its content and does not surrender to exigencies of the market that seeks to invariably routinise sociological knowledge. On the other hand, Sharmila Rege (2000) elucidated the crisis in a discipline, as a result of increasing privatisation of education. In such a situation a discipline faces greater guarding of disciplinary boundaries. The academic community consequently retreats behind protective disciplinary barriers in the face of a crisis. Furthermore, during such times, the borderlands or margins of the discipline are particularly neglected. Rege defined borderlands as contested zones located between, for instance, academy and activism, or between disciplinary boundaries. More importantly, academic borderlands, for instance gender studies, are epistemological borderlands, representing the interface between differing claims to knowledge. Rege called for a sustained dialogue between the mainstream discipline and these borderlands. She argued that attempts, including state-sponsored projects, to make the discipline more gender sensitive have relied largely on adding 'women-centred' courses into the curriculum, as though they were add-ons. There has not been a sufficient and substantial reworking of the conceptual syntax of the discipline with a view to making it more receptive to women's experiences. In fact, she argued that fundamental disciplinary assumptions and borders have not been interrogated in sociology in India, and concepts have not been reworked, and perhaps there is little evidence of a feminist standpoint theory emerging from the context of India. There has been less dialogue between the mainstream and the margins, as also across boundaries. Dialogue across boundaries is essential for the gradual and necessary mainstreaming of knowledge located in the margins. This point was exemplified by Rege's (2002) work on popular performative cultural forms in Maharashtra. She integrated insights from cultural studies, gender studies and sociology in India to study the experiences of *lavani* performers in Maharashtra. The study highlighted the ways in which caste-based cultural forms perpetuate hierarchies of caste and gender and entail restrictions on female dancers' sexuality. This demonstrated how cross-disciplinary borrowings would eventually open up fresh areas of enquiry and bring the ignored margins under more serious critical scrutiny. More importantly, such endeavours could generate an opportunity to debate the notions of sociological anew.

Indeed, the previously marginalised sociology of gender is a significant area within Indian sociology today. There is also the addition of Dalit sociology. But one gets wary of the tokenism fulfilled with these add-ons since there is seldom a debate that can lead to possible methodological innovations and departures from the given epistemological roots. If there was adequate interaction between intellectual history, social thoughts and sociological theories, there ought to be a consequential epistemological departure of methodological significance. Once again, this is a question that does not bother the contributors of Singh's trend report (2014). Moreover, works on less conventional topics, such as literature, music, arts, cinema, popular culture, folklore, performance etc., would not have slipped into isolated islands of disciplinary sub-fields, a euphemism for marginalised attention.[22] Nonetheless, considering the persistent hostility towards works which do not fit in, one wonders whether the emphasis placed on interdisciplinarity in seminars and conferences, is mere lip service. One has to admit this onerous fact despite some of the works by individual scholars attempting a meaningful dialogue across disciplinary divides constitute a ray of hope.

Conclusion

There has to be more than just a conclusion here. And in that spirit, one can recall several sociologists in the past who highlighted the predominance of positivist–structural functionalist approaches in studies and writings. Some also complained about Marxism, as a meta-theory, providing answers to each and every question in sociology because the complex social reality cannot be approached by a singular theoretical way of seeing. Even though there was an urge to think of the future of sociology in India, there was still a tendency to maintain a methodological status quo, mixing methods and techniques, and yet taking for granted the way of seeing in sociology.[23]

By the way of showing the lack of interest in a historical approach in sociology in India, Hetukar Jha (2014) presented an account of the predominant positivistic orientation. This is not to say that there were no research and writings with an historical approach. The point here is that there was a general surrender, intellectual as well as epistemological, to a positivist orientation and structural functionalism, and later, even to a structuralist perspective. Any engagement with these theoretical perspectives and, for that matter, even with a post-structuralist perspective, did not dent the safehouse of sociology, nor did it disturb the epistemological bearings of the ways of seeing. This ought to be a generic starting point even in the lament or defence on the lack of theorising in sociology in India, yet another common motif in the sociology of sociology in India (Chaudhuri and Jayachandran 2014). In the midst of this, there could be a prosaic recognition of the qualitative and quantitative research with specific methods including ethnography. But rarely do we see a homegrown debate on the idea of ethnography in sociology in India. The idea of methodology figures in phrases such as methodological fundamentalism, methodological nationalism and so on. However, they never take to the epistemological tropes where one gets bones and flesh, arteries and cells in the body of what is called methodology. For all practical and discursive purposes, the word methodology connotes 'methods and techniques' or types of research. Rarely does it refer to the discursive terrain where orientation is set; we rarely get an idea about how the sociological way of seeing the issues under discussion is crystallised. At best, this is left for a trend report on the sociology of science where engagement with a scientific question graduates into a technology question. One wonders whether this intellectual division of labour is legitimate, given the fact that every knowledge worker has to grapple with the 'way of seeing' qua 'being sociological' with respect to one's research area of interest. And even within the engagement with science, sociology in India has been delimited in orientation. Sujatha and Sengupta noted, 'In India, social theory of science never took the constructionist path. In the late 1970s, it culled out a unique social theory of science as a powerful critique without violating the integrity and validity of scientific facts, as constructionism did' (2014, 140). The lack of constructionist engagement with science in sociology is indeed reflective of the lack of respect for post-positivist ways of seeing. It is not hard to see that sociology has hardly dwelt on the methodological–epistemological possibilities that were there in the civilisational discourse that the pioneers tried to reformulate at the onset of sociology and anthropology in India. This is, however, with an admission of exceptions, though they are few and far between. The deliberations on the nature and scope of science, efforts to engage with non-Western perspectives and revisiting the philosophy of science, did not find much engagement with the sociological researches and writings. These deliberations appear as isolated islands, area of interest, which does not excite mainstream sociologists and anthropologists in India. Hence, it is rare to see a methodological engagement with the discussions related to the science question, relevant in rethinking ways of seeing in sociology. Some of the philosophers and sociologists underlined such an imperative, for example D.P. Chattopadhyay, B.K. Matilal, J.N. Mohanty, J.P.S. Uberoi, Ashis Nandy, Sundar Sarukkai, Gopal Guru, Saseej Hegde, A. Raghuram Raju, Ravindra Ray, Avijit Pathak, to name a few. Such deliberations offer an opportunity to revisit empiricism, a priori versus posteriori, and the complexity of subjectivity and experiences. Instead, it seems that sociologists and anthropologists have waited for their own Newton for long or have become country cousins of the Western clones of Newton.

In addition, throughout this chapter, we saw that a disciplinary past that allowed a significant degree of freedom eventually came to be corseted into key areas and staple topics; with post-Independence planning and development placed demands on sociology as on other disciplines. Trend reports may celebrate some of the advances. However, the need to maintain the autonomy of the discipline from vested political or market-related interests is also flagged. Moreover, it is very important for contemporary scholars to be sensitive to and respect the largely (inter)disciplinary history of sociology and the intellectual biographies of the predecessors. This calls for a hermeneutic attempt to understand them rather than operating with a logic to unmask and debunk. This particular aspect has been nearly absent in the deliberations on the intellectual history of sociology and anthropology in India. Such chronicles of the discipline seldom reflect on a simple question: What is the way of seeing that dominates sociology in India today? They rarely help in understanding any methodological headway, remote or close to post-positivist dispositions. If at all, one tends to get lost in the tokenism of gender studies, Dalit studies and many such concomitant formations, as a sign of 'greater reflexivity' (Singh 2014, 8), as it were.

To conclude, let's return to the insightful lecture by Ray with which this chapter started. It was a conscientious realisation in his lecture that the idea of *darshan* is present in various embodied thoughts, employed in courses in humanities and social sciences. Yet the notion of *darshan* remains a reinvention in the response to Western knowledge. The language, vocabulary and prejudices of Western epistemology are the means through which we hear of *darshan* in India. As a result, any mention of tradition is without an iota of a relationship with the 'language and practices of everyday' (Ray 2019, 8). In this wake, any idea of swaraj is merely vacuous rhetoric, reacting to the painful realisation of Western hegemony to which our ways of seeing have wilfully surrendered. There is an evident aversion of the traditions, spirituality and metaphysics, along with the relationship of roots and routes, among social scientists. Some see only roots, a fossilised version of tradition, while others see only routes, the socio-cultural vacuum entirely governed by exogenous influences. And thus, sociologists and anthropologists in India seem to have already consigned the project of anti-Eurocentric knowledge to convenient oblivion. In such a situation, a truly self-reflexive sociology in India that could allow an engagement with the fundamentals of the ways of seeing is an imperative.

References

Asad, T. *Anthropology and the Colonial Encounters*. London: Ithaca Press, 1973.

Beteille, Andre. 'Newness in Sociological Enquiry.' In *The Practice of Sociology*, edited by Maitrayee Chaudhuri. New Delhi: Orient Longman, 2003.

Bose, N.K. *My Days with Gandhi*. Calcutta: Nishanta, 1953.

Bottomore, Tom. 'Sociology in India', *The British Journal of Sociology* 13, no. 2, (1962): 98–106.

Chaudhuri, Maitrayee. 'Introduction'. In *The Practice of Sociology*, edited by Maitrayee Chaudhuri. New Delhi: Orient Longman, 2003.

Chaudhuri, Maitrayee, and J. Jayachandran. 'Theory and Methods in Indian Sociology'. In *Indian Sociology: Emerging Concepts, Structure and Change, ICSSR Research Surveys and Explorations*, vol. 1, edited by Y. Singh, 87–135. Delhi: ICSSR and Oxford University Press, 2014.

Cohn, Bernard. *Colonialism and Its Forms of Knowledge: The British in India*. Princeton: Princeton University Press, 1996.

Das, Veena, and J.P.S. Uberoi. 'The Elementary Structure of Caste', *Contributions to Indian Sociology* 5 (1971): 33–43.

Das, Veena. (ed.). *The Oxford India Companion to Sociology and Social Anthropology*. New Delhi: Oxford University Press, 2003.

———. *Structure and Cognition: Aspects of Hindu Caste and Ritual*. New Delhi: Oxford University Press, 2012.

Dubey, S.C. *India's Changing Villages*. New York: Cornell University Press, 1958.

Dubois, A.J.A. *Hindu Manners, Customs and Ceremonies*. Oxford: Clarendon Press, 1906.

Feyerabend, Paul. *Against Method*. London: Verso Books, 1988.

Gouldner, Alvin. *The Coming Crisis in Western Sociology*. New York: Basic Books, 1970.

Gupta, Dipankar. *Nativism in a Metropolis: The Shiv Sena in Bombay*. New Delhi: Manohar Publications, 1982.

Guru, Gopal, and Sundar Sarukkai. *The Cracked Mirror: An Indian Debate on Experience and Theory*. New Delhi: Oxford University Press, 2012.

———. *Experience, Caste, and the Everyday Social*. New Delhi: Oxford University Press, 2019.

Jha, H. 'Historical Sociology in India', In *Indian Sociology: Emerging Concepts, Structure and Change, ICSSR Research Surveys and Explorations* vol. 1, edited by Y. Singh, 20–87. New Delhi: ICSSR and Oxford University Press, 2014.

Jose, George. '"Make It Soft and Easy": The Undergraduate Syllabi in Sociology'. In *The Practice of Sociology*, edited by Maitrayee Chaudhuri. New Delhi: Orient Longman, 2003.

Kar, Samit. 'Remembering A.R. Desai: Marxist Approach to Sociology', *Economic and Political Weekly* 50 (2015): 17.

Madan, T.N. *Sociological Traditions: Methods and Perspectives in the Sociology of India*. New Delhi: Sage, 2011.

———. 'Radhakamal Mukerjee and His Contemporaries: Founding Fathers of Sociology in India', *Sociological Bulletin* 60, no. 1 (2011): 18–44.

Mukerji, D.P. *Diversities: Essays in Economics, Sociology and Other Social Problems*. New Delhi: People's Publishing Co., 1958.

Mukherjee, Ramkrishna. 'Indian Sociology: Historical Development & Present Problems', *Sociological Bulletin* 22, no. 1 (1973): 29–58.

Munshi, Indra. 'Patrick Geddes: Sociologist, Environmentalist and Town Planner', *Economic and Political Weekly* 35, no. 6 (2000): 485–491.

Obeyesekere, Gananath. *The Apotheosis of Captain Cook: European Mythmaking in the Pacific*. Princeton: Princeton University Press, 1992.

———. *Cannibal Talk: The Man-Eating Myth and Human Sacrifice in the South Seas*. London: University of California Press, 2005.

Oommen, T.K. *Charisma, Stability and Change: An Analysis of Bhoodan-Gramdan Movement in India*. Faridabad: Thomson Press, 1972.

———. 'Sociology for One World: A Plea for an Authentic Sociology', *Sociological Bulletin* 39, no. ½ (1990): 1–13.

Patel, Sujata. 'Orientalist-Eurocentric Framing of Sociology in India: A Discussion on Three Twentieth-Century Sociologists'. In *Decentering Social Theory (Political Power and Social Theory*, Volume 25), 105–128, edited by Julian Go. Leeds, Yorkshire: Emerald Group Publishing

Limited, 2013. https://www.emeraldinsight.com/doi/abs/10.1108/S0198-8719%282013%290000025010.

Patel, Sujata. 'Introduction: Ruminating on Sociological Traditions in India.' In *Doing Sociology in India: Genealogies, Locations, and Practices,* edited by Sujata Patel. New Delhi: Oxford University Press, 2016.

———. 'M.N. Srinivas and A.R. Desai.' In *Doing Sociology in India: Genealogies, Locations, and Practices,* edited by Sujata Patel. New Delhi: Oxford University Press, 2016.

———. 'Colonial Modernity and Methodological Nationalism: The Structuring of Sociological Traditions of India', *Sociologial Bulletin* 66, no. 2 (2017): 125–144.

Pathak, Avijit. 'Teaching Sociology: Reflections on Method, Truth and Knowledge'. In *The Practice of Sociology,* edited by Maitrayee Chaudhuri. New Delhi: Orient Longman, 2003.

Pathak, Dev Nath. *Living and Dying: Meanings in Maithili Folklore*. Delhi: Primus, 2019.

Perera, Sasanka, and Dev Nath Pathak. *Intersections of Art, Anthropology and Art History: Decoding Visual World*. New York: Palgrave, 2019.

Ramaswamy, S. *Beyond Appearances?: Visual Practices and Ideologies in Modern India* (*Contributions to Indian Sociology Series*). New Delhi: Sage, 2003.

Ray, Rabindra. 'The Teaching of Darshan and Its Purpose', translated by Satish Deshpande', *Contributions to Indian Sociology* 53, 3 (2019): 1–9.

Rege, Sharmila. 'Histories from the Borderlands.' *Seminar* 495 (2000).

———. 'Conceptualising Popular Culture: "Lavani" and "Powada" in Maharashtra', *Economic and Political Weekly* 37, no. 11 (2002): 1038–1047.

Savur, Manorma. 'The Genealogy of the Discipline in Bombay.' In *Doing Sociology in India: Genealogies, Locations, and Practices*, edited by Sujata Patel. New Delhi: Oxford University Press, 2016.

Singh, Yogendra. *Ideology and Theory in Indian Sociology.* New Delhi: Rawat Publications, 2004.

———. (ed.). *Indian Sociology: Emerging Concepts, Structure and Change*, vol. 1, ICSSR Research Surveys and Explorations. New Delhi: ICSSR and Oxford University Press, 2014.

Sorokin, P. *Fads and Foibles in Modern Sociology and Related Sciences*. Chicago: Henry Regnery Co., 1953.

Srinivas, M.N. 'Sociology in India and Its Future', *Sociological Bulletin* 43, no. 1 (1994): 9–19.

Srinivas, M.N., and M.N. Panini. 'The Development of Sociology and Social Anthropology in India', *Sociological Bulletin* 22, no. 2 (1973): 179–215.

Sujatha, V., and A. Sengupta. 'Knowledge, Science and Society', In *Indian Sociology: Emerging Concepts, Structure and Change,* vol. 1, 135–197. ICSSR Research Surveys and Explorations. New Delhi: ICSSR and Oxford University Press, 2014.

Thakur, Manish. *The Quest for Indian Sociology: Radhakamal Mukerjee and Our Times*. Shimla: Indian Institute of Advanced Studies, 2014.

Thapan, Meenakshi, and Roland Lardinois (eds). *Reading Pierre Bourdieu in a Dual Context*. New Delhi: Routledge, 2006.

Uberoi, Patricia, Nandini Sundar, and Satish Deshpande. 'The Problem: Situating Sociology', *Seminar* 495 (2000).

———. *Anthropology in the East: Founders of Indian Sociology and Anthropology.* Kolkata: Seagull Books, 2007.

Visvanathan, Shiv. 'Interrogating the Nation.' *Economic and Political Weekly* 38, no. 23 (2003): 2295–2302.

9

EPILOGUE OR A WISHFUL MONOLOGUE AT THE EPICENTRE

There is a sense of travesty entailed in an exploration of methodological orientation. It does not make sense since it does not offer yet another formula, a tried-and-tested recipe, following which one can clinically produce a work likely to be accepted by seasoned peers. Such a quick evaluative disposition may be applied to what this book seeks to do. The travesty is akin to the situation and consequences in the nature of academic conferences held today, or research committee meetings as part of the annual gala events, such as the All-India Sociological Conference or the World Anthropology Conference. There could be, however, some exceptions; usually, such larger-than-life academic events organised by one or other societies of scholars seldom provide the space and freedom to deliver a sustained debate, let alone an intellectual dispute such as the one covered in Chapter 5 of this book; in such forums, paper presenters pay a good price to get less than five minutes to speak, during which the chair of the meeting keeps interrupting with, 'Come to your finding, just share your finding, don't give us the debates, don't indulge in theoretical–conceptual discussions'. And the paper presenters return home with a piece of paper certifying their participation. Against such a pessimistic backdrop, this Epilogue constitutes a personalised admission of the scenario that dominates our research imagination and practices. And this is all inspired by an exceptionally optimistic silver lining in a bleak cloud that we can get to see if we allow ourselves a much-needed intellectual repose. With some insightful takeaways from this book, we get to the polemics and pathways available in this Epilogue. And we get to see that the prevalent ways of seeing are causing great damage to sociologists, disabling them to fathom contemporary complexity. Even though there are familiar social issues related to caste, ethnicity, tribe, gender and so on that are crucial in sociology, there ought to be a rethinking on the ways of seeing. The methodological way of seeing is not relevant only to the newly emergent themes of enquiries in sociology. As the chapters in this book have amply underlined, there was always a way of seeing which ought to be recognised, and possibly contested, in twenty-first-century sociology. Hence, there is a perpetual need to conduct, an interrogation into the fundamentals that shape what we invariably call sociological.

This is what Guru and Sarrukai (2019) have exceptionally done through their persistent and persuasive debate on the category of experience. And lately, they have come up with even more nuanced details about the perceptions that govern our idea of social. By breaking down the perceptual world of social into discrete sensory experiences, they have paved an even more ontologised approach to the way we see things in social sciences in general and sociology and anthropology in particular. A refreshingly novel way of seeing arises in which smell, touch, taste and sound create a hermeneutic sensorium, a totality of experiences fraught with interpretative possibilities. By reading the synthesis of perspectives that Guru and Sarrukai provide, we feel capable of putting the idea of the way of seeing in sociology in explicit terms. The way of seeing thus encompasses a variety of sensory experiences, challenging the set normative, comfortable approaches of sociologists and anthropologists. It demands more intellectual–methodological agility than what is available in sociological and anthropological ruminations in India. Merely waxing eloquent about either a crisis or self-fulfilling prophesies, or harping on the foggy idea of quality and rigour, standards and ethics don't lead anywhere. For, in such a way of seeing, as in the debate between Guru and Sarukkai, a hinge for the 'sociological' arises; this is a notion of sociological that does not perform the monolithic exclusion of dubious sensory experience for indubitable sensory experiences. It is not a superiority of the epistemological over the ontological or vice versa. It is about knowing with due respect for feeling and emoting and the overall being. Seeing is thus more than a literal act of seeing; it acquires the significance of the *darshan* that Rabindra Ray (2019, 2) discussed; it entails hearing, smelling, touching, tasting and a host of other sensory sense-making, and therefore it is a holistic exercise of seeing.[1] In this scheme, we engage with the here and now, as well as the there and then. The materiality of the situation under analysis and the intellectual history of ideas unfold together. In this way of seeing, an ideal notion of sociological would be informed by both sophisticated theories and historically conditioned social thoughts, the experiences of the world at large and the academic locations as well, an engagement with the self of the researcher, the seeker of the sociological and the objects of the study in an empirical frame of reference. Perhaps, this way of seeing constitutes a common denominator for the idea of sociological, and that takes care of those who utter the word without any clarity. But for such an ideal state to be, there ought to be an admission of what prevails, and how the prevalent scuttles the novel possibilities in methodological enquiry. This is the mainstay of this Epilogue, which turns out to be embedded in the wishful monologue, seemingly an epicentre of this whole book. Simply, it means the following also presents the whole of the book in a very easy-to-crack nutshell.

Polemic on the Prevalent[2]

Amidst the culture of (how to do) writing workshops (how to do) research symposiums, and such equivalents becoming widespread in academic precincts, one wonders whether they will aid in diminishing any crisis in sociology or if they are, in fact, merely part of the crisis. The question makes sense if placed in the larger framework that this book has explored. There was no expert workshop proposed as a solution to what Gouldner (1971) saw as a coming crisis in Western sociology. Instead, this was meant to see the shadow underneath the lamp; the practice adopted by sociologists looked like that of schizophrenic personalities divided by two modes of being. One was that of a professional sociologist who saw things in an extraordinary way. And the other was a social being which was constituted by the ordinary and the banal. Given the divide, sociologists indulged in a kind of practice of research-writing in which their ordinary self was remotely present. It was a typical piece with sound empirical data and detached intellectual analysis. One may not have replicated, but the Parsonian model of sociological being was of utmost significance. The model alludes to the abstract analytical framework of American sociologist Talcott Parsons, identified with the Theory of Structural Functionalism. As one of the most influential theorists of the twentieth century, Parsons' theoretical model affirmed the relevance of positivism for sociology to deliver generalisable principles.

The pervasiveness of the Parsonian model was despite the fact that Mills (1969) had famously ridiculed Parsons' acumen for arcane sociological theorising. The ridicule of Parsons led Mills to the discussion, in the chapters in this book, on 'issue' or 'trouble' of public significance. To reiterate, a personal issue or trouble is essentially related to the public. Hence, there was Mills' invitation to return to 'intellectual craftsmanship'. The latter emphasised that sociologists must take down minute details, hunches and ideas from ordinary domains of experience into a memo, ledger or diary. The issue or trouble ought to be emerging from what one has gathered as part of intellectual craftsmanship. In this light, one returns to the issue, or trouble, of what research-writing means in contemporary sociology in India. One is aware of the advancement from Mills that comes with the idea of public sociology (Burawoy 2008, 5) or the critical departure from Gouldner that made a methodological headway beyond the antinomies of objectivity and subjectivity (Bourdieu and Waquant 1992, 17). Yet it seems pertinent to resort to polemics in order to diagnose and divulge the trouble or issue with sociological research-writings. Polemic requires a move from the personal to the public nature of discussion on an issue. This essay undertakes that despite an anticipated professional hazard in such an exercise. For, it may amount to doing something akin to 'naming and shaming', a popular mode of public politics in the wake of the ubiquity of social media today. There is a deliberate effort not to slip away in that direction because the objective behind the essay is simply to reflect upon what has become, if not 'unbecome', of sociologists. In that light, the Epilogue implies the relevance of the methodological discussion that this book has offered.

There is a lineage to the discussion on crisis and an emphasis on the quality and rigour in sociology in India. Needless to say, there is a sense of crisis-mongering in the discourse on quality and rigour, a red herring of sorts, which did not amount to understanding concrete processes. That discursive trope ended with a sublime call for pluralising sociology in India (Vasavi 2011, 399). Without taking note of the imperative of the polemical understanding of the seemingly unsurpassable practices, it all seemed to have ended only as programmatic slogan shouting. The diagnosis itself looked incomplete since reading the pulse of crisis-ridden sociology only constituted naval-gazing references. The essential idea of sociology of sociology, a takeaway from the chapters in this book, calls for looking around with an eye at processual peculiarities in the sociological practices in contemporary India. In a polemic framework, the essay seeks to modestly attain this by engaging in a specific discussion on the idea of research, in relation to the act of academic writing, subsequently in connection with the notion of sociological. In logical continuity, the essay arrives at the mathematical, precisely utilitarian, value of publication-oriented research writing. It seeks to show what is missing in the larger popular discourse on the problems of academic publishing—that the idea of research, integral to academic writing, is itself a source of public trouble.

The polemic shall commence with a note on the superiority of written text. A profound apprehension began to haunt the Greek pundits since Plato's articulation in favour of the written text. As history informs us,[3] the Greco-Roman philosophy had an apprehension that the oral is too fluid to be retained in the limited human memory. Hence, the written overcame the spoken. Not to say that the spoken disappeared altogether. Scholastics depended heavily on the spoken. The written, however, conquered the spoken and the heard in terms of significance. Writing and reading preceded speaking and hearing in value orientation. Hence they all wrote and since it was still in an elementary stage, when they wrote, they wrote as if they were talking. In a way, it was interesting that they could not sever the relationship between the written and the spoken. The Greko-Roman philosophers wrote in aphorisms, nuggets and verses as if the written texts were coming straight after the way of communication. The spoken had a spectral presence underpinning the written despite the higher regard for the written. In fact, the intertwined nature of written and spoken has acceptance amongst even the ordinary folks of oral tradition, not only the philosophers. Whether it is the ancient past or the contemporary milieu, we are all *homo-narrans*,[4] inclined to narrating; some take to pen and paper while others, a larger mass, stick to speech. Despite the prevalence of the writing culture, philosophers and sociologists also took up the styles and genres that people used in their conversations. Consider, for example, polemics, a genre of writing that yielded maximum critical understanding, and also the possible growth of science.[5] In this book, Chapter 5 presents an example of polemic as a tool for critical understanding.

But this all began to change very soon, followed in the end by the disappearance of the art of polemics in which we show little confidence today. The change has come to the point where, one wonders, if it is related to a Faustian fear of uncertainty, ignorance and intellectual vulnerability. The change leads to a mode of writing that cannot take the risk of ignominy, vulnerability and a creative play with the raw and cooked. Hence, we mostly get served what's been cooked. It is perhaps so desperately cooked writing that it invariably feels overdone, the research universe emaciated, dehumanised and acultural. The human worldview that is otherwise enchanting, degenerates into an intellectually assassinated carcass in such writings. An exaggeration notwithstanding, a polemic on the act of academic writing that distorts the human worldview to make the writing professional and scientific indulges in over-emphasis. Academic writers who dwell upon research for the premise and details as part of the craft of writing seem to nurse and perpetuate a similar Faustian fear. They want to research and write in such a manner that leaves little respect for even an inevitable kind of ignorance. It connotes intolerance to the creative play of raw and cooked in written narration. The clinical, clear and confident writing discloses the irredeemable fear of playfulness in research and writing. There could be another aspect of the evident confidence in writing a clearly communicated piece. It may be said that it is an ideal condition in which lucid thought finds equally lucid articulation in writing. However, that is not the case since lucidity is at the price of the intellectual liberty to take risks; it is clarity due to the avoidance of writing against the grain; it is writing that does not defy the familiar formulas of writing. The clarity of academic writing today suggests, on the contrary, an irrevocable conquest of an industry of 'predatory journals'.[6] In popular academic parlance, predatory journals charge fees from the authors and do not follow the norms related to quality. As a devil's advocate, in the same breath, one should ask a few hard-hitting questions about some of the so-called peer-reviewed journals too. These questions need to be aimed at the facade of peer reviewing and the editorial practice of inclusion and exclusion of authors who submit their papers. Besides, the political economy of the journals is yet another grey area that awaits critical exploration.

Seemingly this is a natural consequence in an evolutionary scheme of thinking.[7] In the evolutionary scheme of progress, it seems the oral shall be totally dominated by the written; and the written shall be published in a journal for fetching marks for occupational benefits, so the printed dominates non-printed or printed by a lesser-known publisher. The process is a reminder of evolutionary biology: the Neanderthal would be replaced by the Homo sapiens, the species of a bygone age would become extinct, and new types will begin a new race with a unique set of skills at work. Ghastly as it may seem, the idea of evolution operationalises the spatial understanding of progress, in which progress and under-progress are explained away through evolutionary logic. The evolutionary scheme of stages of development has appeared in our thinking on the development of societies as much as about the development of humans. And hence, using such evolutionary logic in a sinister sleight of hand, some exorcists tried to separate childhood from adulthood. These exorcists are the sociologists who believe that the twain shall not meet, binaries shall be sharp, and the break shall be absolute. Using similar logic, there are conceptions of success and achievements in sociological practices. If you want to be esteemed for your achievements, you must not be naïve, sentimentalist, playful, reckless, adventurist, risk-taking, or spontaneously wondering children. You must not dwell upon raw stuff, bold thoughts and even confident conjecturing. A successful man or woman must not be like those children who are yet to join the technically rationalised madness called success.[8] If this is the case with humans in general, how could that 'special' human called the writer be immune to it? How could the tribe of self-congratulatory scholars, also called research writers, stay untouched by the generic disease called successful research and writing? On every occasion when we hear a presentation of a research proposal, or academic writing such as a research paper, thesis or dissertation presented to an 'august' gathering of scholars, we wonder whether scholars really allow themselves to wonder any more. Evolutionary logic has definitely determined the practices of research and writing in contemporary sociology.

The new standard of writing no longer holds to the old tenets of a slow and steady process fraught with the humane vulnerability of a research writer. It is fast, furious and ultimately fabulous writing, in Ninja mode![9] Like the sabre rattling of ferocious warriors, the samurai of the best calibre, a writer's fingers stomp away on the computer keyboard. Words gush out confidently, meanings soar ceaselessly, logic sets out to conquer, and formulas are assured to triumph. It may sound like an ideal dream come true. After all, every writer would cherish an uninhibited flow of ideas, words, phrases, propositions, questions, arguments, and so on. There are ready-made structures of all sorts which you can select as a practitioner of Ninja writing, according to your requirements. So, what is wrong with the Ninja mode? Instead of being an ideal scenario, this dream is metamorphosing into a mass hysteria. Since this essay is mostly a polemic on research writing, it ought to start with a glance through the building block, research. In so doing, the remaining of the Epilogue continues to employ barbed wit and sarcasm. At times, it works better to use high-decibel words and strong meanings rather than mincing words at the cost of this straightforward approach. The issue, the trouble with research, solicits this stance for a diagnostic understanding.

Research, the Enigma of Something and Nothing!

What do we do when we research? A somewhat phenomenological process unfolds. One begins to contemplate the most viable, saleable and feasible issue. Innocently, we call it the selection of a topic or an area of research interest. This is the selection of 'something' that is there but one has to labour to show its relative absence. It is 'something' that one has to research on. Hence, it better be something that is acknowledged as such by the peers in the first place. Let's call this 'something', a name. It is a philosopher's 'a priori' that the philosopher receives from 'somewhere', from 'someone' who has already proven his or her competence to inherit the same. And the peers don't operate with 'nothing' either. They have clarity about what is more acceptable, and what works better in worldly calculations. Various agencies ranging from the funders, fellowships and administrative bodies of higher education seem to be in the background of the choice of an issue. Curiously though, this issue would be called, with all due ingenuity, the researcher's issue.[10] However, the challenge is about how to conceal this bluntness. How to show that this issue, this 'something', is yet to be explored and that it is distinguishable from 'nothing', a non-issue. Intellectualism comes to be an aid in making the simpler issues more profound and complex. A problem is called a problem since it is a problem according to the larger standard set by the peers. There is little personal consideration in the acceptance of the issue, thereby defining a problem for the sake of research. Except that the doer, the vaunted seeker of knowledge, knows that it will please the immediate authority, be it the senior peer, the supervisor advisor, research agencies, the university or in the final analysis, the state. And yet, the researcher will be content, wishfully thinking, 'it is my issue'!

Intellectualism of this sort is like that age-old scientism against which many philosophers and historians of sciences unleashed their respective criticisms. This book attempts to put them together. Be it Popper, the sociologists from the Frankfurt School, or the others such as Kuhn, Feyerabend, Lakatos, they all seemed to have deciphered the problem of scientism. Hardly did they anticipate that there will be a similar anomaly to guide the researchers who would employ concepts, theories, language, jargons and technical terms merely to conceal the vulgarity of the choice. There was nothing against science, as Popper informed us. It was only science's belief in its own supremacy, scientism, that was the bone of contention. Likewise, there is nothing against intellect or intellectual activities. It is intellect's belief in its own supremacy that is the bone of contention here. And in the same vein, it is not against sociologists and anthropologists; it's a problem with their inflated egos and overconfidence in the merit of their work. Researchers intellectualise not because that helps in adding nuance to the issue, topic, questions and assumptions. They do so since they are keen to conceal that the choice that they float as their own is actually not. It is someone's else 'something'. This issue is 'something' since it belongs to the 'to-do' list of a senior peer. It protects the younger scholars from the vulnerability of their own questions, choice and issues. The youth is made to self-doubt so as not to independently think aloud. Who would risk intellectual credibility by pursuing a vulnerable path particularly when the 'somethings' around are sure and certain? Who can play with 'nothing', non-issues, which may be actually a starting point to frame an issue anew? And despite the genealogy of something, we would judge a student for originality, innovativeness, and so on. If any of these are truly to be judged, the researcher should be playing with nothing, the seeming non-issues from where the missing threads could be ferreted out.

Within this 'something', then, unfolds a good drama. It is supposedly a proposed 'something', in a research proposal. An a priori that is being proposed as a possible posteriori. It means research is merely to empirically prove a selected theory, concept, hypothesis, assumption, right or, rarely but in some cases, wrong. Every research proposal seems to wax eloquent about its familiarity with something a priori. Then it eventually says that this a priori is going to be posteriori too. And to say this, the research proposal employs theatrics—framing of questions, hypothesis, clarity of constants and variables, and some kind of exclusive section called 'literature review'. The real world of the people to whom the questions pertain would be marginal. The socio-political context, let alone historical trajectory, would be seldom to shed light on the research universe. Some would do it smartly and some other shabbily. The point is that there is unanimity about this basic formula. The aim invariably is to prove the given a right; prove the a priori as a posteriori; prove the god a god; prove the devil a devil. Popper had elsewhere ridiculed this practice of sociologists. So much of sociological energy is spent in stating the obvious that we are trying to preach to the converts, trying to convince with an arsenal of data those who are almost convinced, more often than not, of course always with exceptions. In a lot of research proposals, this is what we get to see. The proposed work is yet another attempt to prove the might right, as it were. By proving the right, right, you do nothing more than proving the might right. You are, in simpler words, serving the status quo, be it a university, a funding agency, private client, collaborative partners or, in the ultimate analysis, the state. This is, however, a practical thing, as many defenders of formula-based research writing would say. That this is too subjective a complaint, and hence a non-issue. So let's look at it from a distance, or get a little too closer to it. And either way, we stay unsure of the observation.

Whenever this formula is applied, intellectual miscarriage demands attention. We suddenly see that the best pursuit of this formula provides such self-confidence in the seeker of the knowledge, the researcher, that there is no space left to admit vulnerability as innate to the basic idea of research. No vulnerability, no seeking and obviously no step forward from the cold cave of the chained Platonic men who knew no retina-shattering light of truth as long as they were complacent in the shadows. When cavemen first faced the sunlight, they instantly felt the discomfort of stepping out of their comfort zone. You can't sense that you know something unless you have known the ignorance of something. Playing with this Socratic idea, Popper (1963) came up with an insight, to reiterate a point discussed in Chapter 5; ignorance, and the acknowledgement of it, is the vital strength of knowledge. The sense of absence makes it possible to feel its conspicuousness. Popper's interest was to show critical rationalism-based humanism in discussing the idea of ignorance. No ignorance also means no chance to wonder at even the most grotesque, let alone the ordinary mundane world where absence and ignorance, inequality and vulnerability, inclusion and exclusion, revolt and reconciliation are all the norm. Such a recognition of the interplay of knowledge and ignorance, and the intellectual benefits of the same, is scarcely evident in the realm of sociological practices. The notion of success, perfection, feasibility, framing and eventually, the smartness of presentation and articulation dominated the scheme of being sociological. There is no room for goofing up, everything is determined at the very moment you utter the word research. This is the dreadful clarity that characterises the clinically curated show called research. Some may score higher in the performance of this spectacle, some lower; some may not have arrived there yet and someone else might have become an accomplished metropolitan master of the trade. They all hate uncertainty, doubt, vulnerability and intellectual risk. And can there ever be research without risk? All our effort in the research proposal, and through the process of research, is to annihilate any possible risk. No risk in the selection of topic, aka area of research, no risk in the way the questions are framed; no risk in the expected hypothetical assumptions. And hence, we, along with our students, accomplish the intellectual murder of research imagination. Mills cried himself hoarse decrying the grand narratives of the Parsonian kind, advocating for a return to something as basic as 'intellectual craftsmanship' (1959). The latter is not a rocket science. It just requires us to step down from weakly constructed ivory towers. Intellectual craftsmanship calls upon us to be playful and take into account every minute detail of what goes in the shaping up of our research plan. There is a basic framework that a craftsman can follow. Then s/he wanders, exploring a new curve, chiselling a new angle, constructing a new stance, construing a new notion. It entails a lot of cumulative documentation—a memo, a personal ledger, a diary wherein we can willingly note everything from the consequential to the inconsequential. Craftsmanship of this kind demands that we meditate upon the mundane. And see how everything, seemingly nothing, can become something. It enables us to translate an unrelated episteme into a related one. It transforms a fragment into a piece of the whole. Could this happen in formula-based research, which starts with certainty and ending with certainty? There is seldom an intellectual headway in proving the a priori, a posteriori. And, thus, in this process, research seems to be all about finding 'the finding'. There is no utopia stemming from it; no vision on offer nor any sharp logical argument which can make the seeker of the truth troubled, no dispute as a result of this research. This research is as apolitical as an extraordinary prime minister eating an ordinary mango, so to speak.

And Everyone Still Asks, What Is Sociological about It!

Every formulaic research proposal presents the whole idea about the fundamental what, why, where, how etc. Charting a very certain path, it arrives at uncertainty, or pretends to. The proposals end with a paragraph of ethics and validity, both evoking instant vulnerability of the whole draft proposal. Could ethics be something so rock solid as to be immune to temporal–spatial influences in the field? If we can't expect our politicians to be free from corruption, how could we ever be so sure of the ethics of sociologists to be so perfect? This is truly an untenable proposition since we know that we have not been able to find an answer to the probing question of who will guard the guardian. None of the proposal writing workshops held at universities ever venture in these troubled waters. But it is difficult to ignore insightful philosophers who framed this question for us.[11] We are asking the most cunning professionals, sociologists, to formulate for all of us the Bible of ethics in a paragraph, long or short, in a research proposal. It only vindicates that we have killed the basic minimum research imagination of the, ironically, most coveted place—the field. If we had used it, nourishing it with our minds and emotions, we would have known what a volatile world it alludes to. A world that is beyond the control of the most divine, glamorous, know-it-all species of sociologists operates with tentativeness, ad-hocism, uncertainty, the mythology of past and present and socio-cultural politics.[12]

A cartoon[13] on social media shows a tribal community living in huts, watching TV, drinking soft drinks and enjoying all privileges you don't imagine available to the tribe. And then the news about the arrival of anthropologists breaks out. All members of the tribe get alerted. They look out of the window of the huts to verify and sure enough, they spot grim-looking characters heading towards them. This leads to a frantic hustle and bustle within the huts as everyone from the tribal neighbourhood starts hiding the commodities, the privileges, the insignia of transformation, if any. They know how they should look to the visiting anthropologists, what to say to them, and when to welcome them and when not. This is more than a technical phenomenon called the Hawthorne Effect[14] in research discourses. Since, unlike Hawthorne, this suggests a far greater divide between the field and the researcher. This is about the epistemological positions of the two worlds—that of the field and the researcher. From each position, one knows how to pretend, persuade and perform according to the wishes of the other. Both the researcher and the researched oblige each other, answering questions in expected ways, behaving the way a sociologist would like them to behave. The cunningness of the field and the field workers immaculately reciprocate each other.

Someone would say it is just a dubious cartoon with a spurious meaning. Why would anyone take it so seriously and go to the extent of reading between the lines? But this is how the world is, and we are not too removed from this world. We are as happy about consuming the latest goods as anyone else. Let's turn to Husserl via Schutz (1970), who tries to unravel a life world for us. A province where meanings are engendered by all of us, educated or otherwise—the extraordinary schizophrenic sociologist or the ordinary bulldozer driver of Rampura who practised black magic at home.[15] It begins to change when some of us, from this life world, shift to another province of meaning where scientists, theorists, and if you labour efficiently, you can even include sociologists, act and constitute meanings. The phenomenological understanding would be that these special folks called sociologists are only partially involved in this job of the scientific meaning-making process for their substantial half is left behind in the act of translation, from the ordinary folk of the life world into extraordinary folk of the science. Following this translation, you are only a part of yourself when you are in this or that province of meaning. You only operate with certainty, intellect and risk-free tools and techniques, questions and ideas, plan and execution. This, however, may not be the case in the ordinary phenomenologically woven life world. Your research is to find the finding whereas in the ordinary world, the accomplishment of meaning is as much a product as it is a process. Then, how can you be so sure of ethics and validity, particularly when you are dealing in a world fraught with some certainty and some uncertainty? That is, how can you impose your idea of certainty onto the life world of the people who operate with uncertainty though they have their own notion of certainty too. How could you say so conclusively that the man out there is a demon or a god? In the same breath, how could one be so sure that, as a sociologist, one is infallible?

The cap to this, for those who pretend to be all too perfect and hence surely on the path of certainty, is the idea of 'sociological', the central question underpinning this whole book. They all think that they, as formal sociologists, know something called sociological. Do they know for sure the meaning of this intrigue? Methodologically speaking, and not necessarily pertaining to methods and techniques, there are many varieties of the ways of being sociological. We may all parrot the textbook notion. Most of classical sociology is positivist. But would we refuse to see that each theoretical perspective inherently has a different sense of positivism to offer? There is the Comtean way to be positivist which itself, in large part, is a plagiarised version of Saint-Simon's ruminations. Then there is a more robust Durkheimian one, duly supported by systematic practice with elaborate procedure. Indeed, Durkheimian positivism formulated the first ever set of rules for doing sociology and being sociological. And then there are many other varieties including Marxian, geared towards a more nuanced transformative politics surmised in the *Thesis Eleven*. And there is sufficient evidence that Weber's interpretive turn maintains the positivist tendency to fight against the phantoms of the mind. The trinity in the classical sociology shows enough tendency to perpetuate the fear of phantoms, the Baconian idols of the mind. Within positivism itself, one can safely summarise, there are many ways of seeing and hence many ways to be sociological, as discussed in chapters 3 and 4 in this book. This gets better as we hear the exciting orchestra of the positivist dispute in German sociology. Not only scientism gets disputed, so does positivism, and what to say of sociology. A veritable post-positivist turn haunts sociology, scary ideas from the realm of the postmodern gape at them, and we begin to hear the complaint that sociology has, at once, been de-philosophised and de-historicised. And then there is a return to history and philosophy after the Dispute smashes open very many new ways of seeing in sociology. Then, what version of sociological they hurl, when they ask this ultimate, most frequently heard question: What is sociological in a work? It is more than obvious that the idea of sociological is basically a way to guard the territory called sociology, akin to the military of a nation state guarding the whole province with a unique version of curfew in which all the means of communication gets suspended. Much of it dominated the discussion in Chapter 4 in this book.

A sinister scheme unfolds at spurious sites of sociological presentations. Looks like Kuhn's (1962) community of scientists, or our epistemic community or what we also call a department, a centre or a faculty of sociology, are all same in behavioural tendencies at such sites. Each from the herd of senior peers would say a few similar things as their respective comments. Each would mean something else, again as per their respective orientation, pride and prejudices. For example, a senior sociologist might say, 'Why are you looking at the night-hunting process in Bhutan?' Look instead at the gender relations. The student would whimper, 'Madam, night-hunting includes gender relations'. But the commenting sociologist would pay no attention to that. They would go on and on, almost like someone trapped in a tunnel where one heard only one's own voice. In another instance, someone would say, 'Why are you looking at only three films for your analysis? Make it ten.' And someone else will add, 'Why are you so sure about any number of films? Don't mention any number.' Yet another person from the herd of senior peers would conclude, 'You seem to be too confused about your proposed research. You have no clarity about the number of interviewees.' Someone seeks for clarity, while some others demand a suspension of clarity. A student tries to argue, 'I can't have such clarity at the onset of the research since I don't know as to how my field in Bangladesh will unfold and hence I operate with some clarity while I know I cannot anticipate everything in advance.' But this will fall in the deaf ears. The senior peers would instantly declare such research proposals invalid, implausible, infeasible, undoable, and so on. The herd of peers would frown away, saying, 'Should you not have some idea since you come from that place?' The saga entails more fascinating details. Some faculty members would suggest that engagement with theories is essential in a research plan, and some others, particularly those trained in Western universities, would emphasise that all these are dead theories and encourage engagement with contemporary theories and concepts. A good amount of cluelessness characterises the community of senior peers, and it is no wonder that most of the young scholars mostly learn strategies to steer clear of them. Young scholars seldom dispute anything coming from commenting peers. They mostly say, 'I will revise in the light of your very "valuable" comments.' Perhaps, it is a thing of the past when, young or old, scholars disputed each other since they were so steeped in their works and so confident about what they had reasoned with that they could retort, 'Professor! I don't think you have got what my research plan is!'

In such instances, one message is clear. The herd of senior peers seems to have never discussed what research could primarily mean. Perhaps, as they would say, it is not within their 'interest area.' One such instance narrated by an academic friend on the condition of anonymity is worth paying attention to. A sociologist trained in urbanity and awarded a doctorate at one of the top international universities got a teaching job in one of the universities in India. Fresh to the teaching profession, the faculty member was to teach a course on sociological theories. They refused to do so, saying, 'theories is not my interest area.' Ironically though, on the occasions when students present their research proposals, the same faculty member passes comments about the theoretical significance of a proposed research. The faculty member has developed the habit of judging all research proposals from the vantage point of his/her own 'area of interest', 'expertise.' In other instances, some faculty members have been heard saying that theoretical engagement is a waste of time. It has been somewhat accepted that theory building can't be done by sociologists in the southern hemisphere. Research supervisors and faculty members have to sound superior with a variety of articulations. This all appears necessary for the reaffirmation of the power dynamic between the research supervisor and the research scholar. And yet, there would be no consequences. There would be an evident missing link between the supervisor or research advisor and the students. The interactive collaboration between teacher and student is crucial in a young scholar's research. That collaboration has probably disappeared altogether. And hence, the teachers have resigned to the idea of a workshop which, presumably, will remedy all the problems with a student's skills. One never gets to hear whether writing research plan, executing and subsequently writing the draft manuscript is all about acquisition of some technical skills or if there is something more to it.

It is in such a curious condition that various kinds of research is planned and executed these days. We witness it every day in academic spheres, so we hardly ought to be surprised about the mathematics and the aftermath of the publication of research writing. Lately, most of the articulations about the problem of academic publication have been with regard to spurious journals or the merchandise of publishing companies located in some part of Delhi or in Europe. These journals and publishing companies send email invitations to almost everyone in academia for easy and guaranteed publication. Many youngsters fall prey to them. The issue is indeed far graver, hence, the need to continue this polemic.

Research Writing, the Mathematics and the Aftermath

There is more to the experientially substantiated polemic above. The prevalent practice of research does not kill the thing called exception. But then, who cares about the exceptions in a society of spectacle[16] where exceptions, too, are invariably transformed into some kind of spectacle. The activist-academics tend to become 'indignant entrepreneurs'. There is a vivid tendency to conjure a frightful future and show with conclusiveness that your finding is the best finding; this, too, is an offshoot of the whole phenomenological process of research discussed above. You have a utopia, perhaps long forgotten, to be guiding your crisis mongering called research. If this is one kind of mathematics geared to accrue right brownie points for you to emerge as the representative of a select mass, there are other equally interesting variety of mathematics. Continuing with the cunning calculation of the research process is the mathematics entailed in research-writing. This is writing that would not leave any sign of the creative intellectual mess which one may have encountered and recorded in diary or elsewhere—if one was honest about the encountered accounts. Research with in-built uncertainty would not get a plan and simple finding. It would lead to a discursive terrain, fraught with challenges and full of possibilities. On this terrain, a researcher would take bold guess, try out hunches, logically develop arguments, provoke debates and posit new pathways for future research and a transformation of the world, including oneself. But research which was about 'something' against 'nothing', certainty against vulnerability, finding against discourse, would seldom deliver anything more than data. Method begets method and such kinds of research beget findings and data. Following the scheme of an empirical 'shudra', inferior to theoretical 'brahmins',[17] it seems most of the research writings become a testimonial of the flaws of research intentions. Since there is no element of vision, utopia or alternative ideas involved in the prevalent paradigm of research, we don't get them in return. We did not invest anything other than what we got. We invested 'something', we got 'something'; this almost vindicates the theory of 'no risk no gain'. There is little room in there to accommodate anything counter-inductive, as it were. Then again, paradoxically, we ask our students, what is original in this research, what is new about this finding, and how is this more refreshing than others? We did not throw the baby in the pool and still we are asking them to learn how to swim. To learn to swim, the aspiring swimmer has to be pushed into the pool. We failed as research advisors and we are offering research students various palliatives such as research writing workshops and author workshops. We are roping in the professionals from publishing companies to teach our young scholars and academics about the basics of academic writings. One wonders whether some of our best teachers wrote so badly without doing any such workshops.

Getting back to the trouble, such clinical research writings are for various stakeholders. Publishers, funders, bodies and agencies that regulate universities, the market and, of course, the state. The most formulaic research yields the most formulaic research writing that gets space in the formulaic journals. There is a new breed of formulaic journals, which we earlier referred to as predatory journals. But then, the so-called non- predatory journal need not be devoid of their own formulas. The doubly blind peer- reviewed journals are no less. They say the proof of their quality and standard is the rejection rate. The more they reject, the higher their quality and standard. This is something we learnt from an unusual work of Robert Merton (1971) in sociology of science on the structure of refereed journals. Or did we? Perhaps we need to ask this question to the editors of the various journals. Any discussion on academic publishing tends to celebrate the idea of quality and standards and laments any mediocrity. Who can contest this? But the point is that in the euphoria of the celebration and unity in the lament, we mostly forget that quality and standards could be a logical correlation to the formula-based research writing. Some academics are very good at following the formulas while others aren't. Who can ask for the kind of arguments, quality of debate, and the merit of hunches and bold guesses that underpins research writing? Everyone in professional academics is more than willing to get measured by the measuring tape and scales, which are determined elsewhere. At times, we hear that the marketing team of reputed publishers determine the title as well as some part of the content of a book. Copy editors suggest what should be added and deleted from various parts of the manuscripts. And if you don't abide by the suggestions, you are in for an irresolvable limbo. Even though the blind-anonymous reviewers of your work, commissioned by the publishers, have recommended the publication of your manuscript, the publisher may decide to quietly sit on it for the simple reason that the author does not look like an abiding type, or the author does not have explicit loyalty to the eminent peers in professional academics. The way risk was avoided at the onset of the research, it shall be done in the aftermath when one is preparing the manuscript. No bold play of ideas is allowed, nor is there the liberty to say that this work is never a finished one. It is so rare to read a work which could critically unearth the fakeness underlying sociological research in our time. And hence, there need not be any anxiety about the sociological status of a work. We adequately train our young scholars in intellectual timidity and submissiveness; we keep reminding them through the phenomenological process of research discussed above that they should not walk the unsafe terrain; our whole stress during their research writing is to weed out any sign of intellectual ambition, adventurism and risk-taking. A common comment on most of their manuscript we generously give, as do the anonymous referees of journals and publishing companies, is to 'tone down'. The supervisors, or interchangeably research advisors, become academic editors during the process of research itself. This is unfortunately an academic editor, rather than the ideal imagination of a research advisor who could be an interactive collaborator, in a research work and research writing in the aftermath. Academic editors ensure that the mathematics of what is acceptable and unacceptable, right and wrong, good and bad, publishable and unpublishable is at the forefront in the whole process. They don't enable a researcher to cope and deal with the inevitable vulnerability of the seeker of knowledge. Nor do they orient academic writers to contest a reviewer's mistaken judgement, if any. Instead, they ensure that any sign of acknowledgement of the vulnerability is removed from the beginning of the research to the publication. If at all, there will be fashionable articulation of the difficulties one faced in doing research. There would be hardly any relationship between the difficulties faced and the arguments developed. For, the arguments, if any, would be too conclusive to be in tune with the vulnerability. In order to hide such vulnerability of the researcher, and the volatility of the field, they would add more titles in the literature review, a few more names dropped, the bibliography growing humongous. From the first sentence to the last sentence of the monograph, what we read is some or other citation. It is a series of references that make an 'academic referenced' work respectable. Seemingly, ironies such as this characterise 'academic referenced' work.

Thus, in Lieu of a Conclusion

The idea of sociological solicits a thorough critical engagement with various methodological strands from the history of social sciences. This book has eclectically curated such a trope, which may enable furthering the quest, since ways seeing are ever multiplying in this age of an intricately mediated social world. When post-truth, Anthropocene, artificial intelligence and such epochal issues are prevalent, there can be only many beginnings of various debates on methodology.

One could only think of a polemic doing service to the recognition of what we have become and where we are headed. In the backdrop of the pithy picture of the sociologists in this Epilogue, one can recall Bertrand Russell's ridicule about the problem of writing in sociology. He said that sociologists might write like the following:

> Human beings are completely exempt from undesirable behaviour-patterns only when certain prerequisites, not satisfied except in a small percentage of actual cases, have, through some fortuitous concourse of favourable circumstances, whether congenital or environmental, chanced to combine in producing an individual in whom many factors deviate from the norm in a socially advantageous manner. (Russell 2009, 35)

This whole humbug can be simply put, without a care for political correctness, as Russell does in the following:

> All men are scoundrels, or at any rate almost all. The men who are not must have had unusual luck, both in their birth and in their upbringing. (35)

The philosopher's dig is indeed to be dug deeper, and then perhaps one goes backwards in this essay to fathom the reasons why the dig makes sense. One also ought to be going backwards to the previous chapters in this book to discern the relevance of the methodological discourse. This is what the essay has tried to do, though with careful avoidance of the names of individuals and institutions; they have been named in the previous chapters in this book aplenty. At times, through acrimonious polemic laced with instance-based reasoning, the essay has dared to call a scoundrel a scoundrel. And at times it lets loose the rawness of energy, emotion and intellect in recounting the experience of the issue, trouble, problem. Since no experience is a total exhaustion of the possible reality, neither is this essay, and nor is this whole book.

References

Adorno, T., G. Adey, and D. Frisby. *The Positivist Dispute in German Sociology*. London: Heinemann, 1976.

Basu, Kanti, and Anjan Ghosh. 'In Defense of Serious Polemics', *Social Scientist* 10, no. 10 (1982): 56–63.

Bourdieu, P., and L. Wacquant. *An Invitation to Reflexive Sociology*. Chicago: University of Chicago Press, 1992.

Burawoy, Michael. 'Open Letter to C. Wright Mills', *Antipode* 40, no. 3 (2008): 365–75. http://burawoy.berkeley.edu/PS/Open%20Letter%20to%20Mills.pdf.

Connors, Robert J. 'Greek Rhetoric and the Transition from Orality', *Philosophy & Rhetoric* 19, no. 1 (1986): 38–65.

Das, Veena. 'Sociological Research in India—The State of Crisis', *Economic and Political Weekly* 28, no. 23 (1993): 1159–1161.

Debord, G. *The Society of Spectacles*. Paris: Editions Buchet-Chastel, 1967. https://www.marxists.org/reference/archive/debord/society.htm.

Deshpande, Satish. 'Crisis in Sociology: A Tired Discipline', *Economic and Political Weekly* 29, no. 10 (1994): 575–576.

Gouldner, Alvin. *The Coming Crisis in Western Sociology*. London and Delhi: Heinemann, 1971.

Guru, G. 'How Egalitarian Are the Social Sciences in India?', *Economic and Political Weekly* 37, no. 50 (2002): 5003–5009. https://www.epw.in/journal/2002/50/perspectives/how-egalitarian-are-social-sciences-india.html.

Guru, Gopal, and Sundar Sarukkai. *Experience, Caste, and the Everyday Social*. New Delhi: Oxford University Press, 2019.

Huxley, J. 'Natural Selection and Evolutionary Progress', *Nature* 138 (1936): 603–605.

Jha, Hetukar. 'Indian Sociology in Crisis: The Need for Regional Orientation', *Sociological Bulletin* 54, no. 3 (2005): 396–411.

Kuhn, T. *The Structure of Scientific Revolutions*. Chicago: The University of Chicago Press, 1962.

Mills, Wright C. *The Sociological Imagination*. New York: Oxford University Press, 1959.

Nietzsche, F. *Beyond Good and Evil*. London: Penguin, 1973.

Niles, John D. *Homo Narrans: The Poetics and Anthropology of Oral Literature*. Philadelphia: University of Pennsylvania Press, 1999.

Pathak, Dev Nath. 'In Pursuit of Spectacle of Success: Implications of the Dominant Rationality in the Domain of Education', *History and Sociology of South Asia* 9, no. 2 (2015): 126–145.

Pathak, Dev Nath. *Living and Dying: Meanings in Maithili Folklore*. Delhi: Primus, 2019.

———. 'Idea of Research-Writing in Sociology: Polemics on the Loss of a Transformative Practice', *Sociological Bulletin* 70, no. 2 (2021): 147–163. https://doi.org/10.1177/0038022920970303.

Pathak, D.N., R.K. Roy, B. Das, et al. *Seeing South Asia: Visuals Beyond Borders*. London and New Delhi: Routledge, 2022.

Popper, Karl. *Conjectures and Refutations: The Growth of Scientific Knowledge*. London: Routledge, 1963.

Ray, Rabindra. 'The Teaching of Darshan and Its Purpose' (trans. by Satish Deshpande), *Contributions to Indian Sociology* 53, no. 3 (2019): 1–9.

Russell, Bertrand. *The Basic Writings of Bertrand Russell*, edited by Robert E. Egner and Lester E. Denonn. London and New York: Routledge, 2009.

Srinivas, M.N. *Social Change in Modern India*. Berkley and Los Angeles: University of California Press, 1966.

Vasavi, A.R. 'Pluralising the Sociology of India', *Contributions to Indian Sociology* 45, no. 3 (2011): 399–426.

Wagner, Helmut R. *Alfred Schutz: On Phenomenology and Social Relations: Selected Writings*. Chicago: Chicago University Press, 1970.

Zukerman, H., and R. Merton. 'Patterns of Evaluation in Science: Institutionalization, Structure and the Functions of the Referee System', *Minerva* 9 (1971): 66–100.

NOTES

Prologue: A Provocation for Pluralism in the Way of Seeing in Sociology

1 Though ten to fourteen are often named as the main Upanishads, there is also mention of 108 to 200 Upanishads. The main ones are *Isha, Kena, Katha, Prahsna, Mundaka, Māndūkya, Taittirīya, Aitareya, Chāndogya and Brihadāranyaka*.

2 See Katz and Egenes (2015, 31).

3 Thich Nhat's guided breath medication is available at https://www.youtube.com/watch?v=XHvtIcaD194 (accessed on 20 September 2023).

4 See Rumi's famous poem, 'Only Breath', available at https://allpoetry.com/Only-Breath (accessed on 20 September 2023).

5 A compilation of teachings and practices of Thich Nhat is available at https://plumvillage.org/#filter=.region-as (accessed on 20 September 2023).

6 Fromm (1955) presented a psychoanalysis of historically evolved fear of freedom that plagued the psychic structure in modern times and underlined the mechanisms of escape from freedom through an illusion of individuality and turn to authoritarianism.

7 The Gulbenkian Commission Report sought to present a case for restructuring the social sciences so as to address contemporary concerns.

8 To know more about the foundation, see https://gulbenkian.pt/en/ (accessed on 20 September 2023).

9 For more details, see https://iwallerstein.com/ (accessed on 20 September 2023).

10 Fromm (1955, 3).

Chapter 1: The Ordinary and the Extraordinary in the Scheme of Sociological

1 Elsewhere an interplay of ordinary and extraordinary led to a liberating authorial experience, in Pathak (2021).

2 Raju (2013, 3) recounts a similar story where the guru is named Paramanandayya.

3 This was the conceptual mainstay in Pathak (2021, 2022).

4 Banks (2001) for an elaborate understanding.

5 See for example, Banks and Morphy (1997) and Banks and Ruby (2011).

6 In Burawoy (2021).

7 A reading of Burawoy along these lines was in Pathak (2022).

8 See Wright (2010).

9 See Wright (2020).

10 Among many, there are Das (1993), Deshpande (1994), Jha (2005) and Vasavi (2011). However, one ought to remember that Bottomore (1962) anticipated the crisis in sociology in India fairly early on.

11 See Madan (2003) as well as Thakur (2015).

12 For a discussion, see Pathak (2018).

13 This is quoted from Partha Nath Mukherji's introduction to the proceedings of the conference. It is available at http://www.isa-sociology.org/colmemb/national-associations/en/meetings/reports/SouthAsia.html (accessed on 7 October 2015).

14 Patel (2006) presented an elaborate critical appraisal of the advent and tenacity of binaries in sociology. In a different context, much before Patel, Obeyesekere (1963) proposed a critical departure from binaries and deciphered the intermixing of the Great Tradition and Little Tradition in understanding the dynamics of Sinhala Buddhism.

15 The phrases such as Methodological Dualism, Methodological Monism, Reflexive Sociology are in upper case in the original.

16 I intend to suggest the debate on sociology in crisis in India that has received many interventions. However, there are little evident changes at the level of practices, be it teaching programmes or research.

17 Todd Gitlin deemed sociology paled by 'the bloated puffery of Grand Theory and the microscopic marginality of Abstract Empiricism' (2000, 233).

18 Gitlin (2000, 196).

19 Gitlin (2000, 197).

20 Gitlin (2000, 198).

21 Gitlin (2000, 211–212).

22 Keeping the tradition of critical reasoning intact, there is a significant critique of Mills' imagination that is worth noting. Alleging a 'reverse orientalism', Denzin observed this about Mills: 'he saw ordinary people as "the other" whose life he could objectively describe and explain through the tools of the classical theorists. His imagination served to legitimate a version of institutionalized sociological practice that interpretive sociologists today wrestle with. It cast American society as a giant theatre where the performances of ordinary people could be read from the privileged perspective of a bourgeois sociological aesthetic' (1990, 13).

23 This issue has been discussed at length in an essay that introduced a conversation between sociologists and an art historian, Parul Dave-Mukherji. I am borrowing some of the understanding from Pathak (2015).

24 There have been a few noticeable attempts to systematically understand the contribution of Mukerjee to sociology in Indian context. See for example, Thakur (2015) other than Madan (2003, 2011).

25 For example, see Das (1993) and Deshpande (1994).

26 David Pocock and Louis Dumont debate is an oft-quoted starting point for this discussion. The idea is not to present an exhaustive list of who did what. But to pick a thread conducive for the argument.

27 For more on the quest of a regional framework to explore the indigenisation of sociology, see Mukherji and Sengupta (2004).

28 Elsewhere, Thakur (2015) has read this as the ambivalence of the Indian mind in its encounter with Western modernity, much akin to Pathak's (1998/2015) discussion that unravels paradoxes and possibilities of modernity in Indian thought system.

29 This was the title of the editorial co-authored by Louis Dumont and David Pocock (1957) in the inaugural issue of the journal, *Contributions to Indian Sociology*, which led to a debate participated by ranks and files of sociologists and anthropologists. For a descriptive account, see Madan (2011).

30 A.K. Saran was perhaps the earliest to express discomfort with the Dumont-Pocock on sociology of India. However, it persisted, as Andre Beteille clubbed this with the anti-historical perspective, and Satish Deshpande deemed it a book view rather than a field view of Indian society. The book-view alludes to a kind of armchair scholarship in which fieldwork based ethnography is not central. See Madan (2011, 224).

31 Bailey is supposed to have asked, 'Is there an Indian chemistry', as quoted in Madan (2011, 226).

32 A comprehensive, self-reflective summary of some of the key debates spanning the lifetime of D.N. Dhanagre serves the intended purpose. See Dhanagre (2014).

33 Partha Nath Mukherji's (2014) Foreword to *The Writings of D.N. Dhanagre* underlines the conspicuous absence of such debates.

Chapter 2: Persistent Precursors: A Philosophical-Scientific Backdrop

1 This is quoted from 'Some Thoughts about Bertrand Russell', in Russell (2003, xxxi–xxxii). The note below the poem mentions, 'Written in 1897 by Lady Russell, grandmother and guardian of Bertrand Russell, as quoted in Earl Russell's (Bertrand Russell's elder brother, Frank) *My Life and Adventure*, London: Cassell & Co. Ltd., 1923'.

2 For a salty detail that could enable asking a question whether the Copernican Revolution was indeed the first revolutionary moment in the history of science, it is worth reading a recent contribution by Wootton (2016).

3 It is curious to read together Kuhn's *The Copernican Revolution: Planetary Astronomy in the Development of Western Thought* (1957) and *The Structure of Scientific Revolutions* (1962). This aids in understanding that prior to the Copernican moment, there were other equally significant contributions, which could build up an idea of science.

4 One is tempted, on this note, to venture into the area of history and sociology of science in colonial and postcolonial India. This is a reference-heavy domain that has brought forth many fascinating details about the systematic process of decline of local sciences in colonial India, the relationship of modern scientific and technological endeavours with polity and economy, and modern science as a manifestation of Empire's pursuit of the colony. See Kumar (1995), Nandy (1990), Alvares (1979), Dharampal (1971), Habib and Raina (1989) among several others.

5 One can think of the propositions made by Dharampal (1971), Rahman (2009), Alvares (1979) and the discussion by Kumar with reference to such materials.

6 This is, however, not to suggest that science and technology were victims of colonial science, an imported force. It was also, as acknowledged by

many, due to the caste structure in which theoretical and practical aspects were separated along the lines of purity and pollution. It is interesting to look at one of the earliest accounts on this: Ray (1909) and Chattopadhyay (1986).

7 See Raina, Dhruv, 'Postcolonial Narratives of Modern Science in the Making: The Exchange of Scientific Knowledge between India and Europe (1700–1950)', http://www.ssoar.info/ssoar/bitstream/handle/document/17272/ssoar-2006-raina-postcolonial_narratives_of_modern_science.pdf?sequence=1. This indeed resonates the discussions in various other sources, including Basalla (1967), Baber (1996), Raina (2003), among others.

8 There is a curious case of K.C. Paul, known as a Geocentric Theory man, who sticks to his subversive theory in spite of rejections and ridicule. See https://scroll.in/magazine/901353/one-mans-four-decade-long-mission-to-convince-kolkata-that-the-sun-revolves-around-the-earth (accessed on 20 October 2022). Also, there is a documentary film worth watching, *The Geocentric Man*, https://www.youtube.com/watch?v=lAzubmp1s4k (accessed on 20 October 2022).

9 Wootton (2016, 576) helps in recalling this and provides an exhaustive bibliography of works along these lines.

10 One can recall the moral and political anarchy of fifteenth-century Italy, which witnessed the importance of Machiavelli's doctrines alongside important works in art and literature.

11 Bierstedt (1978). Also see http://www.columbia.edu/acis/ets/CCREAD/etscc/kant.html (accessed on 20 October 2022).

12 When Luther came to know of Copernius' theory, he scoffed at it, and so did Calvin.

13 Pythagoras is renowned for contributing the famous formulation to Euclidean geometry: the sum of (the areas of) the two small squares equals (the area of) the big one. In algebraic terms, $a^2 + b^2 = c^2$ where c is the hypotenuse while a and b are the legs of the triangle. See http://www.cut-the-knot.org/pythagoras/index.shtml (accessed on 20 September 2022).

14 These tidbits on Newton are from Bierstedt (1978).

15 'Isaac Newton', The *Stanford Encyclopedia of Philosophy*, https://plato.stanford.edu/archives/fall2008/entries/newton/ (accessed on 20 August 2024).

16 This idea, also referred to as cogito, according to Russell (2003, 517), was advanced by St Augustine. However, it acquired much prominence in the Cartesian meditations.

17 As expected, being a rationalist himself, Russell was vocally uncomfortable with Hume's alleged 'carelessness and inattention'. Russel notes, 'his skepticism is insincere as he can not maintain in his practice', and furthermore, 'the growth of unreason throughout the nineteenth century and what has passed of the twentieth century is a natural sequel to Hume's destruction of empiricism' (2003, 611). Of course, he names Rousseau, Schopenhauer and Nietzsche, along with Hume for weakening reason.

18 For a broad account on creative imagination associated with romanticism, see Engell (1981).
19 This point is explored in detail in Das Gupta (2019).
20 See http://www.columbia.edu/acis/ets/CCREAD/etscc/kant.html.
21 See http://www.columbia.edu/acis/ets/CCREAD/etscc/kant.html.
22 Also see Bottomore (1989) for a more detailed account on the Frankfurt School. The Vinenna Circle was a group of scientists who propagated mathematical logic-based empiricism in which there was a little room for synthetic a priori. See https://plato.stanford.edu/entries/vienna-circle/ (accessed on 30 September 2022).
23 Interestingly enough, unlike many other theorists, philosophers read Merton's Sociology of Science too, and that too without any negative reaction. See Richardson (2004).
24 In the sense that Max Weber held Puritanism as a force behind the type of character structure which fostered the development of capitalism. For more on this, see Cole (2004).
25 This meant that the most eminent of scientists who collaborated would earn the lion's share of the credit despite the small amount of work in a collaborative research and findings. See Merton (1968).
26 See Vaudeville (1964).
27 See https://rekhta.org/urdudictionary?keyword=anal-haq (accessed on 20 December 2022).

Chapter 3: Predecessors and Precursors: A Case of Sociology before Sociology

1 This fascinating paradox of sociology to offer a critique of what underpins it, viz., modernity, is convincingly elucidated in Nisbet (1967, 17), and happens to be at the core of most social thoughts emerging from postcolonial South Asia; one such substantive account is in Pathak (2015).
2 Pathak (2004) explores a possibility in terms teaching and learning sociology in India.
3 However, for all technical and methodological reasons, it may not be untenable to propose that Durkheim is akin to a disciplinary father who gives it a concrete shape in terms of research questions and ways of seeing. See Durkheim (1960) for a discussion on *précurseur*, which means forerunner.
4 Though Zeitlin (1968), upon which this part of the discussion in this chapter relies, notes the significance of Giovanni Vico whose contributions shall be deemed equally significant in the history and advent of sociology.
5 The reference to this classical work is through the online source, https://www.marxists.org/reference/subject/philosophy/works/fr/montesqu.htm (accessed on 1 September 2022).
6 For more along these lines, see Berlin (1980) and Jones (1994).
7 This is based on an observation by Berlin, that, 'by temperament Montesquieu is an empiricist who seeks to explain everything by naturalistic means wherever and whenever he can' (1980, 137).

8 See Montesquieu (1752), https://www.marxists.org/reference/subject/philosophy/works/fr/montesqu.htm (accessed on 1 September 2022).
9 Quoted from Montesquieu (1752).
10 Jones quotes Durkheim in a footnote (1994, 2).
11 Rousseau's *Discourses on the Sciences and Arts* is analysed in Gourevitch (1972).
12 Related to this, Voltaire is quoted to have said, 'never has so much intelligence been employed in order to render us stupid'. See Marshall (1978, 421).
13 These are *Discourses on the Sciences and Arts* and *Discourses on the Origins of Inequality, Polemics, and Political Economy*.
14 Quoted from the online version of the *Discourse*, https://www.stmarys-ca.edu/sites/default/files/2023-03/arts.pdf (accessed on 1 September 2022).
15 See http://www.latindictionary.org/latin/english/meaning/Vitam_impendere_vero (accessed on 1 September 2022).
16 Marshall (1978) and Orwin (1998) have amplified this paradox respectively.
17 In a critical note, Marshall notes, 'Rousseau's defense of ignorance against the Enlightenment is enigmatic. It corresponds neither to the views of the learned nor of the common man, yet it has something to do with his theory of practice' (1978, 424).
18 Quoted in Zeitlin (1968, 28–29).
19 Orwin (1998) is of the view that Rousseau chisels a version of Socrates, different from Plato's, that leads to celebration of ignorance. Here, I dwell upon Orwin for the information about the epistemological proximity between Rousseau and Socrates, rather than the distance between the two which may be an analytically valid reading.
20 Marshall (1978, 428).
21 Quoted from the online version of the *Discourse*, https://www.stmarys-ca.edu/sites/default/files/2023-03/arts.pdf (accessed on 1 September 2022).
22 Quoted from Marshall (1978, 438).
23 Quoted from Marshall (1978, 439).
24 With due dismay, Robert Nisbet noted in a significant footnote,

> No single, systematic work exists on the conservative anti-Enlightenment of 1790–1830; nothing that deals with this movement in any way comparable to the countless treatments of the Enlightenment; nothing that seeks to do justice to the time period or to the geographical distribution of the conservative movement … there are fortunately some excellent works on the emergence of conservatism in individual countries—chiefly France and Germany…. (1978, 113)

25 Nisbet (1978, 89).
26 Nisbet (1967) develops his discussion on sociological tradition along this line.
27 Quoted in Zeitlin (1968, 39).
28 See Zeilin (1968, 40).

29 See Nisbet (1952, 1967, 1978).
30 Interestingly enough, for Durkheim (1958), Saint-Simon was a more credible a founding figure.
31 Quoted in Zeitlin (1968, 57).
32 To get a detailed sense of the utopianism, it is worth referring to Saint-Simon (1975).
33 To reiterate an earlier note, it is worth mentioning that Giddens too reaffirms, 'Comte plundered Saint-Simon's ideas in constructing his own system, a matter of great acrimony in the relations between the two thinkers after Comte broke away from the tutelage of his mentor' (1978, 239).
34 Quoted in Zeitlin (1968, 75).
35 Along with Giddens' (1978) discussion, for a brief overview of the history and broader contour on the Vienna Circle, it is worth referring to the encyclopaedic entries. I am dwelling upon https://plato.stanford.edu/entries/vienna-circle/ (accessed on 7 August 2017).
36 Giddens (1978, 249).
37 Giddens (1978, 254).
38 I am paraphrasing the tenets of positivism culled out by Delanty and Bryman, and quoted in Mukherji (2000, 18–19).
39 This shall be taken up in the latter chapters of the book. Often, this means a turn to the paradigms of constructivism. But then, this could also mean something larger. I am being informed by Alexander (1990), though Giddens (1978) presented a thorough literature survey on the topic.
40 See Giddens (2009), though this scheme of appearance is also due to the centrality of the concept of capitalism.

Chapter 4: Return to the Trinity: Sociological in Marx, Weber and Durkheim

1 One can refer to any of the known works on the epic, such as C. Rajagopalachari (2010), Meera Uberoi (2005) for the convenience of translated work. I am reading this portion from the Mahabharata published by Gita Press. And I have employed it elsewhere for a witty critique of the educational spectacles, see Pathak (2015).
2 Elsewhere Burawoy (2021) defends the canonical significance of the trinity, and yet finds equally important place in the realm of classical for W.E.B. Dubois.
3 See Tiryakiyan (1979), Giddens (2009) among others.
4 See Bottomore (1979), Giddens (2009) among others.
5 Giddens (2009, 65). But this is to be taken with a pinch of salt, for any thought in the classical sociology, and in sociology in general, does not seem to be entirely free from propaganda.
6 Giddens (2009, 67) suggests that biological concepts were only metaphors for Schäffle, which Durkheim made too literal in employing as analogy for the social concepts.
7 See Barberis (2021).
8 See Chapter 2 in this book.

9 This observation comes from Jones (1994, 15).
10 Durkheim's sociologism 'an epistemological revolution' of some sort, emphasises, 'knowledge is a function of a priori structures which are societal in origin and imparted to the individual in socialization process' (Tiryakiyan 1979, 210).
11 See Tiryakiyan (1979), Giddens (2009).
12 Tiryakiyan (1979, 202).
13 This is informed by Bottomore (1975 and 1979).
14 One can also refer to York and Clark (2006).
15 Quoted in Giddens (2009, 1).
16 Giddens cites Georges Gurvitch in a footnote towards this (2009, 2).
17 While many Marxist scholars tend to consider the *Economic and Philosophic Manuscripts of 1844* and *The German Ideology* as the works coming from a young, little less scientific and naïve Marx, it makes sense to agree with Giddens' (2009) proposition that these works set most of the thematic issues that Marx was going to discuss in his works, including *Das Capital*, in the future.
18 See https://www.marxists.org/archive/marx/works/1844/manuscripts/labour.htm (accessed on 1 March 2021).
19 Needless to say, all such words are important conceptual category in Marxian literature, and the purpose is not to discuss these concepts, instead to show the way Marx arrives at them, by following a scheme that engenders a unique rationality in Marx's way of seeing.
20 See https://www.marxists.org/archive/marx/works/1844/manuscripts/labour.htm (accessed on 1 March 2021).
21 See https://www.marxists.org/archive/marx/works/1844/manuscripts/labour.htm (accessed on 1 March 2021).
22 See https://www.marxists.org/archive/marx/works/1845/theses/ (accessed on 1 March 2021).
23 In this sense, perhaps Weber can be deemed relatively less propagandist. He is unlike Durkheim who sought to show the possible order in a vulnerable industrial society, and Marx who persuaded to see the potentially alienation free world though a transformative struggle. But is Weber really without a propagandist goal? Is it not propaganda, of the new Christian world, to see everything through the category of vocation and calling that pertain to the Protestant Spirit? I am leaving these questions unaddressed, for they have been addressed aplenty in several other works.
24 See Weber (2009).
25 Since students tend to like the lectures, and such teachers, which vends opinion on burning issues of national concern, Weber notes furthermore,

> Everyone knows, however, that these vital questions of our national life cannot be discussed with full freedom in German universities. In view of the fact that certain value questions which are of decisive political significance are permanently banned from university discussion, it seems to me to be only in accord with the dignity of a representative of science to be silent as well about such value-problems, as he is allowed to treat. (10)

26 Weber (1968, 24) acknowledged that the decimal system came to existence in India but it did not give birth to sophisticated modern system of arithmetic, bookkeeping or rational calculation.

27 See in Chapter 2 of this book.

28 Weber notes the gradual development of the rationalist notions in Calvinism with the suggestion that 'no priest', 'no sacraments', 'no Church' and finally 'no God' had any role to play in the pursuits of a free individual in vocation (1968, 104).

29 One can also take a quick note of the opinion of Bryan Turner who, in the Preface to the Gerth and Mills edited book, says, 'It is reported that in a discussion with Oswald Spengler in February 1920 Weber said that the moral stature and honesty of a present-day scholar might be measured by their attitudes towards Nietzsche and Marx' (2009, xxvii). One can say that Weber sociologises Nietzsche as much sociologically recasts Marx. And thereby, he becomes what many have called, 'liberal in despair', as well as 'philosophical anthropologist of despair'.

30 Quoted in Gerth and Mills (2009, 55).

31 I have employed this premise for a critical discussion on success oriented educational ideology elsewhere. See Pathak (2015).

32 See http://www.greeka.com/greece-myths/king-midas.htm (accessed on 2 October 2022).

Chapter 5: The Dispute(s): Science Revisited, Sociology Rethought

1 See https://www.britannica.com/topic/New-Left (accessed on 20 September 2023).

2 The references to Dispute in title case is meant to highlight its historical importance.

3 See Gedo (1980).

4 See Chapter 1 of this book. Mills' critique of empirical abstractions in contemporary sociological research, juxtaposed with a critique of the positivistic predisposition towards the grand narratives, is relevant till date.

5 See Guru (2002).

6 This includes the debate between Gopal Guru and Sundar Sarukkai, which has been subtitled as an *Indian Debate on Experience and Theory* (2012).

7 Frisby (1976) offers a lucid account in a detailed introduction to the English translation of the Positivist Dispute in German sociology. Also see Keuth (2015).

8 Detailed in Samuels et al. (2003).

9 Quoted in Frisby (1976, xxiv). Everyone did not, however, accept the idea of value-neutral sociology and the debate continued till the outbreak of the First World War.

10 Discussed in Chapter 4 of this book. For more, see https://plato.stanford.edu/entries/vienna-circle/ (accessed on 20 September 2023).

11 As elucidated in Giddens (1979) and Bottomore (2002).

12 The Frankfurt School was established by a decree of German Ministry of Education in 1923 and was affiliated with the University of Frankfurt, as discussed in Bottomore (2002).

13 See Bottomore (2002, 15).
14 Horkheimer's speech was titled 'The Present Situation of Social Philosophy and the Tasks of an Institute for Social Research'.
15 A more detailed discussion on this is in Popper (1963, 44–55).
16 In this regard, it shall be further noted that Popper distinguishes Socratic doubt from Cartesian doubt. While Socratic doubt reaffirms the presence of ignorance due to the uncertainty of human knowledge, Cartesian doubt is all about arriving at certainty. See Popper (1963, 21).
17 For a simpler version on the virtue of Popper's Theory of Refutation and Falsification, see Williams (2012).
18 There was another round of debate between Jürgan Habermas and Hans Albert in 1963–1964.
19 Scientism was, as Habermas (1976) more precisely defined, science's belief in itself.
20 See Frisby (1976, ix).
21 This is a conclusion that Keuth drew, saying, 'In the dispute about positivism, critical rationalism had the better arguments, in fact the only valid ones, but critical theory exerted much more influence on a broad, mostly academic public' (2015, 167).
22 The functionalist concept of systems is accredited to many, including Talcott Parsons in sociology, which received critiques from various quarters, including Mills' (1959) famous barbed wit against the grand narrative.
23 Anglo-American philosophy, interchangeably called analytic philosophy, is the work of European thinkers who immigrated to the US during early twentieth century.
24 A simple takeaway from the trio's engagement with Popper's Theory of Falsification is offered in Williams (2012).
25 Mukherji (2000, 21) helps in understanding this aspect of Kuhn.
26 So much so that Feyerabend acknowledged Lakatos' encouragement in the Preface of the book *Against Method*. Also to be noted, the manuscript of the book was lost in London and recovered by Lakatos with the aid of the Interpol. Being a rationalist, though ironically called a fellow anarchist by Feyerabend, Lakatos was keen that the Feyerabend thesis comes to light. See Feyerabend (2010: xvii) and Motterlini (1999) for the relation and debate between Lakatos and Feyerabend.
27 Richter (1997) said that Dadaism is known to have emerged as an artistic response to modernism in art in Switzerland (Zürich) and the US (New York) sometime in 1915 and subsequently spread over Europe. This was an aftereffect of the First World War geared to question logic, rationality, reason and aestheticism of a modern capitalist society. In affinity with the radical left, the Dadaists disclosed discontent in their arts, music, songs and public discourses. Some of the well-known Dadaists in Germany and Switzerland were Hugo Ball, Hannah Höch, George Grosz, André Breton, Philippe Soupault, Emmy Hennings, Tristan Tzara, Jean Arp, Marcel Janco, Richard Huelsenbeck, Sophie Taeuber and Hans Richter. Dadaism promoted a way of thinking, seeing and doing that assumed immense popularity.

28 Mukherji (2000, 22) makes an interesting comparative reading.
29 Feyerabend quotes Chinese thinker Chou Shao.
30 For more on Bohr, see https://plato.stanford.edu/entries/bohr-correspondence/.

Chapter 6: Post-Positivist Ways of Seeing: Resurgence of Experience

1 See Chapter 5.
2 Being aware of the allegation that the Eurocentric theories of experience did not draw upon Indian, Chinese and African sources of discussion, Guru and Sarukkai (2014) underlined that phenomenological tradition in India as well as in western philosophy offers plenty on the omnipresence of subjective.
3 Hermes were known as messengers of gods in Greek tradition whose objective was to deliver the Biblical interpretation of the hidden meanings in the scriptures. And with the Enlightenment, the hermeneutic philosophers shifted their attention from the Biblical scripture to the human world to interpret meanings. For more details, see https://plato.stanford.edu/entries/hermeneutics/ (accessed on 9 September 2023).
4 See Chapter 2.
5 Discussed in Chapters 4 and 5.
6 It is partly echoed in the Chapter 5 too. For more, see Adorno et al. (1976).
7 This is what Wagner (1970, 1) noted in his introduction to Schutz's phenomenology.
8 See Chapter 2 for a discussion on the Cartesian preoccupation with Cogito.
9 Garfinkel noted in a footnote that only the works of Alfred Schutz are the exception in sociology and deal with these questions. He also acknowledges that his understanding of everyday activities dwells upon Schutz's. See Garfinkel (2011, 36).
10 For a discussion on this, see Wolff (1978, 538).
11 For an overview of feminist standpoint theory and its advancement in the wake of postmodern challenges, see Hekman (1997).

Chapter 7: Intrigues of Experience(s): Return to Reflexivity

1 The rendition of the ghazal is available on Youtube at https://www.youtube.com/watch?v=EsTaHa1x-GU (accessed on October 20, 2023). The translations of such verses are mine, unless stated otherwise.
2 The song is available at https://www.youtube.com/watch?v=pueoTXV6FLY. (accessed on 20 October 2023).
3 For more information, see https://www.imdb.com/title/tt3614516/ (accessed on 20 October 2023).
4 The copy of NCF-05 is available at http://www.ncert.nic.in/rightside/links/pdf/framework/english/nf2005.pdf (accessed on 20 October 2023).
5 Idea of connecting text with experience of the learners was central, from Freire (1972) to Hooks (1994).
6 Indeed many, including Gopal Guru and Sundar Sarukkai (2012), complain of the relative absence of experience in modern theorising.

7 Nandy (1983) presented a detailed and riveting psychoanalysis of colonial minds.
8 As discussed in Madan (2000, 2011).
9 Guru (2002) made this provocative but substantiated observation.
10 A substantial cross-section of discussion is available in Chaudhuri (2004).
11 This was a mainstay of discussion in Jayawardena (1986).
12 Here, John is informed by Radha Kumar's work (1993).
13 As discussed in Sangri (1995).
14 See Chaudhury (2004).
15 Laxmi Murthy with others documented some of the instances of mobilisations. For more details, see Murthy (2017).
16 More details are available at https://www.mkgandhi.org/gandhiji/42harijan.htm (accessed on 20 October 2023).
17 As discussed in Pathak (2016).
18 Take a look at Matilal (1992) for more, and for a simpler synthesis, see Ganeri (2001).
19 Cited earlier with reference to M.N. Srinivas (1976) and T.N. Madan (2000).
20 A critique of such predispositions was in Cohn (1996) and Asad (1973).
21 The quote is from Madan (2011, 175). I had asked something similar to sociologist Susan Visvanathan who straddles both the worlds of anthropology and fiction with equal ease. Her answer has, till now, been agnostic.
22 See Chapters 5 and 6.
23 As discussed in Clifford and Marcus (1986).
24 It is worth re-reading writing culture debate in the light of recent intervention, such as Zenker and Kumoll (2010).
25 Marcel Mauss popularised the idea of total social fact in his anthropological discussion on the phenomenon of exchange of gifts in archaic societies, whereby total social facts are facts that 'set into motion in some cases the totality of society and its institutions … and in others a very large number of institutions' (Mauss 2002, 10).
26 In an elegant footnote, Wacquant quoted Bourdieu and Marleau-Ponty to weigh the proximity of their insights. Bourdieu is quoted to have said, 'The body is in the social world but the social world is in the body', and Marleau-Ponty stated, 'Inside and outside are wholly inseparable. The world is wholly inside and I am wholly outside myself' (1992, 20).
27 To various critics who held habitus as a conceptually blurred and metaphorical usage, Bourdieu's answer was a quote from Wittgenstein: *if a concept depends on a pattern of life, then there must be some indefiniteness in it* (Wacquant 1992, 23).
28 Upanishad literally means sitting near (the teacher) and learning. The claim about the number of Upanishads varies from source to source, indicating a range of 108 to 200. However, two of them have been counted as the most prominent, *Brihadarnayaka Upanishad* and *Chandogya Upanishad*. The *Brihadaranyaka Upanishad* means sitting in the great forest (with the teacher) and learning. This instance is also discussed in Pathak (2018). See

http://www.britannica.com/EBchecked/topic/266312/Hinduism/59824/The-Upanishads.

29 For more details, see https://plato.stanford.edu/entries/shankara/ (accessed on 20 October 2023).

30 In Sanskrit it is, '*Yad Hridayam Hridayamiti Hridayashtha Budhdhi Ruchyata*' (reproduced from memory, translation mine).

31 In Sanskrit, it is, '*Hridayen hi Satyam Janati*' (reproduced from memory, translation mine).

32 This particular adage is accompanied by '*Dwitiyat wai bhayam bhawet* and '*Ekaki na ramte*'. It means, 'I fear an existence apart from me', and 'I dislike being only one', respectively. The resolve of this tension is '*Sa dwitiyam echhet*', meaning, 'Hence I want somebody apart from me'. The wisdom is singularly expressed in '*Eko aham bahusyam*', meaning 'I am one yearning and becoming many'.

Chapter 8: Diehard Devils: Myopias and Utopias in Sociology in India

1 For an epistemic notion essentially associated with the Indian philosophy and Hindu religious worldview, see https://www.britannica.com/topic/darshan (accessed on 20 October 2023).

2 For the anatomical meaning, see https://www.merriam-webster.com/dictionary/myopia (accessed on 20 October 2023).

3 Though the dictionary meaning is negative in nature, Mannheim deemed it a positive aspect of knowledge, that is, a reality-transcending device (see Chapter 6).

4 See for example, Rege (2000); Srinivas and Panini (1973); Uberoi et al. (2000); Patel (2016); Madan (2011); Singh (2014).

5 This oft-repeated information is in many chronicles, including, Mukherjee (1973).

6 We will return to this with reference to Jha (2014); Chaudhuri and Jayachandran (2014); Sujatha and Sengupta (2014).

7 Srinivas and Panini (1973); Singh (2004); Uberoi et al. (2007); Patel (2016); Thakur (2014) among others inform us about this.

8 See Obeyesekere (2005).

9 See Obeyesekere (1992). Both, Shahlin and Obeyesekere had different interpretation of the Hawaiian deification of Captain Cook, revealing the distinction of the ways of seeing eomplyed in their respective interpretations.

10 For example, Das and Uberoi (1971) presented a critique of Dumont's central axis to show the overly simplistic binaries of pure–impure.

11 Madan (2011, 226–227).

12 See Das (2012).

13 See Guru and Sarukkai (2012, 2019).

14 For more details, see Savur (2016); Srinivas and Panini (1973); Madan (2011); Jose (2003); Patel (2016); Uberoi et al. (2007).

15 Many treatises reflect on this issue in sociology, such as Uberoi et al. (2000); Patel (2016). However, in this regard, it's also pertinent to recall Asad (1973) and Cohn (1996), the main sources that inform sociologists

in India about the encounter of sociology and anthropology with colonial modernity.

16 See Perera and Pathak (2019).

17 A visual turn was visible in a special issue of the journal that made an edited compendium. See Ramaswamy (2003).

18 Patel (2016) points out the role of the University Grants Commission of India in the standardisation processes.

19 Patel (2017) deemed sociology playing into the agenda of a nation state, and thus methodological nationalism.

20 See Das (2003) on the roles of the international funding agencies.

21 A.K. Saran presented a critique of this much earlier. See Madan (2011).

22 Chaudhury and Jayachandran in Singh (2014).

23 This was glaring in a speech delivered by M.N. Srinivas (1994).

Chapter 9: Epilogue or a Wishful Monologue at the Epicentre

1 This was at the core of a discourse in Pathak et al. (2022).

2 An anticipation of the ideas in this section was in Pathak (2021).

3 See Connors (1986).

4 See Niles (1999).

5 It is worth recalling an unusual discussion by Basu and Ghosh (1982).

6 Lately, this has been a common concern that journals without academic credence facilitate paid publication of substandard quality. A website also maintains a list of such journals, https://predatoryjournals.com/journals/ (accessed on 5 August 2019).

7 A famous essay—almost notorious in discursive terms—by Huxley (1936) is worth recalling. See at https://www.nature.com/articles/138603a0 (accessed on 5 August 2019).

8 See a polemic on the spectacles of success and education in Pathak (2015).

9 There is a visible industry for Ninja writing. Crash courses, lectures and training workshops promise to enable the participating candidates to become smart writers. A Google search delivers manifold results on this: https://www.google.com/search?q=Ninja+writing&rlz=1C5CHFA_enIN782IN786&oq=Ninja+writing&aqs=chrome..69i57.3195j0j4&sourceid= chrome&ie=UTF-8 (accessed on 5 August 2019).

10 In the Positivism debate in German sociology, Karl Popper discussed this as the pursuit of issue by ideologically converted followers. He underlined the ideological reasons why one selects a problem. See Adorno et al. (1976).

11 Nietzsche (1973) is one such iconoclast, as it were.

12 As discussed in a previous chapter in this book, with reference to Bourdieu and Waquant (1992), that is, configuration of the field as a domain of power relations.

13 Titled *The Far Side* by Gary Larson. See https://anthropology.net/2007/09/14/watch-out-the-anthropologists-are-coming/anthropologists-anthropologists/ (accessed on 1 July 2019).

14 The online dictionary gives the meaning of this phrase, as 'a positive change in the performance of a group of persons taking part in an experiment or

study due to their perception of being singled out for special consideration'. See https://www.dictionary.com/browse/hawthorne-effect?s=t; though, it appears as one of the most negative consequences of the technological mediation in social research.

15 Srinivas' (1966) discussion on the government bulldozer driver in the remembered village called Rampura, who practised black magic upon return from formal profession, is very suggestive. It prompts us to think whether sociologists are any different.

16 This is unabashedly guided by Debord (1967).

17 This provocative insight is borrowed from Guru's (2002) critique of non-egalitarian social sciences in India. Though his scheme is too simple to be applied without further critique, it does give an inroad.

INDEX

ABOUT THE AUTHOR

Dev Nath Pathak is associate professor and chairperson of the Department of Sociology at South Asian University, New Delhi. He has been endowed with several fellowships and grants, including by the Charles Wallace Trust and the Indian Institute of Advance Studies. He researches and writes on performative expressions and cultural politics in South Asia, epistemological issues in social sciences and the sociology of literature and art. Some of his monographs include *In Defence of the Ordinary: Everyday Awakenings* (2021) and *Living and Dying: Meanings in Maithili Folklore* (2018) and some of his edited books are *Another South Asia* (2018), *Performative Communication: Culture and Politics in South Asia* (2017), *Investigating Developmentalism: Notions of Development in the Social Sphere*s (2019), *Seeing South Asia: Visuals Beyond Borders* (2021), *Neighbourhood and Neighbourliness in Urban South Asia* (2022) and several research articles in journals. He also edits a journal *Society and Culture in South Asia* (co-published by Sage).